The Universal Service Desk (USD)

Implementing, controlling and improving service delivery

The Universal Service Desk (USD)

Implementing, controlling and improving service delivery

BRIAN JOHNSON AND LÉON-PAUL DE ROUW

IT Governance Publishing

IT Governance Publishing Ltd
Unit 3, Clive Court
Bartholomew's Walk
Cambridgeshire Business Park
Ely, Cambridgeshire
CB7 4EA
United Kingdom
www.itgovernancepublishing.co.uk

Formerly published as *De servicedesk – Spin in het facilitaire web, third edition* in 2018 by Vakmedianet.

First published in the United Kingdom in 2020 by IT Governance Publishing.

ISBN 978-1-78778-148-1

ABOUT THE AUTHORS

Brian Johnson has published over a dozen official titles in the IT Infrastructure Library (ITIL®) and a total of more than 30 books. He is the author of many books about best practices in business and IT. He designed and led the programme for ITIL version 2, which is widely used in the Netherlands and throughout the world.

Brian has inhabited many roles during his career, including vice president, lead architect, director and consultant.

One of his current roles is as chief architect at the ASL BISL Foundation. The Utrecht-based Foundation provides guidance on business information management to a wide range of public- and private-sector businesses in the Benelux region. It publishes best-practice guidance and, together with certification bodies, provides education and examinations. Brian is chief architect for the redesign of all guidance and will be the author of new strategic publications.

Léon-Paul de Rouw studied technical management and organisation sociology. He worked for several years as a consultant and researcher in the private sector. Since 2003, he has been a programme manager with the central government in the Netherlands. He is responsible for all types of projects and programmes that focus on IT and business (outsourcing, implementation and change).

In general, his interests include policy development, innovation, design and implementation, and management, mostly in the field of IT. Because of this, in addition to his professional career, he also writes, teaches, consults and delivers workshops and masterclasses.

Léon-Paul's previous books were primarily written for professionals in their field, including IT demand-supply and facilities management. The books have since been used by a number of institutions as guides and textbooks and have also been incorporated into postgraduate courses.

ACKNOWLEDGEMENTS

While writing this book, we were very fortunate to have the reviews, help and support of many people. For this version we especially mention Wil Gooskens, Merle Laterveer and Tim van Leeuwen, Breda University of Applied Sciences; and Ron van Haasteren and Renske van der Heide, Topdesk.

We would also like to thank Katinka Pani-Harreman, Sanjay Nair and Shriram Bharathwaj for their helpful comments during the review process.

So now, all that's left is for us to offer a few definitions and a few ideas about getting started on a USD.

CONTENTS

INTRODUCTION

What is the universal service desk (USD)?

The USD directs the bundling/combining and delivery of user or customer calls and by default, is the front office intermediary between customer and delivery organisation, or 'back office'. The USD can be found anywhere, internal service organisation (IT, facilities, HR etc.), as a customer service centre (call centre, help centre etc.) for any enterprise, or as a temporary single point of contact for events, incidents, requests or large scale interventions. Depending on whom you consult, the USD has its own language, approach and good practice.

For example, if you mentioned the USD to someone in IT, they will refer to something like ITIL® as a 'best practice' and assume it focuses on IT. The facts are that USDs (or service/help desks) existed long before IT and in many different guises, most often focusing on the needs of employees (internal customers), with regard to their needs such as having a canteen with tea and coffee, or a desk and chair or maybe a pencil or three. In this stone age the original name for this concept was facilities management (FM).

And so came the idea that people from outside the organisation (often called, erm, people, or customers or citizens) need somewhere that they can use to make enquiries or to report problems that need to be addressed in order to work, or to access services (internal or external). FM is applicable to a great variety of services, and it covers many of the principles and processes documented in specific USDs (such as ITIL or VeriSM or whatever IT practice you preach), so this book does not focus on 'best practice' though it is certainly covered; the primary focus is service management in the broadest sense, and professional attitudes to the provision of services.

In the wider world, professional FM, as an interdisciplinary business function, has the objective to coordinate the demand and supply of facilities and services within public and private organisations. The term 'facilities' means something that is built, installed or established to serve a purpose that, in general, is a very tangible asset that supports an organisation.

FM covers an extensive range of professions and services. Here are just a few which it can apply to:

- Real estate (properties and buildings);
- Technical infrastructure;
- Heating and cooling;
- Lighting;
- Transportation;
- IT services;
- Networks;
- Furniture; and
- Janitorial services, and many other user-specific equipment and appliances.

A service desk has long been the preferred gateway for customers for reporting incidents or problems, making requests or calls and for a whole host of services relating to their needs.

But the USD is not a term only reserved for facility management or IT. In this day and age the USD is a practical and efficient tool that many disciplines use to streamline service management, both internally (in many departments, including HR, finance and IT), or externally (in areas like customer call centres, and municipal desks that answer civilians' needs and requests and so on).

Despite its breadth, the primary focus of the USD is service management, in the broadest sense, and the establishment and maintenance of professional attitudes for service provision. Although there are many different options, the basic structure and principles used to organise the USD are the same across all disciplines. In accordance with this fact, this book discusses the essentials of any USD, whatever the purpose.

Part 1: The USD – purpose and approach

INTRODUCTION

What is a USD? What are the products and services you will be delivering through the USD? What are the essentials of these products and services? How can you design and build a USD? What do you use the USD for, an internal help desk or an external call centre? Who are your customers?

If your answer is, "Whatever is written in the ten commandments of ITIL, IT4IT, COBIT or VeriSM, ISO 41000 or any other standard or framework", think again. Businesses (whether they provide services like banking, insurance, government regulation, or whether they make millions of rubber patches for tyres) require help with business issues first and foremost and not on the provision of test environments, or how many angels you can get on top of a pin that certifies you attended some waste-of-time event or other.

See anyone from the business at that IT event? We thought not.

The questions above will be addressed in the first part of this book. The USD will be presented as a guide to structure the demand process according to the front office to back office principle. The USD will be considered as a concept that comprises a virtual USD (delivered via the Internet), a call centre function, a physical desk and some form of account management. All components must be considered as a coherent entity. Of course, your enterprise will decide the precise form and structure of the USD. Some organisations may elect to create all distribution channels to focus on maximum service delivery, while others may choose, for example, to provide only a service portal.

Tight fisted so and so's…

CHAPTER 1: THE USD IN THE ENTERPRISE

In general, enterprises require that all service processes relating to customers are handled in line with the perspective of the customer. This does not happen when the favourite framework of the IT organisation or department becomes the goal, rather than the tool. Focusing on the customer's perspective usually means that all services offered through the USD should be streamlined for efficiency and channelled for ease of access.

After reading this chapter, the reader will become acquainted with the subject of the USD and concepts of service delivery. Readers will understand how this book is structured. It is intended as a guide; it is not intended that you plough through every word and pass an exam that certifies that you know where to find a word in a diagram, but that you have no clue what to do about it.

1.1 Demand-oriented USD

The USD directs the bundling/combining and delivery of customer calls (or how to ignore them until they go away, your choice). The USD is, in essence, a concept relating to services or service delivery. In some organisations, a USD may not have a physical location; really, there is no need to have a USD physically in place (such as a bureau or a bunch of IT types with fancy headsets and nice shiny badges of credibility). For example, public services for municipalities and service centres for consumer support which are often wholly automated. A USD can exist as a telephone-based help desk (for your IT types), or as a portal on the Internet or intranet. A USD is not always a physical entity at a location where callers are seen, assessed and sent on their way. Large outsourced USDs are the exception to this rule; although in these cases, greed dictates that many staff work from home in foreign lands (such as County Durham), and get paid a pittance, and have to pretend their name is Derek or Jeff or Pierre or whatever.

In summary, the USD has many appearances.

There are many names for a USD (come to that there are many names for those staffing the USD but most should remain unpublished); you can have:

- Contact centre;
- Call centre;
- Service centre;
- Support centre; and
- Help desk or just front office.

In this book we use 'USD' because it makes money.

No, we use USD because it should relate to demand-oriented working and where the customer request is a starting point. The USD is a key component of demand-oriented working (we said that twice to make sure you'd notice). The *concept* of the USD originates from the management concept of front and back office. This *principle* states that the demand and needs of the internal customer provides guidance within legal and policy constraints.

Of course there are many definitions of the USD. Here are some examples:

- The central point of contact for services that respond to enquiries from internal customers;
- The single point of contact;
- The internal customer contact centre;
- A functional unit with employees who identify and resolve service incidents. Contact may be made by telephone, intranet or automatic reporting;
- A single point of contact within an organisation for managing customer incidents and service requests[1];
- A central department in an IT or business organisation. It may be a comparable department in an organisation, like a call centre or help desk. The USD is also a function that has been described in ITIL; and
- A contact centre; that is a coordinated system of people, processes, technology and strategy that opens, makes available, and admits information sources and expertise, through chosen and qualified communication channels that make possible interaction and add value for the customer and the organisation.[2]

For this book, we practice the following definition of the USD:

> The point of contact/central node of the enterprise where the customer can be admitted/can pose any and all questions and calls about (internal) service delivery. The USD then takes responsibility for appropriate action for the satisfaction of the customer in line with service level agreements.

Notice that this definition does not say anything about conforming to any framework or 'best practice'; service management should focus on the person at the other end of the enquiry, not on 'best practice'.

In this book, we show you how a USD within a demand-oriented organisation can be designed and implemented in a pragmatic and organic way. After all, the basic steps of demand-oriented working is acceptance of the customer question, registration of it, following up on it and to deliver a response as appropriate.

1.2 Why do you want a USD?

Enterprises need to react faster and faster to developments in the market or, in government, to societal changes. As a result, working flexibly in terms of time, place and capacity is a necessary condition to stay in business. The USD organisation/support adds (almost always invisibly), to the ability of the enterprise to provide business services. One development is that many enterprises want to provide employees the space to optimise their productivity.

---

[1] Knapp, D, *A Guide to USD Concepts*, Boston, MA: Course Technology, 2010.

[2] Cleveland, B, *Call Centre Management on Fast Forward: Succeeding in the New Era of Customer Relationships*, Colorado Springs, CO: ICMI Press, 2012.

Enterprises are increasingly tying to meet highly individual needs: maybe one employee wants to work at home while the other is a happy worker when they work while others are sleeping. One will a want a room, others like to work anywhere, anytime with their laptop.

An enterprise's USD:

- Is part of the professional service delivery that is directed by the enterprise;
- Provides many advantages. A USD makes it easy to efficiently streamline processes in ways that meet the needs of internal customers. As a result, tasks in back offices can be organised more efficiently, rather than being 'fixed' over and over again;
- Has a clear point of contact for the internal organisation for support so that employees can focus on their own tasks;
- Prevents arbitrary decisions being made within the enterprise about the provision of service support; and
- Ensures that all user enquiries are centrally collated within the enterprise and are forwarded to the right place in (or outside the enterprise) for resolution.

Many enterprises already have a USD or USDs, or something that looks quite like one: if it looks and smells like a USD, then it probably is one.

The role and function of the USD will evolve further and become more important as organisations and their employees learn to work in the new digital world. In other words, life is going to get more complicated in the office and someone will need to be on hand to help.

In the past, a business could focus provision of standard offerings with regard to how support was offered to internal (and external) customers. Today, businesses need to adapt to the individual needs of employees, workplace support and customers. However, despite this increase in scope, businesses cannot allow their total costs to increase. On the contrary, there is more need and demand to decrease costs. So, we have the usual paradox of getting higher service quality for the same or lower costs. The importance of the USD becomes higher as it has a central role in this strategy. This leads to the need for further improvement and development of the USD.

The USD needs to create generic solutions to customer enquiries and incidents in order to increase efficiency. The USD has the potential to act as a spider in the web of an enterprise, and to facilitate the resolution of most internal and external customer enquiries. Such a service requires a solid functional base to serve as a source of information for all, and to store and interpret data to promote innovation.

Example: A complete USD

The USD is the central point of contact for the business organisation where every employee (and/or customer) can submit their questions, problems and reports. From here, the call or report will be followed up and a decision taken regarding the follow-up. If necessary, the call will be escalated to other parts of the organisation. The USD should be founded on close cooperation with colleagues from other parts of the organisation e.g. IT, human resources, finance.

Enquiries or calls will be driven through the intranet where possible (through the service page), email and, of course, via phone – and in some cases at a counter where *real* people *actually* exist. On average, there will be around 300 enquiries a day through all channels.

In this example, the USD is needed to provide information about all available services and products. Products and services delivered by the USD, and included in the products and service catalogue, may encompass: mobility (taxi bookings, car hire, air and train tickets), enquiries relating to infrastructure (furniture, trolleys, mechanical and building problems, room reservations and receptions) and information about organisational services (IT, HR, Payroll). The USD also coordinates the delivery of all services to new personnel, including the creation of employee accounts and the provision of furniture, access passes, laptops and mobile phones etc.

1.3 The USD for service management

In this book, we focus on all aspects of the design, construction, improvement, innovation and further development of a USD. Other important aspects, such as the implementation of the USD, and the functioning of the USD and its employees, are only covered briefly in this book. Why? Because the ultimate success of the implementation and functioning of any USD is always dependent on organisational competencies and the actions of individuals.

In this regard, it is important to ask early on: Is the person making enquiries through the USD organisation a user or a customer? Any discussion about customer orientation and being 'customer centric' leads inevitably to new questions. The dilemma for the USD function is that 'it' wishes to be customer centric, but at the same time sets conditions and constraints about customer choices.

When we talk about customer centric in terms of service delivery, we actually mean that the USD should be demand-oriented and that it should adopt a customer friendly attitude and approach as key principles. It is also important that this customer friendly attitude and approach works within policy constraints, as well as with organisational principles and strategies. Demand orientation is really the key issue. The demand, (and the need behind it), is taken from the perspective of the service delivery.

In this publication, we will discuss 'the complete USD', and it will be up to the reader to decide which elements are the most use to them. A choice can be made from the integral design so that the elements concerning design, construction, improvement or further development of the current USD can be assessed and weighted.

Your USD might focus on handling simple enquiries e.g. defective furniture, a lousy coffee machine or requests for a meeting room. However, it could also be used for the coordination of a new employee entering the organisation (onboarding), taking care of all the necessary needs for expatriates, or delivering services to external clients in addition to internal personnel. The principles are the same for all types of USDs, the scaling is the major difference.

Dealing with internal customers differs from external dealings in a number of ways, including that some internal agreements for services will be in place that are not likely to be legal, they will be, shall we say, fraternal? External customers will generally be formally contracted to a service, with legal obligations on both sides.

The USD is part of the totality of internal and external service delivery. Depending on the focus, we can discuss the principles of the USD in relation to any service organisation, whether internal or external. A service organisation could be an IT department, facilities management function, service support centre or any other sort of service provider. As a 'catch all' we use the word 'service organisation' to mean all of these instances. And of course, service organisations, and USDs, are usually highly IT driven (unless your business has not evolved since 1948)…

1.4 For whom is this book written?

The book is written for students and those working in any guise of service management (facility management, IT and HR service management, customer services etc.), the service desk industry and employees of the service desk sector. Students can use this book to understand the components that relate to a USD. The guidance in this book aims to help people become better prepared for working in service desk practices. This book offers insight, help and advice for further development, value improvement and professionalisation of the service desk sector.

1.5 Structure of the book

This book comprises three parts. In the first part, the principles and conceptual structure including products and services of the USD are discussed. It is advisable to read this first part before reading other chapters. In the second part, all the different components of a USD are discussed in detail. Each chapter in this part can be read separately. Finally, the third part concentrates on the context in which the USD is positioned. The following subjects are covered here:

- Quality of service;
- Considerations when implementing the USD;
- Management and control; and
- Quality improvement.

The chapters in the third part can also be read separately, depending on your needs and interests (and how quickly you become bored).

Table 1.1 provides a quick summary of the subjects covered in each chapter.

Table 1.1: Where to Find a Subject

Chapter 1, 2 and 5	Underlying principles of any USD and a generic approach to build and improve an USD.
Chapters 3 and 4	Customer, users and services of a USD.
Chapters 7–15	Components of the USD.
Chapters 17–21	Context of the USD: USD as part of management and control, contract management, when an USD is successful, quality management, implementation and change.
Chapters 22	Practical tips and tricks to improve the USD.
Chapters 6, 16 and 24	Use cases.
Chapters 23 and 25	Future of the USD and summary.

Examples are included to assist the unimaginative (i.e. anyone who ever copied an SLA from some idiot claiming they are all the same, the SLAs, not the idiots. Mind you, even idiots vary in that a better class of idiot can be found the higher you go up the hierarchy, no more intelligent than the average idiot, but with the power to really screw things up), and with luck our imagination will help you to understand the practical implementation of the USD. At the end of each of the three parts, there is a specific chapter concentrating on a use case. In these examples, you will see that each USD is different but that the underlying principles are always the same. We end the book with a discussion about the future and its possible impact on the USD, as workplaces change from physical entities to virtual workspaces. Should be fun!

Navigation

After the introduction in *chapter 1*, *chapter 2* will explain the meaning and concept of the USD. In *chapter 3*, we focus on the attributes, categorisation and delivery of products and services from the perspective of supply and demand.

Understanding the attributes and behaviours of customers and customers' groups, within their specific workspaces and environment, is important for demand-oriented service delivery. Therefore, in *chapter 4* we delve into the issues and needs of the customer, and the function and the impact of this on the USD.

In *chapter 5*, we bring all the different strands together and provide an approach for developing, designing or improving the USD. Part one ends with *chapter 6* discussing the service desk of Breda University of Applied Sciences (BUAS).

In *chapter 7* we start with the description of the service management software (SMS). The SMS often forms the beating heart of IT service management or facility management, and it provides full functionality for the support of a USD – it is important to remember that the USD is an IT driven business service.

In *chapter 8*, we cover the service portal, the virtual USD. In *chapter 9*, we focus on call centre functionality. In *chapter 10*, the physical desk is described in detail and, in *chapter 11*, we focus on the role of account management as an important partner of the USD. In *chapter 12*, we cover the essential success factor for the USD: employees of the USD (a USD will never fully function without the right people on board). In *chapter 13*, we discuss USD processes in general, as well as the processes that mediate between the USD and the back office, and the management of these processes.

Chapter 14 focuses on the information needs of the USD and the dependency for adequate information from other departments. In *chapter 15*, we cover the many different components that come together to build, organise and improve the USD.

Chapter 16 (part 3) describes the position and role of the USD as part of management, and outlines procedures for controlling USD organisation. *Chapter 17* describes the indicators used for measuring the success of a USD. *Chapter 18* focuses on contract management and the role of the USD in it. In *chapter 19*, we describe the criteria for a successful USD. Next, in *chapter 20*, you will learn how quality management can help you make improvements based on these indicators.

Chapter 21 is about the approach to change, improve or build the USD through project management. Of course, sometimes you do not have the time or the possibility to start with an improvement plan or strategy, you need to start on the fly. Therefore, in *chapter 22* we offer you 30 practical tips and tricks to implement USD improvements immediately. In *chapter 23* we explore possible developments of the workplace and the consequences for the USD, and part three ends with another use case in *chapter 24*.

Finally (at last you might say), the book ends with *chapter 25*, a summary of the USD development as an interface between supply and demand.

After that take a strong drink, a deep breath and try to relax.

CHAPTER 2: THE USD AS A CONCEPT

The USD as a concept constitutes a coherent aggregate of intranet, phone, email and digital document handling, desk and account management. The demand process is structured according to the front office/back office principle. After reading this chapter the reader will be aware of the definition and meaning of the USD for the enterprise, which tasks belong to a USD and how the USD can be considered in such a way that it is applicable as concept in all enterprises.

2.1 What is a USD?

The USD is the central point of contact for the service organisation. It accepts all customer enquiries, calls and tickets; qualifies them as specific tasks and services and, where appropriate, hands them over to other parts of the enterprise (or to other providers) for resolution. In most cases, the USD takes ownership of the customer question (the demand) and pursues the progress of any resolution through to the satisfaction of the customer. In consequence, additional tasks for the USD include monitoring the progress of any actions, informing and advising the customer about the status of the call and ultimately, closing the customer's ticket. Where closure is not possible, the USD may maintain a log of known errors.

2.2 Tasks of a USD

The USD for customers and users is the central point of contact. This is different in any enterprise. The principal tasks of a USD are listed in *Table 2.1*, instantiation is dependent on the capabilities and requirements of your enterprise.

Table 2.1: Tasks of a USD

Tasks
• Receives enquiries (intake), both standard and non-standard • Manages complaints, expressions of preference, information requests, incidents, problems • Provides information (first line customer advice) • Monitors output on the basis of contract or service agreements • Manages the products and service catalogue • Reporting • Relationship management and account management • Product and process management • Contract management • Quality management • Ensures enquiries are pursued thoroughly and correctly • Monitors external and internal developments • Collects information • Monitors and oversees progress

2.3 The USD and front office

The USD is responsible for the collection and coordination of customer demands; it is therefore 'the front office'. The back office (which could be internal or outsourced functions), is responsible for proper and complete resolution.

The USD is therefore often seen as managing the back office as a proxy for the customer.

To manage the customer demands and escalate issues to the appropriate area of the enterprise, the USD needs to structure the intake of enquiries in an efficient manner. The USD of a service organisation therefore has five functions:

1. Taking care of the structuring and orchestration of the customer demand (the enquiries);
2. Starting the delivery process (once the enquiries have been received);
3. Managing the integrated completion of the services;
4. Monitoring internal and external developments (for example, by collecting management information); and
5. Presenting the professional face of the service organisation.

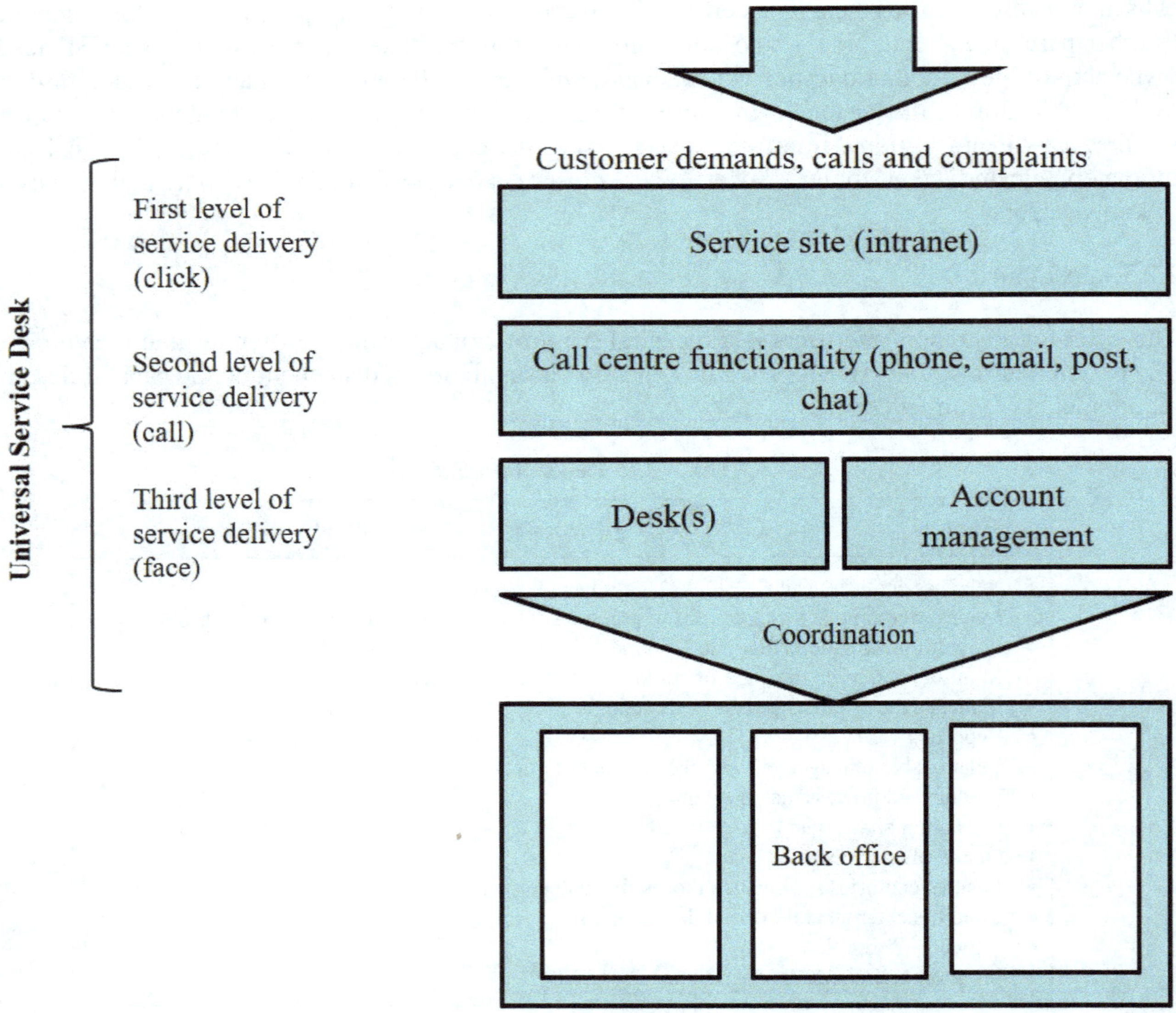

Figure 2.1: Concept of the USD

The drawing in *Figure 2.1* illustrates the relationship between the USD and the back office. The USD comprises two layers: a layer of coordination and a layer of service delivery. In the layer of service delivery, contact is made with the consumer, client or customer, and products and services are delivered.

In the layer of coordination, the customer demand will follow a defined process and will be escalated to the back office as appropriate. This coordination layer forms the internal organisation of the USD: the employees, the equipment, management instruments and all of the facilities required for the USD to function (perhaps including strong alcohol and counselling).

To meet enterprise goals (which should be set out in a contract or service level agreement), the USD needs to work closely with the back office. This relationship should be clearly defined, as well as evident in the way processes are arranged into working agreements and tasks, and automated or manual procedures.

Layers of service delivery

The layer of service delivery comprises three levels:

1. A virtual 'mailbox-office' on the intranet/Internet service site – this is the first level of service delivery, sometimes known as 'click' or level 0 support;
2. Call centre functionality (phone, email and digital post) – this is the second level of service delivery or level 1 support, sometimes known as 'chat' or maybe even 'natter' (or choose your favourite word for people moaning); and
3. Physical locations (desk or desks) and account management – this is the third level of service ('face') delivery, also named level 1 support (it is the place where actual assault can take place if the service is poor).

Example: Division between USD and account management

In practice, USD functionality and account management are often divided. This has to do with the differences in competences needed (knowledge, behaviour, skill) and partly because of the different stakeholders within the enterprise. The USD focuses mostly on the operational service delivery. This means that products and services can be standardised.

For tactical and strategic product and services enquiries, where requests might cause substantial changes and therefore substantial costs, most often the account management function is used. In larger organisations, account management might be further subdivided where service management takes control of tactical requests (perhaps identified by the estimated time needed for resolution or the estimated cost), and account management for strategic requests where criteria determine the necessary escalation.

Depending on the ambition and size of an enterprise, the USD might be responsible for the entirety of a given service or simply a single part.

Demands from customers can hit the service organisation through any of the different layers. Directing traffic to the intranet or Internet offers excellent possibilities to cover a large area of the total services through a standard approach, and ensures that much of the service delivery can be handled automatically. Besides the automation, users should consider the 'Martini approach' as being a benefit (the possibility to make their enquiries 'anytime, anyplace, anywhere').

The physical location, too, can have different appearances. Sometimes different locations are chosen depending on the type of services that will be provided. However, it is wise (even if simply for logistical reasons) to place these together in one geographical spot (like a service plaza). The management structure will dictate how interdisciplinary and multidisciplinary activities and locations will take place.

In cases where more contact with the consumer is necessary (or maybe less), or more clarity about the desired services and where standard offerings fall short, account management should take over.

The different levels of service delivery can be complementary to each other. In some cases, services will be offered on all three levels; in other cases, only one of the channels is best suited, perhaps help desk support over the phone. When a problem is caused by software or hardware it is not recommended (and highly unlikely), for customers to walk to a counter for service. It is much more practical to phone the help desk, where more often than not, they will take immediate action to solve the problem. There may be some specific cases where visiting the desk is mandatory, for example when requesting a user ID.

An organisation can choose to use all distribution channels, or only one or two, depending on the organisation's need and desired quality of service.

Example: Customer at the desk

Ever been kept waiting while a clerk takes a call? Well, unless a service contract stipulates something else, someone standing at a service desk counter should always be attended to first, and callers should be placed on hold or asked for a number where they can be reached.

A client on the phone can never see how busy it is at the desk (unless they happen to be using FaceTime).

Layers of coordination and back office

Calls from customers will be taken by the USD and need to be recorded and processed, and sometimes they will require action in the back office. The processing of the call depends on the management and monitoring procedures, and the enterprise (of processes and procedures) between the USD and back office. Back office can be divided into different levels of support, but mostly levels 2 and 3 are distinguished. In practice there are several versions for functional or organisational implementation of the USD.

Often, the desk's employees also take care of some of the call centre tasks. In these situations, a distinction can be made between the first and second lines of support. The first line of support is responsible for the desk and takes care of emails but takes no calls by phone. The second line of support does not work at the desk but takes phone calls as their principal task and can provide backup to the desk.

In some cases, the call centre functionality is situated at a location removed from the service desk. This is also the case for account management functions and sometimes for management oversight of the entire function.

Keep in mind that account management is often not considered part of USD management. It can have a different responsibility, or perhaps be absent completely. In the last case, (especially in smaller organisations) these account management tasks are undertaken by senior employees or USD management.

From a conceptual point of view, account management tasks should ideally be part of the responsibility of the USD function. When the different levels of service delivery are not managed unilaterally, their coordination, synchronisation and tuning become more difficult. As a consequence, this leads to a lack of clarity for customers (who do I call? Ghostbusters?) and a reduction in the quality of services.

The way in which the resolution processes are actioned and managed depends on the organisation of the back office. Fundamental to the design of delivery of services is that standard processes are followed wherever possible. Of course, not all questions or calls by customers can be foreseen. Therefore, agreements must be made about the coordination between front office and back office or redesign/work around of the processes to avoid problems with delivery of specific services.

Example: Channelling customer questions

Customer demand may move through many different channels and may even go directly to the back office, despite efforts to eliminate such action. It will be the task of the USD manager to arrange the process in such a way that the demand is channelled to the right place in the back office when a call is processed by the USD (routing methodology). In all cases, the swift and comprehensive resolution of enquiries or problems will be valued most by customers.

2.4 Process of service delivery

Coordination tasks of the USD include:

1. Receiving and recording the call, and understanding the issues (resolving the call where practical);
2. Providing information about products and services;
3. Handling, controlling and delivering products and services;
4. Directing the call to the back office and/or account management for resolution (routing);
5. Monitoring progress and closing; and
6. Reporting on performance and quality with regard to the action taken.

1. *Receiving and recording the call*

A customer can place a call at the USD in different ways: service portal, phone, email, digital post or by visiting the desk. The USD employee can also settle a call in different ways. Depending on the nature of the customer question, the USD employee will accept the call, record the enquiry and, where the resolution is known, resolve the enquiry.

2. *Providing information about products and services*

When a customer has an enquiry for the USD, the USD clerk checks whether the request can be handled directly (for example, an enquiry or the reporting of a visitor) or whether the question should be recorded and processed in the back office. In some organisations, the USD is set up to resolve as many enquiries as possible immediately; others are set up merely to record enquiries and process the action elsewhere.

Whether a request is handled directly is, of course, also dependent on its urgency or its special nature. If the boss is stuck because of an elevator malfunction, then action would be immediate; leave them there for as long as possible. Well, that would not be the action but we all would like it to be the action (or inaction). In the event of a disaster or emergency of some kind, such as large-scale water damage to computer facilities, regular activities might be shelved while the focus is shifted to the coordination of recovery activities.

3. *Handling, controlling and delivering products and services*

Once a call is taken by the USD, it is important that the employee becomes the owner of the enquiry. This means that all data relating to the enquiry must be complete and clear. All essential information should be identified using a predesigned, computerised entry screen according to specified procedures. We should always avoid a repeated call to the customer to complete missing information.

4. *Directing the call to the back office and/or account management*

Of course, not all calls can be handled and delivered by the USD. When the USD cannot process the enquiry, it must be redirected to account management or the back office. Each contact needs to be routed and distributed to the right place. To do this, the back office and USD must have an established agreement about the division between front and back office.

5. *Monitoring, progress and closing*

Monitoring progress is an important responsibility of the USD. The customer should always be informed in a timely way about the situation, especially when it takes time to resolve and to close an enquiry. It should be easy to track the status of all enquiries. A management information system (MIS) or service management software (SMS) can be a great help with monitoring progress. Within IT, it is often called an IT service management tool; while within the service management world, the SMS is usually a specific service desk software tool or part of an integrated software suite that includes an asset management or a view of the configuration management database (CMDB). In the facility industry it is called facility management information system (FMIS).

In the call centre, usually the SMS is the contact centre software in conjunction with the customer relation management system (CRM). Upon completion, the USD or the back office must close the call. If necessary, the USD must make sure that after care is offered.

6. *Reporting on performance and quality*

The USD should have, based on its position in the organisation, access to all operational information concerning requests, calls and status of requests/calls, and understand the quality of delivery. Next to that it will have direct contact with users and can check how the USD organisation is perceived. The information a USD reports will be an important part of all management information for the manager.

In *Table 2.2* there is a simplified fact sheet of the proceedings of a call. This sheet can be used solely with text or combined with symbols.

Table 2.2: Example of a Simplified Fact Sheet 'Standard Calls'

Activity	Commentary	Change in MIS
Intake and input data	USD employee receives call.	Standard calls are already formatted in the MIS so data can be entered.
Ask questions	Employee asks standard question to determine the right solution.	Questions that can be asked are available on screen.
Urgent	When a call is urgent the subcontractor or contractor is notified at once to start immediately.	In a standard call, the subcontractor or contractor will be known.
Agent in back office controls new orders	A work order is automatically created.	Agents can read orders in working order module.
Report back	After actions, the back office notifies their completion by signing of the work order.	Also report back when no timely solution is available. Contractor notifies cause and solution on the working order. When lead time changes, report to customer.
Close and reporting completion	USD employee closes call and sends completion message to customer.	Report completion.

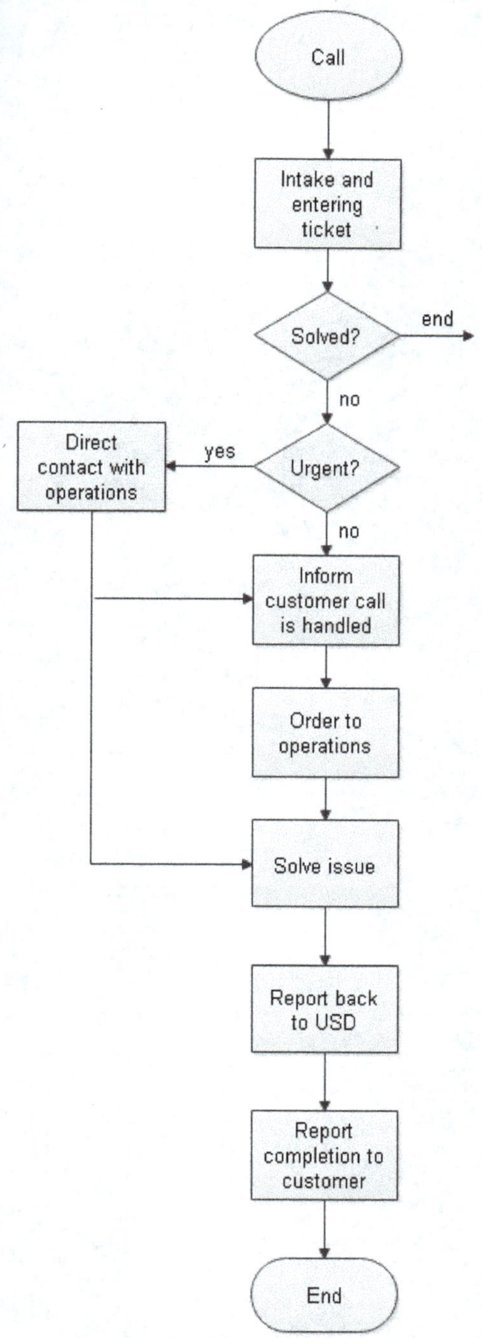

CHAPTER 3: DELIVERING PRODUCTS AND SERVICES THROUGH THE USD

Products and services that are offered by the USD depend on their attributes, on the choices made in relation to service quality and on the nature of the enterprise (whether the preference is the 'all in one USD' or a 'hub-and-spoke' distributed set).

A smart classification of products and services, and the way they can be requested, helps to efficiently organise demand and delivery. In this way, it is possible to bring about an effective balance in matching specific customer demand and generic standardised service delivery.

After reading this chapter, the reader should understand the attributes of the USD (or enterprise USD products and services) from the perspective of demand and supply, and understand the difference between the USD customer orientation and the back office's product and services orientation. Using this information, you will be able to define the process of matching requests to the delivery of products and services in the enterprise.

3.1 Smart classification of products and services

In order to classify the services offered, we must first understand the services. It is not wise to try to run a shop without knowing what you sell, and it is relatively simple to list your products. In some instances, it may be possible to find and reuse templates of standard products. Take a look at the listing in the European FM ISO 41000 series or the IT standard ISO 20000, and also look at guidance about creating products and a service catalogue.

The services mostly comprise a combination of specific physical products and more intangible services. Typical services:

- Are often intangible, for example, reservations made. Services often occur in combination with goods that have a tangible character; cleaning services are a good example: a cleaner performs activities and uses machines. In this case, the service is the clean environment; the result of the service can be seen, but it is not exactly tangible as an offering.
- Consist of a series of activities, for example, the request and delivery of purchased items. The process comprises a series of actions where the end product is the delivery of the purchased item. The quality of service is assessed on the basis of the quality of the delivered goods (for example, an office chair), and the manner in which the process was executed (via the purchasing department).
- Are often directly produced and consumed, for example, the handling of an information request, reservation or call.
- Include customer participation (at least to a certain extent) in the provision of services, for example, during the creation of access passes with a passport photo.
- Can be personal as a result of customers' participation. When the customer actively participates in the service process, we can respond to individual customers. In every case, services are only performed (and therefore manufactured) at the moment the customer requests the service.

Service management defines services in many ways (including as intangible or impermanent), and describes a heterogeneity of services and interactive consumption. The outcome is that the way in which products and services are looked at and the way in which they are assessed qualitatively depends on the perspective. The person responsible for providing the service, for example a relocation service, will mainly concentrate on the effectiveness and efficiency of the move. For the USD, the relocation may only be part of a larger renovation which also includes other services such as cleaning, wall movements, adjusting electric cabling and so on. The customer will not be interested in the individual parts at all. They want a solution, for example, the lack of space in the office which will be exacerbated by bringing in 50 more IT specialists. The renovation is an annoying but necessary part of the entire issue.

Thus, customers (the demand), request (USD) and delivery (partly USD, partly back office) have different interpretations of products and services. The nature of products and services also has consequences for the way in which the overall service and delivery of the service are organised. For example, the individual customers or departments will only have to deal with a renovation as an incidental part of life in the office. There is, therefore, no need for them to have expertise on this subject.

For 'building management' in the back office (which is often more involved with renovations and relocations), it is important to organise this service or event efficiently and effectively. Often the back office does not immediately take into account additional services that have to be delivered, for example, where part of the service that has been outsourced and where contract management is assigned to the USD. If this example, back office is product-oriented and will specialise in building management as a holistic service.

Clearly, however, the USD cannot solely specialise in 'building' management because it must be customer-oriented across a wide range of issues. The USD must keep an eye on the broad spectrum of all products and services, and possible aggregations, associated with customer demand. The USD is the point that links the specific demand and the supply, which is regarded as generic for the back office components involved. Therefore, the USD must translate every question into the available services: the better a USD translates, the faster and more effective its work will be.

How can the USD achieve this? The USD could create separate procedures and agreements for all products and services of the service organisation in terms of handling, financing and mandate. However, this is cumbersome, especially if the USD does not work exclusively for one particular service but also for diverse components of the enterprise other than facilities, for example IT, or a multifunctional business centre. Keep in mind the point about having one central desk or hub and bespoke arrangement. In that case, hundreds of products and services will soon be your responsibility and separate procedures for each product and service will not work.

A practical way to meet the various objectives is to make a nested set of agreements for both the demand side (the customer side) and the supply side (delivery side) for product and service categories, grouping several products and services as appropriate. For each group, agreements are made concerning the way in which products and services are classified and handled and under what conditions. Based on the groupings, consideration can then be given to how products and services can be applied for, how they can be delivered and how they relate to each other.

The two ways in which they may be classified are:

- Classification from the supply side (on the basis of complexity or budgeting); and
- Classification from the demand side.

3.2 Classification from the supply side

From the supply side, the products and services are divided along two axes: the degree of complexity (operational, tactical or strategic) and the method of budgeting (which we will term 'basic services', 'basic-plus' and 'additional').

Operational, tactical and strategic

In our first classification, the demand for products and services is distinguished according to the complexity level: operational, tactical and strategic. The customer demand can therefore be considered at each of the three levels:

1. Customer demand at the operational level involves the delivery of products and services that are highly standardised and for which the handling processes are more or less fixed. Standardised means that the characteristics of the product or service are known.
2. Customer demand at the tactical level relates to products and services which, although within a functional area (department), require additional specification. To this end, an intake interview must be conducted by an expert.
3. Customer demand at the strategic level relates to products and services that are both cross-functional and custom-made. These are usually new to the service and may only be requested once or sporadically. Sometimes these products and services still have to be developed. In situations involving these sorts of products and services, the customer has a problem for which no solution or work process is currently available (as the prophet Bono once said, they still haven't found what they're looking for).

Examples:

- **Operational:** Requesting a promotional gift or information brochure is simple and can be typified as operational.
- **Tactical:** Applying for ICT support is limited to one department but it requires more information regarding the content of the ICT systems and the extent of the support.
- **Strategic:** Initiating the support of a new business unit involves more than one department of the enterprise and therefore can be characterised as strategic in nature.

Basic, basic-plus and supplementary services

In addition to the division of operational, tactical and strategic, a classification can also be made according to the nature of products in relation to financing. In this second classification three categories are distinguished, namely:

1. Products from the basic services;
2. Products from basic-plus services; and
3. Products from the supplementary services.

Basic service

Basic service (basic package) refers to products and services that are offered to all customers by default. Generally, these are products and services for which customers have little or no influence on the costs. The basic service is the minimum support required by management for an effective and efficient primary process. A characteristic of the basic service is that management has approved it for the benefit of all users. For the basic service, therefore, no agreements have to be made with individual customers. In fact, they have no choice regarding the nature and quality of the agreements made (think about Microsoft® Office being distributed to everyone: you have no choice and good luck requesting changes).

Basic-plus service

Basic-plus service provision consists of standard products and services where the customer has freedom regarding the quantity and level of what is purchased, but not regarding its form. For example, you can request a specific number of workstations or smartphones but only from specific model ranges. Basic-plus is standardised as much as possible: the standard is determined in conjunction with the customer and the product owners. The budget for this service lies with the customers.

Supplementary services

In addition to the products and services mentioned in the basic and basic-plus package, the on-demand internal services can provide additional services that are not specified. Sometimes these are described as customised services. With these products and services, the customer is free to determine the content and the scope. Additional products and services are provided at a pre-agreed rate.

Example: Cost control

Think about an enterprise very much focused on cost reduction, that means standardised where possible. In general, the quality and price of the products and services are fixed. Customers mainly affect the volume. That is why the agreements are divided into a structural service and 'one-off' service. The structural services are divided into basic services and structural extras. The basic level has been determined on the basis of a minimum requirement and is included in the standard price.

What must be regarded as a structural extra is laid down in a supplementary contract. This concerns for example, more surveillance, extra opening hours or higher frequency of cleaning. Sometimes it is necessary to deviate from the standards if there is a one-off service, which occurs among other things in projects and renovations. These are charged separately.

When these two divisions are placed opposite each other, nine cells are created. The matrix is shown in *Table 3.1*.

Table 3.1: Indicators of the Characters of Products and Services

	USD (through intranet)	Account or Service Management Specialist (possibly via intranet)	Strategic Account Management or Standard Management
	Operational	**Tactical**	**Strategic**
Basic Service	• Meeting room reservation • Standard workstation • New employee induction • Technical maintenance and management • Intake purchase advice request • Signal deviations on products and service catalogue • Incidents/requests	• SLA report • Drafting of purchasing advice • Discussion of deviations from the products and service catalogue	• Drafting, assessing and establishing of the products and service catalogue, and service agreements or contracts. • Discussion of audit report (with management) in relation to contracts and budget, number of disruptions and number of new employees, etc.
Basic-plus Service	• Meeting room reservation with standard catering • Intake: different office furniture • Intake: application for relocation and/or refurbishment • Intake: request regarding support purchasing process • Intake: IT components (smartphone, laptop, software and any additional requirements)	• Report number of deliveries for standard catering. • Connecting with customer to discuss preferences. • Drafting quotations, purchase orders, project plans, inspection reports and numbers of deliveries, etc.	• Coordinating when drawing up the project plan and applying for tenders. • Drawing up a project plan and coordination on request, including quotes and execution. • Drafting an advice plan for relocation. • Control of execution.
Supplementary Services	• Intake: meeting room reservation with exclusive catering • Intake: application for a new office or additional office space • Intake: application concerning a new workplace concept • Intake: request relating to extra USD capacity for an event or project		• Control of execution. • Connecting with customer to discuss preferences. • Drafting an advice plan. • Coordinating with the customer regarding new or additional requirements (for example, a new department or an expansion). • Drafting an advice plan or a project plan and coordinating on quality and time commitment.

The operational products generally do not require additional explanation. This makes the delivery processes easy to standardise and to use an SMS. These kind of products and services can therefore be handled via the USD or the intranet. The products and services from the groups of basic-plus products sometimes require additional agreements with the customer. The USD is not always suitable for this.

This is true also for products and services that are strategic in nature, especially if they are also categorised as supplementary. These instances often require special agreements, sometimes at board level.

In other words, if we want to properly capture and expand the total range of customer requests multiple inputs are required, and each input must correspond to the specific needs of the customer.

Example: USD responsibility

Operational products are usually handled by the USD. When a product or service is more tactical in nature, other solutions are chosen, such as account management. In addition, specialists often need other (perhaps external) specialists for tactical or strategic projects.

3.3 Classification from the demand side

One solution for the customer

It should be self-evident to customers that they get a total solution for a given request. The separate subprocesses behind the request does not matter to them. The customers perceive service from a different perspective than that of the service organisation or IT service desk or whatever. For example, a 'relocation', 'a renovation' 'a change to IT' or a 'new employee' as a request will lead to different parts of the back office going to work. The dependencies between the different sub-processes must be properly arranged and coordinated so that customers are unaware.

It is the USD that takes over customer demand and then divides the overall request into components of smaller products and services, which are then individually released to the back office. Accordingly, it is possible to standardise on a product level by dividing a demand into its most logical units. These units are termed 'building blocks' (unless you prefer Lego® bricks).

Products and services are building blocks in the total service provision

The range of products and services offered by the internal service provider can be built up from separate units (simple products and services), and then aggregated into larger groups (multiple products and services). In accordance with their type, building blocks can be either single or multiple in number.

Single products and services are the smallest individual units and they are available from one functional area. These single products and services also act as the building blocks for multiple products and services.

Multiple products and services consist of a combination of simple products and services (a combination of building blocks), that are logically related from a user perspective. These products and services provide a total solution in situations due to their combination of all required single products and services. For example, office, desk, computer, company card, transport scheme, employee savings, etc., together form the multiple product 'introduction package' in a situation where a new employee begins to work. The multiple product 'workplace' – consisting of a desk, chair, cupboard, trash can, telephone, computer, etc. – is offered in these situations that will require internal and/or external needs.

Note

The term 'multiple products and services' in this book are also referred to as composite or integral products and services.

Multiple products and services often consist of simple products and single services. If for the sake of brevity we speak of multiple products, this concept also includes any service elements present therein.

Think about this example: The customer is confronted with a 'situation' and wants a 'solution'. The USD translates the situation into a combination of products and services. Products and services (the building blocks) must be combined for each situation, and that combination will always be at least slightly different.

Examples of situations other than those mentioned in the foregoing paragraphs with their possible solution components are: 'I need transport from a to b'; the building blocks for the solution might include bicycle, transport ticket, taxi, driver. Good luck getting the CEO to ride a bike, but you never know. The focus of the enterprise services (internal, external or both), determines scale and the possible range of customer interactions.

As one more example, we can use an 'I need a meeting' request. In this case, products and services such as the reservation of a room, the cleaning of the room, the shifting of tables and furniture, catering, audio-visual support and other elements can be combined. *Table 3.2* provides a concise summary of common situations.

Table 3.2: Examples of Requests

Requests
• Transport to and from abroad • Information about employment conditions for the introduction of a new (temporary) employee and/or the departure of a (temporary) employee • Network or specific IT problems relating to services or access to services • Workplace set up • Working at home • Giving a presentation or organising a meeting or event

Every situation involves a range of possibilities regarding requests. The example in *Figure 3.1* makes it clear (using the example of requesting a meeting), that different types of needs and questions exist, and the USD must, therefore, offer a combination of products and services to meet the customer's wishes.

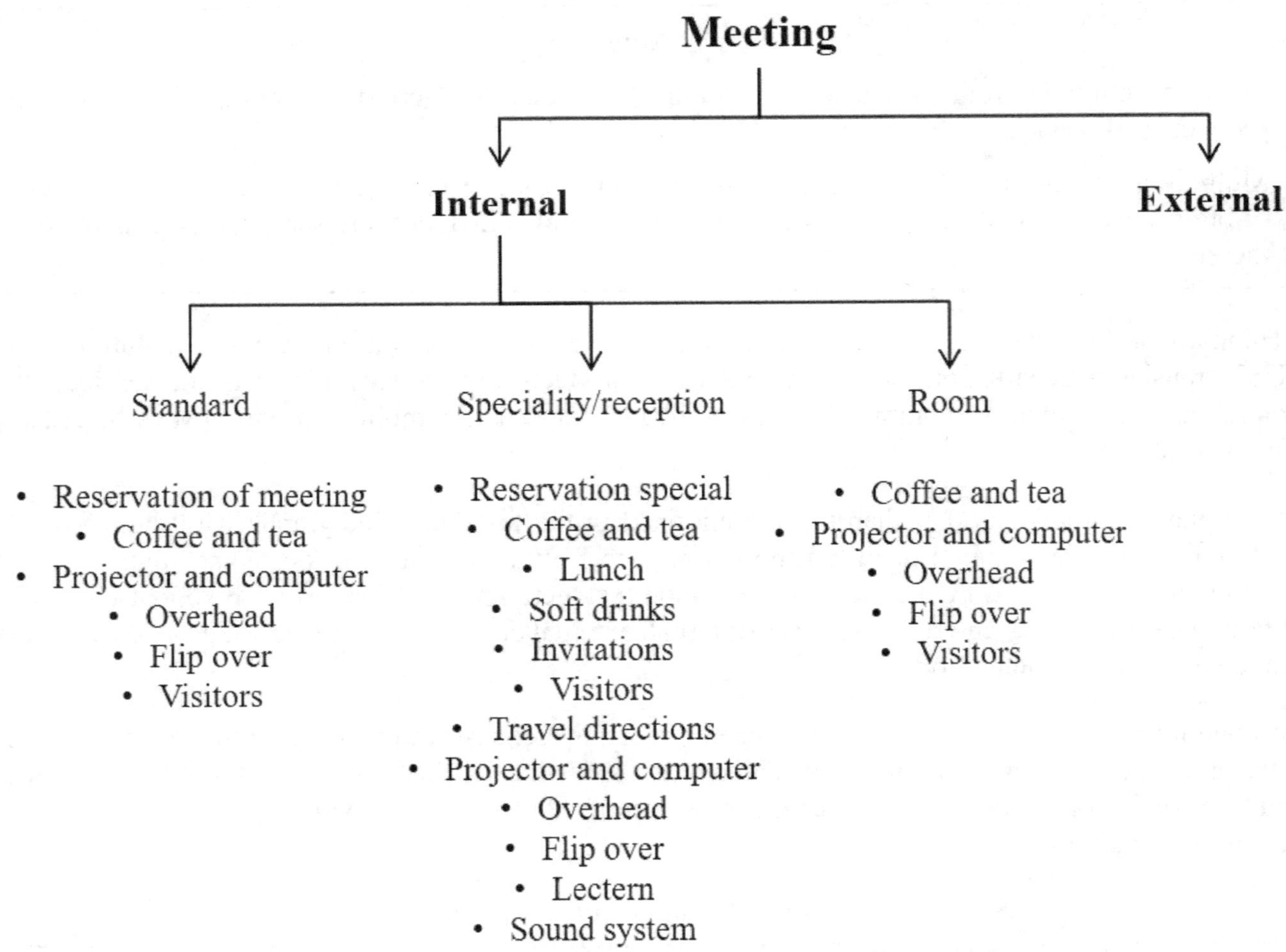

Figure 3.1: Building blocks for the multiple product meeting

The design of a USD should make it possible to structure the various options, making it easier for the service organisation to tailor the service as well and as efficiently as possible to the demand. In the case of introducing a new employee to the workplace, numerous variants are also possible. Every situation requires its own set of existing products and services tailored to the specific location.

In some more complex situations, products and services from multiple departments will have to be combined. An example of this is shown in *Figure 3.2*, in which virtually all supporting departments are involved.

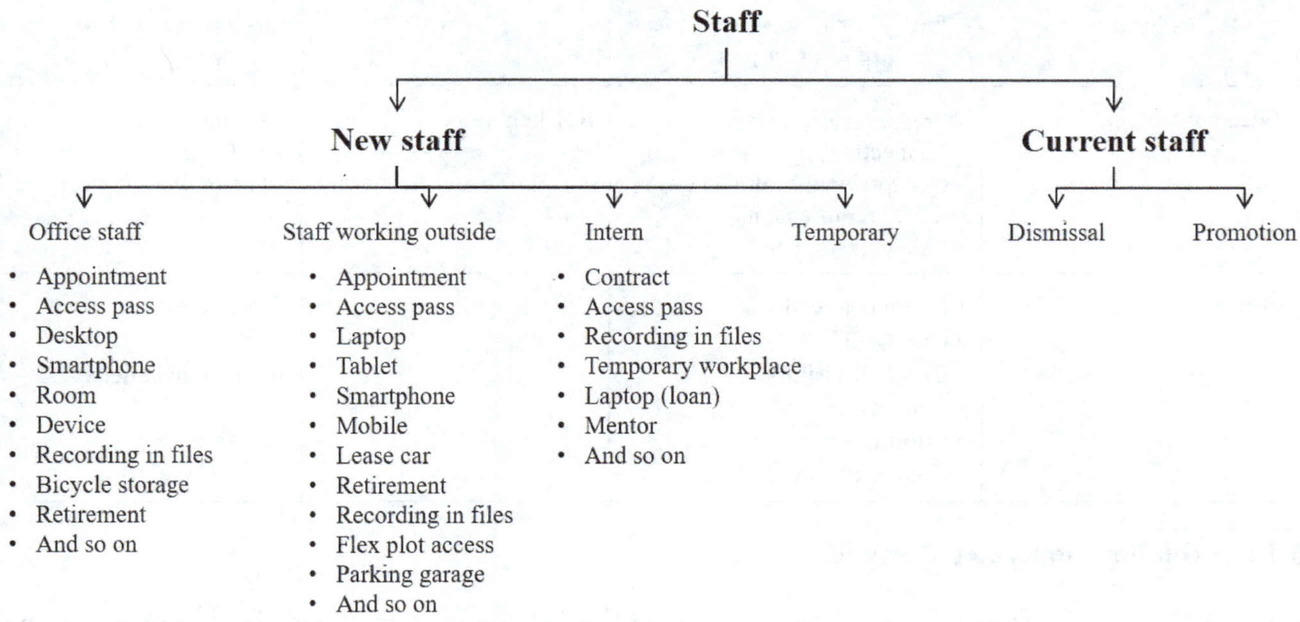

Figure 3.2: Introduction of new staff

As we have said before, requests arise from the needs of customers. It is up to the USD to recognise this need and translate it into a demand that can be handled with optimal effectiveness. Essentially, the USD must be able to recognise whether the situation or request can be handled by a fixed structure or whether a new structure is needed. Fortunately, in practice, there are many requests that can be filled in with a more or less fixed combination of products and services. Usually ten to fifteen multiple products and services are the maximum. *Table 3.3* shows the most common multiple products with examples of their building blocks and the departments involved.

Table 3.3: Common Multiple Products and Services with Examples of Building Blocks

Multiple Product	Partial Products (examples are not complete)	Owner	Departments Involved
Employee attendance	• Change employee file • Salary data • Set up a workplace • Credentials • Company pass	USD	• Facilities • ICT • Communication • Finance • Personnel
Relocation or refurbishment	• Move hardware • Customise employee file • Adjust telephony • Cleaning • Customise nameplates	USD	• Facilities • ICT
Workplace	• Purchase furniture • Digital workplace environment, including hardware (PC, tablet, etc.)	USD	• Facilities • ICT

Multiple Product	Partial Products (examples are not complete)	Owner	Departments Involved
Video conference	• Prepare teleworking connection • Occupational health and safety requirements • Telework support	ICT help desk	• Facilities • ICT • Personnel
Meeting	• Room reservation • Overhead • Check in visitors • Catering • Information • Computer and projector	USD	• Facilities • ICT • Communications

3.4 Combining supply and demand

By bringing the demand together from the perspective of the customer and the supply from the perspective of the service providers (back office), the USD can realise two different goals:

1. To determine the best form of execution and delivery of the services; and
2. To standardise and simplify the processes between the USD and the back office.

Determining the best form of execution and delivery of the services

The level at which service is provided depends on the type of products and services; this will once more be dictated by scale and market. For example:

- A room reservation, the reservation of a laptop or an information brochure can be requested via the intranet.
- Special lunch provisions or help desk support can be requested via telephone or email.
- The ID card (employee card) must be picked up at the physical counter because a (digital) photo must be taken.
- A requested purchase advice is reported, and the USD forwards the question to the back office.

When allocating the products and services to specific service levels, the following principles are therefore used:

- Depending on the desired quality of service and the desired manner of handling, products and services are identified at a specific level.
- For cost control reasons, products and services should be supplied at the lowest possible service level. Thus, a service is delivered via the intranet as much as possible, providing relief to the second and third levels of service.
- Products and services delivered at a lower level must also be available at a higher level. For example, if the USD is not accessible via the network, some services must be available for request by telephone or at the physical desk. However, some services cannot be offered via the intranet

because the physical presence of the customer is required for these services (think of the ID card for which a passport photo is required).

Will the principle always hold?

It is not always possible to apply this principle: making everything at a lower level available at a higher level too. If a demand is handled directly via an intranet application, this service cannot be delivered in the event of a network failure. Consider, for example, the delivery of manuals or reports.

Standardise and simplify the processes between USD and back office

The level to which a product or service is allocated also depends on the customer demand. The nature of customer questions is related to product or service. There is a great diversity in products and services (information, problem reporting, requests for services or products, general advice, IT, communication advice, tendering, purchasing advice, network support, workplace design…). Generally speaking, concrete, tangible products can be discussed (room reservation, a new laptop, furniture) and certain more complex, less tangible services (purchasing advice, refurbishment). Each product or service can be characterised in performance terms such as number of hours, number of pieces of equipment, size etc.

For more strategic products and services, the customer needs both more support on the formulation of the service and more information about the nature of the product or service. For more operational products and services, the handling follows fixed procedures and the characteristics of the product or service are also more fixed.

It is the task of the USD to translate customer-specific needs and questions into as many standardised products, services and processes as possible. The better they are capable of doing this, and the better the underlying service organisation can handle these, the higher the added value of the USD in customer-oriented service provision.

The nature of customer demand dictates how it is handled, whether by the USD, the back office, or a combination of both. It is therefore important to make clear agreements about the handling of a request and about the role and responsibilities for both the USD and the back office. As mentioned earlier in this chapter, it is possible to make a distinction between basic and basic-plus services and tailor-made assignments. In the case of basic-plus services or custom orders, after the initial intake of the USD, a project leader is often responsible for the entire chain and also acts as the first point of contact for the customer during the process. With basic services, there is often a lack of clarity about who has responsibility or which role should be performed. From a customer's perspective, it is logical that the USD is the point of contact for any questions or complaints relating to customer demand. After all, if you contact the customer service of your provider to get an appointment, you may also need to call customer service to discuss your question or complaint if your initial request is not fulfilled.

However, this is not always self-evident. Often there is a referral to the back office without further role of the USD. This is then called the 'pass-through' role. If you want to prevent this and give the USD a clear position, it is important that there are clear agreements about role and responsibility. This does require a few things from both the USD staff and the back office staff. They will have to make agreements about which communication moments there are for a customer request and by whom.

CHAPTER 4: THE USD CUSTOMERS

Users of the USD should be considered customers for internal services. External users would be very surprised if they were not. Customers can be categorised in customer groups/ segments. One of which will inevitably be 'awkward…'. Each segment has its own attributes. The added value of the USD is that it can act as a central portal to any question on service products and services.

After reading this you will understand the implications of being a customer of the USD, what the added value of the USD is, and how customer groups can be segmented. With luck, you will also clearly understand the conflict and tension created between expectation and experience of the USD's quality of services.

4.1 We are all individuals

In supply-oriented service support customers have little or no influence on the service (this is the "you can get any colour you like so long as it's black" model). If service support reflects a demand-oriented organisation, then the customer's needs are taken as the starting point in the service provided.

There are three primary forces that stimulate this process. In the first place, these are the changed requirements imposed on business operations and therefore on service support. After all, enterprises must react faster and faster to developments in the environment. Flexibility in time, place and capacity are uppermost to remain competitive. The service support environment provides an important element of the conditions.

Just think of the changes that have taken place in workplace design, telephony and catering. On a more basic level, the nature of the standard workday has changed significantly. From twelve to two was the normal accepted opening time for taking lunch (and go back a few years, imbibing more than a few restorative alcoholic beverages…). Now the enterprise is embracing flexible hours, working wherever you want, paternity and maternity leave, 24 hour service in some instances and the opening hours (as well as facilities such as catering), have to be adjusted accordingly.

A second primary force is the emancipation of the customer. Customers are becoming more and more articulate and their needs are becoming increasingly individual. Some even use the word 'emancipate.' They are also better informed. The consequence is that they also demand more. In general, customers are looking for more ready-made and rapid solutions, lower costs and fewer problems with the use of goods and services. In other words, they demand higher added value. Prima donna bunch…

How often do we notice in our own enterprises that the standard device or the prescribed model of mobile phone no longer suffices? More choice that is adapted to the personal situation or taste is the need. External customers also require choices; rarely do they like multiple menu options offered on the phone that get in the way of speaking to a (possibly) real human.

Thirdly, technical innovations, particularly in the field of information technology, drive new services. Blockchain and the Internet of Things (IoT) will change things as dramatically as the iPhone and GPS.

The changes and the expanding options are expressed in the desire for more time and location independent work. As a result, the influence on the physical working environment is reduced because some people like to work from home, yet this causes the design of the digital work environment to increase. Every customer is unique and needs to be responded to. This requires serious adjustment and the need to be flexible from the service organisation and therefore from the service manager.

External customers also demand access from varied locations; geography is not a barrier and neither is the excuse of design limitations; design for access means access for everyone, regardless of their physical or mental capacities.

4.2 The user as a service customer

In the first chapter we talked about the confusion of concepts that can occur when clients of the service organisation, in particular the USD, are discussed. The concept of a 'customer' usually assumes that the customer is someone who pays and is free in their choices about the nature and scope of the services that are requested. In general, this is not the case for the enterprise's internal employees. The choices about the level and nature of the services are made by a small group of employees in the enterprise that manage the budget for services, or exercise control over it. Therefore, a distinction is made between clients (the budget holders) and the users (those who purchase services).

By and large, it would be a surprise if external customers were not paying, even where some charges are hidden. A contract with a major service supplier might be utilised through a service catalogue and your enterprise might have negotiated various pricing options, but the individual may never see these costs. For example, do you know what you pay to use Microsoft Word or PowerPoint?

Clients, customers and consumers

For now, the distinction between clients and users is sufficient. In *chapter 17*, the distinction is further clarified when the USD is discussed in relation to the service organisations' control cycle. From the perspective that the service organisation brings supply and demand together, three parties are distinguished on the demand side of the service organisation:

1. General management (client or owner);
2. Customers (customers or clients); and
3. Users (consumers or customers).

Certainly, users influence service quality and their behaviour often determines the way in which the service organisation acts. For example, if a user is dissatisfied with a change, it can and often will be reversed. However, users should also understand that they cannot choose the colour of the furniture like they can in their own homes, and that recliners with built-in TVs are not in the catalogue. Critically, the way in which this sort of limitation or refusal is communicated will determine a user's reaction: If users are not helped well or are treated rudely, they will always look for alternatives, possibly outside of the enterprise.

The service offer of the service organisation comprises combinations of concrete physical products and the more elusive services. A characteristic of the services is that both employees of the USD and customers (users) of a service, play a major role in the way in which users experience service, and thus also the quality of the products and services. That is why there are several arguments that claim ALL users of services should be regarded as customers. It is therefore necessary to talk about the USD as the main entrance of the customers for the services.

4.3 The added value of the USD

The USD is the visible access to the service organisation. The strength of the USD is that it takes over the demand from customers, or at least can adequately inform customers and turn product-driven services from the back office into customer-oriented services. The various users and clients must have the idea at all levels within the enterprise that the USD matters, that it helps them to carry out their work and will solve the problem that they (think) they have. A characteristic of the customer perspective on support services is that customers do need them; that said, they also do not want to spend time working with support because it distracts them too much from their own workload.

Support becomes a necessary evil that customers use to achieve their own goals. For a client who wants to arrange meetings they do not want to spend any time talking about needs; there are expectations that support will ensure that a meeting can be arranged at the desired location, visitors have easy access, tele-conferencing will work, the room is clean and the coffee is ready without fuss. Another example is when a new colleague starts. In this instance, an access pass, ID card, workplace and user account are arranged so that the new colleague can actually start work on the first day. This is also true where these services are obtained through third parties.

The knowledge of marketing helps us to better understand the nature of the relationship between customer and service provider. Schiffman and his colleagues studied the behaviour of customers with the aim of realising a successful relationship between customer and service provider.[3] Their research notes that at least four conditions must be met to achieve this result:

1. Added value for the customer;
2. A high level of customer satisfaction;
3. Strong client confidence; and
4. Customer retention (a structure that ensures that the customer comes back).

1. Added value for the customer

The added value for the customer, sometimes called 'customer value', can be considered as the ratio between their perceived or experienced benefits (economic, functional and psychological) and the resources (money, time and effort) that are available to obtain these benefits. A good example is the willingness of customers to pay more in a Michelin star restaurant because they have more money than sense. Sorry, that should read because expectation about the experience is better. They want to pay less at the chip shop because they have lower expectations here, for example about the quality of the food, the service, and the fact that Trevor and his Dad never wash their aprons.

In the case of the USD, customers want to know that they can in any and every case receive a satisfactory answer. This can also mean a 'no', but the way this is told (frameworks or guidelines) is important for acceptance ('No idea', 'try somewhere else' or 'take a wild guess' are sometimes perceived as a little offhand). Situations in which internal customers experience that they are dealing with a USD that has little knowledge or opportunities to really help, mean that from the perspective of customers the added value of the USD is low.

2. A high level of customer satisfaction

The experience of internal customers after taking the service must be in balance with their expectations. In the example of restaurants, customers have completely different expectations of satisfaction at a

[3] Schiffman, L.G., Kanuk, L.L., & Wisenblit, J, *Consumer Behavior*, French's Forest, NSW: Pearson Australia, 2010.

Michelin star restaurant, than at McDonalds. The experience divided by the expectation is greater than, or equal to 1. If the experience is equal to the expectation, the customer is 'normally satisfied'. If you exceed expectations, customers will experience good service. If the experience is less than expected, customers will experience poor service and dissatisfied customers will complain.

For the USD, it is not enough to promise something or just say 'computer says no'. Promises made by the USD must be fulfilled. That is why the USD and the back office must cooperate effectively. Of course, it helps when customers are (or can be) made aware of the quality to be delivered.

The reality is that the USD is in a conflict. It does not determine all of the criteria for services. Should general management decide that something less luxurious than heated and cooled seating in the company car must be selected, then often the USD will be seen by customers as responsible for such a wicked and unreasonable decision. Communication and transparency are therefore extremely important. Internal customers understand if something is not possible, as long as they are informed well in time. Unless it is the latest iPhone, then of course that is just not acceptable.

3. Strong client confidence

Closely connected with customer satisfaction is customer confidence. The challenge for gaining a strong customer trust is to maintain confidence in the enterprise in its products and services by providing a consistently positive experience. If you retain the trust of the customers, you lay the foundation for a long-term relationship with which loyalty is strong, even if things go less smoothly. If the USD has consistently worked on customer satisfaction from the start, and that does not disappoint, customer confidence will increase accordingly, especially with active users ('heavy users', such as heads of business offices and secretaries). A relationship of trust with the USD is important for a strong image of the service organisation. These users must always be confirmed in their trust with the USD.

4. Customer retention

The customer needs to find that most products and services are clearly defined, easily available and working. With regard to counter services, that the entrance door is open, the light is on and the coffee machine is working. The service company, internal or external, does not receive any applause for this. The trick is to exceed customer expectations, which the customer experiences as added value. This is difficult enough, because you do not get many opportunities to exceed expectations.

Some examples and opportunities are:

- Taking care of a large meeting with absolutely no customer issues regarding network reliability.
- Organising and executing a contingency plan for IT testing with zero disruption to operations.
- By surpassing expectation, trust is created and customer retention is simple.

The USD must be a reliable partner in communication for the customer and must therefore have the correct information and the mandate to make agreements or commitments.

Customer retention not only stands and falls with the mandate of the USD, but also with the customer-oriented and approachable attitude of the USD staff. If customers like to contact the USD and the USD staff knows their business, confidence increases.

4.4 Customer groups

In order to build up the customer relationship as well as possible, it is necessary to have appropriate knowledge of the different customer types. This also means that there are internal customers who have power and mandate, not so much because of their function and formal position, but because of their informal knowledge and expertise and their influence. In many enterprises, this informal group determines whether or not matters really come together. When these customer groups call on the USD, it is important to respond adequately. Politically influential customer groups should always be on the radar. In government bodies in the UK, the letter from MPs sent on behalf of a disgruntled citizen is a very good example.

Customer groups can be described in two ways:

1. By role or function; or
2. According to the nature of the work environment.

Customer groups by role or function

The following customer types (see *Table 4.1*) can be described for the service organisation: the internal employee of the enterprise, the internal specialist, secretariats, contacts, managers, back offices and management organisation. You can use the colours (green/red) to indicate whether a contact channel is available. Of course, depending on the tasks of the USD the list needs to be adapted to, for example, external customers.

Key:

P	Phone
@	Email
I	Internet/intranet
D	Desk
(green)	Channel is available
(red)	Channel is not available

Table 4.1: Customer Groups According to the Nature of the Work Environment (example)

Type of Customer	Contact Frequency	Attribute	Contact Channel (P@ID)	Focus	Particularities
Employees	Low	Generic support.	P @ I D	Do not know the specifications of the service. Above all, they want the problem to be solved.	Make relatively little use of the USD. Handling according to schedule.
Specialists	Low	Specific support on specific services.	P @ I D	Provide the technical background to the service (sometimes better than the USD).	Make relatively little use of the USD. Processing is urgent.
Secretaries	High	Generic with a focus on services relating to things like meetings and visitors.	P @ I D	Know the enterprise through and through. Can be ambassadors of the USD.	Make extensive use of the USD. Handling according to schedule.
Official contacts	High	Specific support by one named service.	P @ I D	Know the specifications of the appointed service. Know the backgrounds of the services often better than the USD does.	Make extensive use of the USD. Handling according to schedule.
Managers	High	General support.	P @ I D	Do not know the specifications of the service. Above all, want the problem to be solved.	Make relatively little use of the USD. Processing is urgent.
Back offices	High	Explanation of complaints, preferences, information, malfunctions and feedback status.	P @ I D	Search for the best solutions together. No promises from the USD that the back office cannot deliver.	Make extensive use of the USD. Processing is urgent.
Retained organisations/ intelligent customer/ demand-supply organisation	Low	Specific questions about quality service.	P @ I D	Know the specifications of the service. Above all, want information about the quality of service.	Make relatively little use of the USD. Processing is urgent.

A classification of customer groups can also be made on the basis of the different working methods and environments within which work is done. In *Figure 4.1*, customer groups are made visible along two axes: 'knowledge based' (or procedural) work, and work that occurs at a fixed location or peripatetic location.

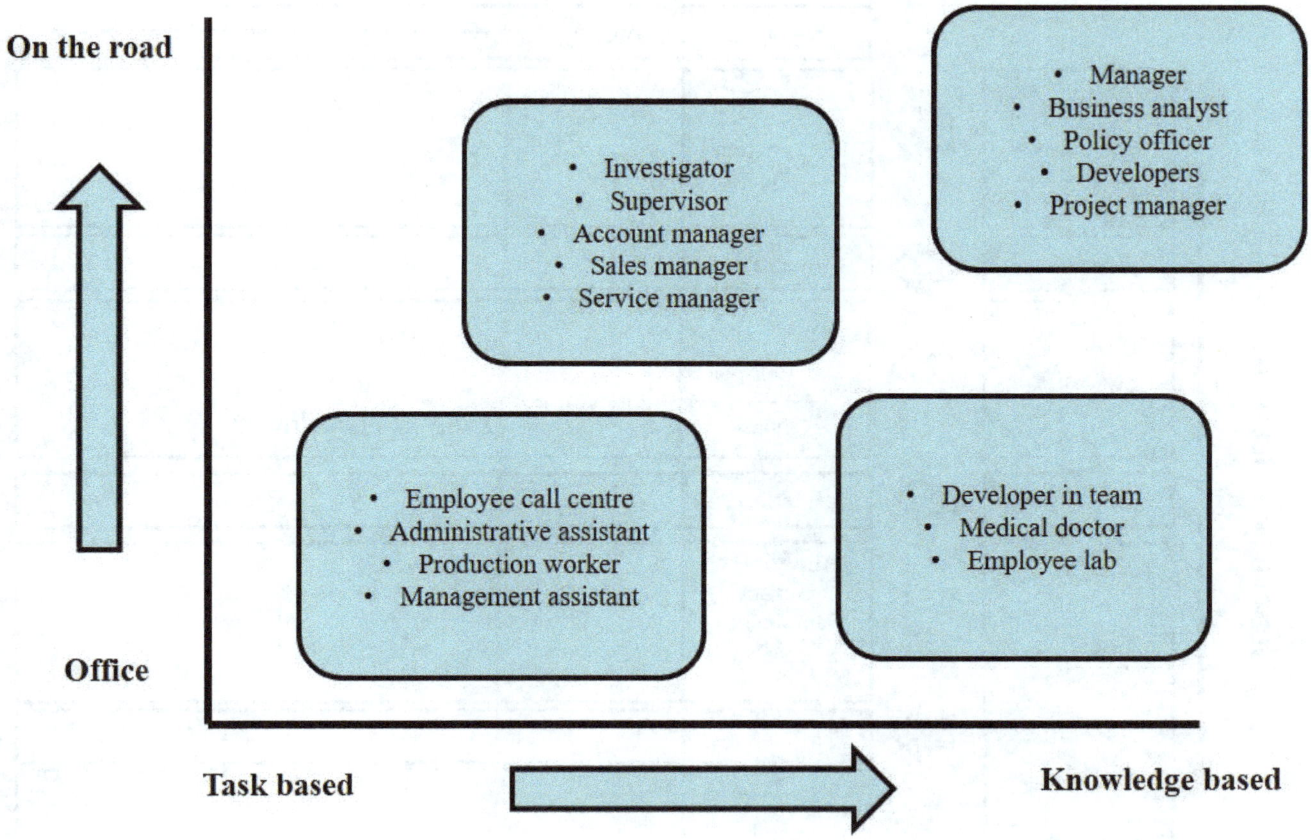

Figure 4.1: Customer groups according to the nature of the work environment

4.5 Insight into what your customer wants: the customer journey

How will you understand your customer or user? Although there are many different approaches, we favour an adapted approach that was first proposed by G Lynn Shostack, and later explored by others.[4] It will help you structure, design and align all activities and transactions as they unfold over time starting when a customer knocks on the USD-door. A standard service blueprint approach does not exist, but in essence there is an agreement on two aspects that are always clarified: the user journey over time and the main activities and processes in a front-back office process.

Use the generic service delivery process to analyse a request. A request is made to the USD (front office), that in cooperation with the back office leads to service delivery. Service delivery is of course being developed with output in mind. Between the three there are interactions that must be explored to understand what interfaces will be needed (portal, desk, agent, automated procedure, etc.). A certain part of the service delivery will be visible to users that make a request for a particular service. In the blueprint method, this is called the 'line of visibility'.

In *Figure 4.2* we show the blueprint template:

[4] Shostack, G.L., "Designing Services that Deliver", *Harvard Business Review*, January-February 1984, p. 133-139, 1984.

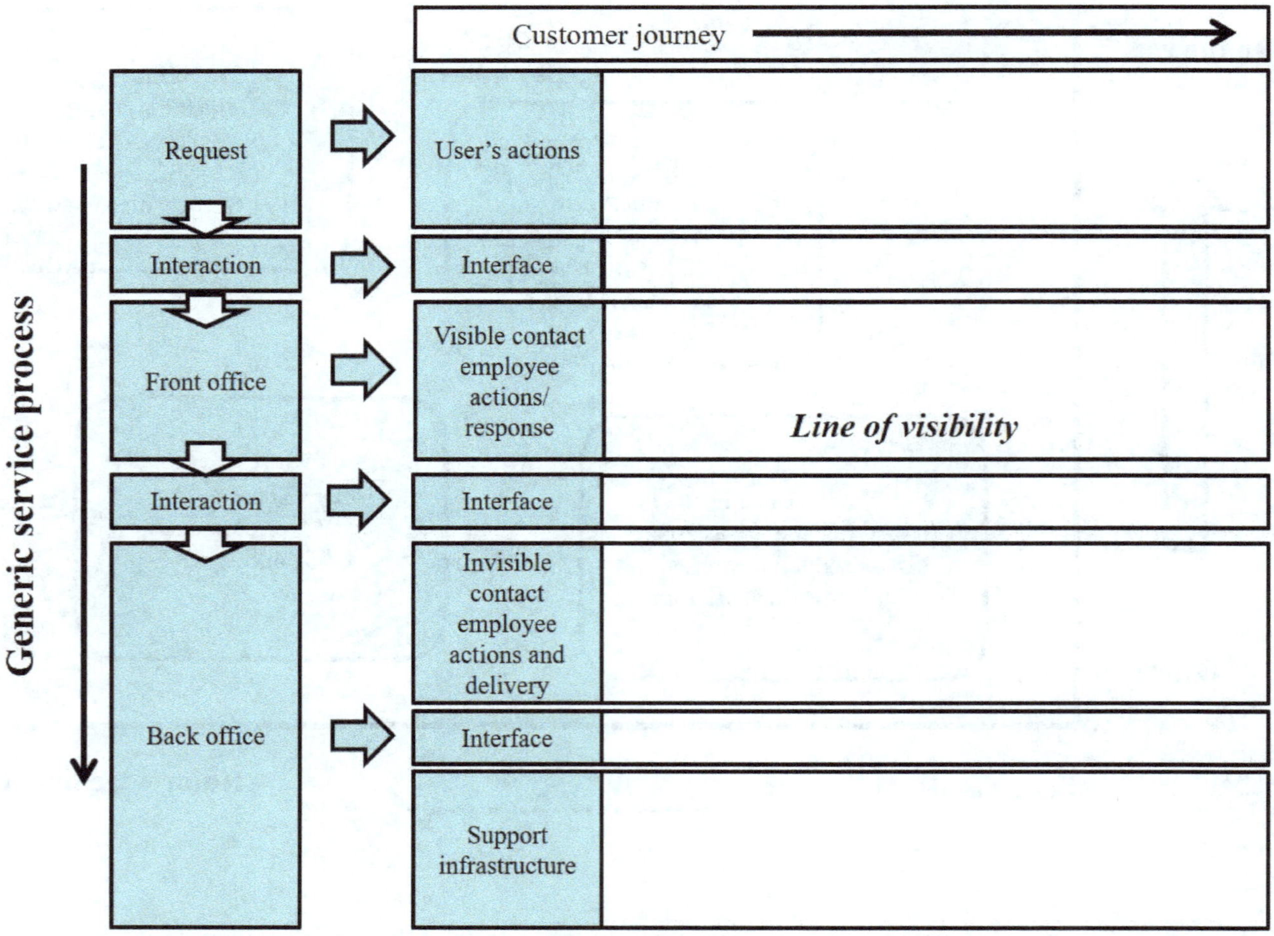

Figure 4.2: Service blueprint template in business service design

On the vertical axis, the timeline, or more specifically; the customer journey is plotted. Services have different stages: awareness (a call to action), the start of the action and a road of trials, reaching of the goal, and afterwards (return to the ordinary world). Thus, in many respects they are like stories. This provides a simple framework that helps the participants structure the user journey and experiences, and helps them to understand and perhaps even influence, their behaviour.

Table 4.2: Questions You Can Ask to Understand the Customer Journey

Stage of The Customer Journey	Questions You Can Ask
Awareness (the call to action)	Where do the users come from? What experiences have they had with the offered services prior to engaging with the USD? And what are their expectations? Think about customers' experiences and requirements.
Start of the action	How did the USD engagement begin, and how do users approach the start of the service?
Road of trials	What sort of experiences will the user have? What are the possible obstacles? What issues and failures might occur? What is the level of complexity and what is the lead time? Ultimately, what happens to the customer?

Stage of The Customer Journey	Questions You Can Ask
Reaching the goal	How do customers get what they want?
Afterwards (return to business as usual)	Is there aftercare? Remember, past customers can be future customers, and customers will tell many others about their experiences. Good reputations spread quickly, so analyse feedback.

It is up to you where to start but the most common starting point is when somebody reports at the USD, and from there you work on the actual understanding of the request, process and delivery, building up the high-level service design between the different layers that can be distinguished between the generic service delivery processes. You should begin with having a possible set of outputs and user mandatory and desirable requirements in mind. You probably need to brainstorm and think about different possibilities. Sometimes you can continue based on assumptions about given platforms or situations. You make a choice and start sketching the service activities. Remember you can always change or start anew. Starting for the first time with a new design invariably is trial and error.

Having settled on the initial concepts, you must flesh out the core. You work from the inside to the outside and build up the other layers with specific activities and processes. When the service design of the USD process is relatively simple, you may finish within one or two hours; however, innovative or complex situations need much more time.

Of course, when coming up with issues that should be part of the design but do not fit, create a waiting room, parking lot, or whatever name you wish to give it. In the 'waiting room' there will be any information that you want or need to use in the final design but are currently struggling to clarify or place.

For a simple and effective approach, you should make sure to use participants to help structure, investigate and analyse the USD service delivery process. That will make it easier to understand the USD customers and users and to implement improvements.

4.6 A few words about quality of service

For a long time, quality was mainly related to the characteristics of a product or service. Quality-enhancing measures were mainly aimed at limiting expenditure and improving the quality of products and services. Today, it is established that a heavier and more intelligent use of the service organisation components is necessary (see also Boomsma & Van Borrendam;[5] Grönroos).[6] The services of the USD generally come about in close cooperation with the customers. The characteristics of the service require that a customer often participates in the service process. This is how customer-oriented thinking was introduced within service organisation. As a result, quality can be translated into meeting the expectations of the customer. This 'demand-oriented approach' within the service organisation means

[5] Boomsma, S. & Borrendam, A. van, *Kwaliteit van dienstverlening*, Alphen aan den Rijn: Samsom, 2000.

[6] Grönroos, C., *Service Management and Marketing: A Customer Relationship Management Approach.* Chichester/Hoboken, NJ: John Wiley & Sons, 2000.

that the users are regarded as customers and that their service needs are proactively translated into the service offer.

This also means that the quality of the service is not only determined by the physical (or technical) quality of the product or service, but also by the way in which the service is provided (treatment, understanding, expectation, lies, etc.). This is termed 'functional quality'. The quality of service perceived by the customer arises from the difference between their expectation and experience. Grönroos has done a lot of research into this and has proposed a scheme that shows how the customer's perception of service quality is created.[7] *Figure 4.3* outlines the situation of the USD.

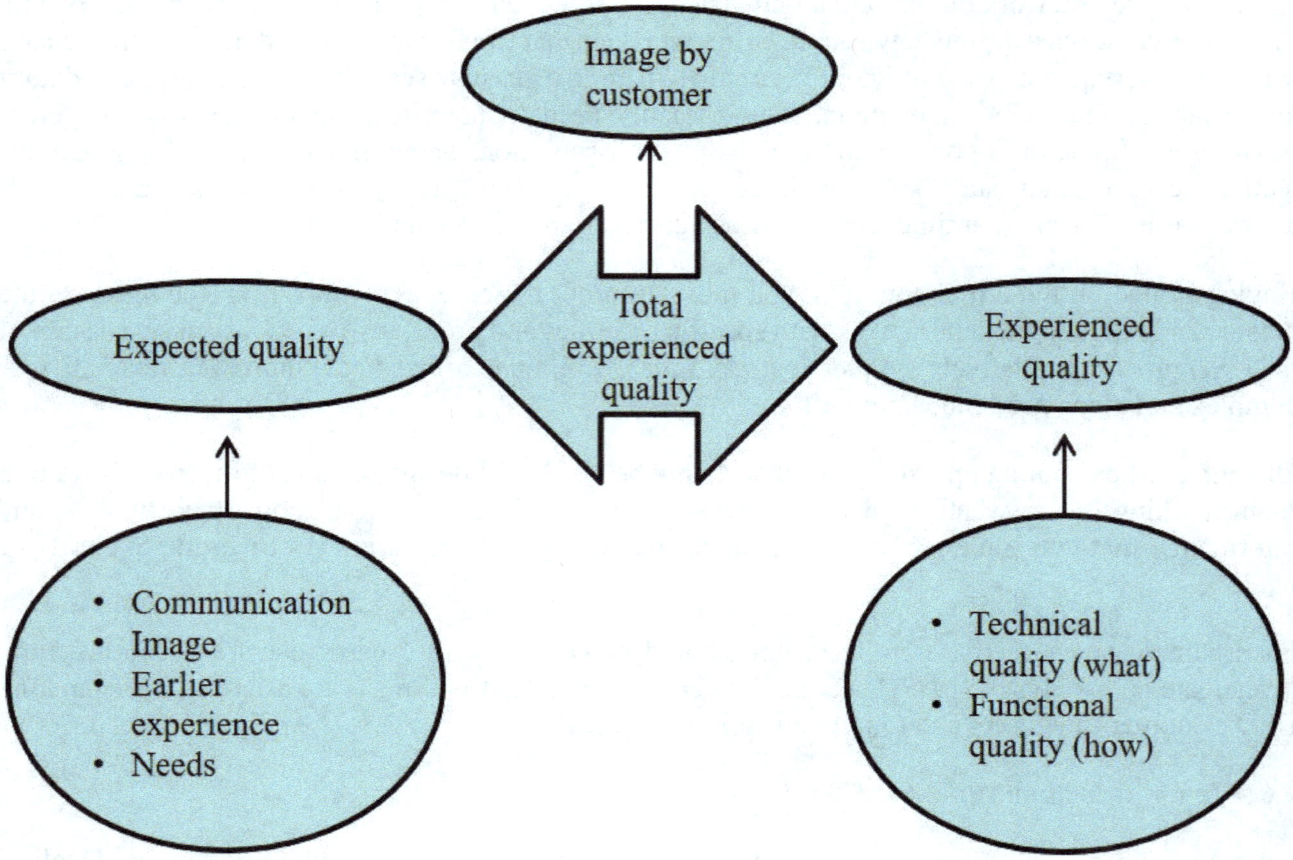

Figure 4.3: The total perceived quality of the service via the USD (after Grönroos, 2000)

The customer's image of the total perceived quality results from the comparison between the expected quality and the perceived quality. The experienced quality comprises the technical quality of a product or service and its functional quality. The technical quality is the outcome or the result of the use of the product. Let's use meeting rooms again as an example: the actual location with associated facilities has been arranged, visitors have been notified and the request has been handled correctly.

---

[7] Grönroos, C., *Service Management and Marketing: A Customer Relationship Management Approach*, Chichester/Hoboken, NJ: John Wiley & Sons, 2000.

In addition, there is also the functional quality. This is determined by the interaction between the USD employee and, later, the back office employees and the customer; it includes the way people have been spoken to, the behaviour or the manner of the interaction, and so on. This also applies to the accessibility of, for example, the internal service site or the telephone service.

Example: Effect of bad experience

According to marketing knowledge, the rule of thumb is that bad experiences are discussed an average of eleven times. Good experiences are considered 'normal' and are discussed an average of three times. If one in 20 employees has a bad experience, then the bad news in an enterprise of 120 employees is retold 66 times (120/20 × 11). The effect of a bad experience should not be underestimated. (Shakespeare said it first, "The evil that men do lives after them / the good is oft interred with their bones"[8] – and he was only worried about the town crier and the odd peasant able to read the proclamation nailed on a wall).

A great deal of research has been done into the perceived quality of customer service and how this can be measured. One of the best known is the ServQual instrument of Zeithaml, Parasuraman and Berry,[9] specially developed to be able to measure quality in the broadest sense of the word. Using this instrument, the various aspects that influence the final image for the customer can be mapped. In *chapter 9*, aspects of the quality of services for the call centre function (second level of service) are identified and derived using the ServQual method.

4.7 About customer expectations

What expectations can an internal customer of the USD have? If the expectation is not realistic, for example much too high, then the USD can never excel. This is also one of the difficulties of providing services. The service company has many products and services that are also known as 'dis-satisfiers' (as opposed to 'satisfiers'). Products or services that function as satisfiers have characteristics that lead to positive reactions from customers simply because their expectations are low. Not unsurprisingly, products and services that are dis-satisfiers do not have these characteristics.

Services that do not function as satisfiers are rarely appreciated; think of office cleaning: no one notices when the office is clean (and free from mouse droppings and crisps), only when it is not clean. Hence, we call them 'dis-satisfiers'. Nevertheless, the USD can exert much influence on the expected quality by communicating well, building a positive image within the enterprise and being able to deliver its services as well as possible. However, leaving 'NO MOUSE ****' signs all around might not be the best way to do this. Keep in mind that the USD has a signalling function for account managers and management when the service fails to deliver what has been agreed.

---

[8] Shakespeare, William, *Julius Caesar*.

[9] Zeithaml, V., Parasuraman, A. & Berry, L.L., *Delivering Quality Service: Balancing Customer Perceptions and Expectations*, New York: Free Press, 1990.

Example: Hospitality and the USD

If you exceed the expectations of the customer, you are actually engaged in hospitality. Hospitality is seen as an important part of service management. Not only external customers must be received in a hospitable manner, but internal employees also deserve a high level of service. Attitudes of employees to customers and service are central. The employees of the USD, as the faculty of the service organisation, have an important role and give immediate meaning to hospitality in practice.

In addition, the requirements and wishes of customers are constantly changing. Improvement of services leads to appreciation in the first instance. However, habituation soon arises and requirements are often adjusted (usually upwards…). Nevertheless, based on analyses of customer feedback, customer satisfaction surveys and customer experiences (see also Cleveland, 2012),[10] it is known which dimensions contribute to a high customer expectation.

These are:

1. **Be accessible:** The service should be easily accessible, waiting times short, opening hours practical and logical (e.g. during lunch hours or in the morning); physical and virtual accessibility should be arranged through multiple channels; service levels should match; response times should be fast; and 24 hour service and self-service options should be available.
2. **Be polite:** This means friendly, with respect and taking into account the feelings and the perspective of the customer. The need to repeat information, transfer unclear information on the phone by a computer (interactive voice responses) and hard to find phone numbers, URLs and email addresses, should be avoided as much as possible. Think of the failure of the notme.gov website.
3. **Be responsive:** Ensure that contacts are handled adequately and that as much as possible can be dealt with directly at the request of the customer. In concrete terms, this means having knowledge of the status of deliveries, of previously made agreements, of changes, purchases and the like.
4. **Be fast:** Speed has to do with the service level, with the response times to correspondence, and also with being aware of the most recent interactions (independent of the channel through which the interactions have proceeded). Response times to emails of 24 hours or more cannot really be justified anymore.
5. **Provide well-trained staff:** Knowledge and skills of the USD and back office employees should be adequate. Employees should know what they are talking about. Promises made should be fulfilled.
6. **Tell the customer what to expect:** 'Being clear' is an important tool when it comes to managing customer expectations. Information about delivery time and correspondence receipt confirmations, in which for example processing times are indicated, are appreciated. Such communication should not be overlooked.

---

[10] Cleveland, B., *Call Centre Management on Fast Forward: Succeeding in the New Era of Customer Relationships*, Colorado Springs, CO: ICMI Press, 2012.

7. **Make and deliver on promises:** Ensure that agreements, stated response times and the like are complied with. Focus processes and support systems in such a way that the promises can be realised. Do not make commitments that are difficult or impossible to realise. Ensure that processes are measurable, in such a way that on the basis of insight into process performance real commitments can be made, and it also becomes clear what needs to be worked on in order to better meet the requirements of customers.
8. **Do it right the first time and be reliable:** Prevent customers from having to 'repeat' enquiries and make 'one stop shopping' and 'once-and-done' a reality.
9. **Monitor the contacts:** Respect the customer's request by carefully monitoring each contact, for example, in the processing of requests and of information obtained from the contact, in the fulfilment of appointments and in the welcoming of new customers in the form of service contacts or calls.
10. **Trade with integrity and responsibility:** Corporate social responsibility or sustainable business has become an important requirement of customers with respect to their suppliers. Corporate values are the basis of socially accepted positioning. Ultimately, however, it is the contact with customers who have to make this positioning an important part. Mistakes can easily be punished mercilessly through, for example, online consumer forums and other virtual communities.

CHAPTER 5: FROM DESIGN TO REALITY

This chapter explains the concept of the USD as an integral front office for the service organisation. We also discuss the design and development of improvements to the USD, for example the hiring and training of staff.

Five phases are posited, each with a number of steps. We begin with ambition and the necessary tasks, and end with an operating USD. After reading this chapter, the reader should understand the approach to creating, developing and improving a USD.

5.1 Action plan: from design to realisation

An action plan structures thinking and development. You can compare this with building a house. Not the USD, for sure we cannot compare a USD to a house, except for the sleeping occupants, we mean just the principles. When building a house, you would not start with the roof when you have not built the foundations; (unless you are a mollusc, or maybe a tree dweller, or Salvador Dali). First, you need to establish the goal of the USD and what products and services will be offered and then you can commence building. To design, build or develop a USD you will need to take the following steps:

Ambition and tasks

1. Formulate goals and mission

Tune USD and back office

2. Document an inventory of products, services and resolution processes
3. Document an inventory of common customer questions and needs
4. Identify any matches (or obvious omissions) between customer demand and products and services
5. Understand and synchronise USD and back office activities and processes
6. Select channels and technologies
7. Coordinate the current USD activities to ensure they are efficient

Design

8. Manage, design and organise the USD

Building and construction

9. House the USD
10. Build the information function
11. Build the virtual USD
12. Design the call centre functionality
13. Organise account management
14. Organise the USD human resources

In use

15. Go live with the USD

An optional item 16 is 'find someone to blame if it all goes wrong'.

Figure 5.1 shows the action plan of the different tasks (phases and steps) to build or develop a USD.

5.2 Step 1 – Ambition and tasks

1. Formulating goals and mission

The design of the USD begins with the strategic principles. As we have said, front office to back office principles are the Bible; however, that should not restrict choices regarding ambitions of the USD. The mission and goals of the USD must be carefully formulated.

A mission statement needs to be simple, short and easy to understand (and not nicked from the Internet).

Here are some questions to help you formulate the mission:

- What are we good at?
- What is our reason for existence?
- Who are our commissioners, users and customers?
- Which competencies and capacities are unique to us?

The mission should be described in goal statements. The goals should concern the quality of service and creating an efficient and effective operating organisation. These goals set a frame (or blueprint) for the final design of the USD. The goals will be used to populate a strategic plan that will focus on necessary resources (people and capabilities). Of course, the mission of the USD should fit with the mission and goals of the enterprise. It is of little value to have a USD which focuses on customer intimacy when the enterprise is only interested in operational excellence. The mission and goals of the enterprise will in a perfect world exist somewhere and can be used to ensure some form of business alignment. Or for a laugh, you can tell the business that the IT framework/model/method *xyz* is an instrument of business alignment. For a real hoot try telling them *xyz* is an instrument of business integration. Always good for a laugh…

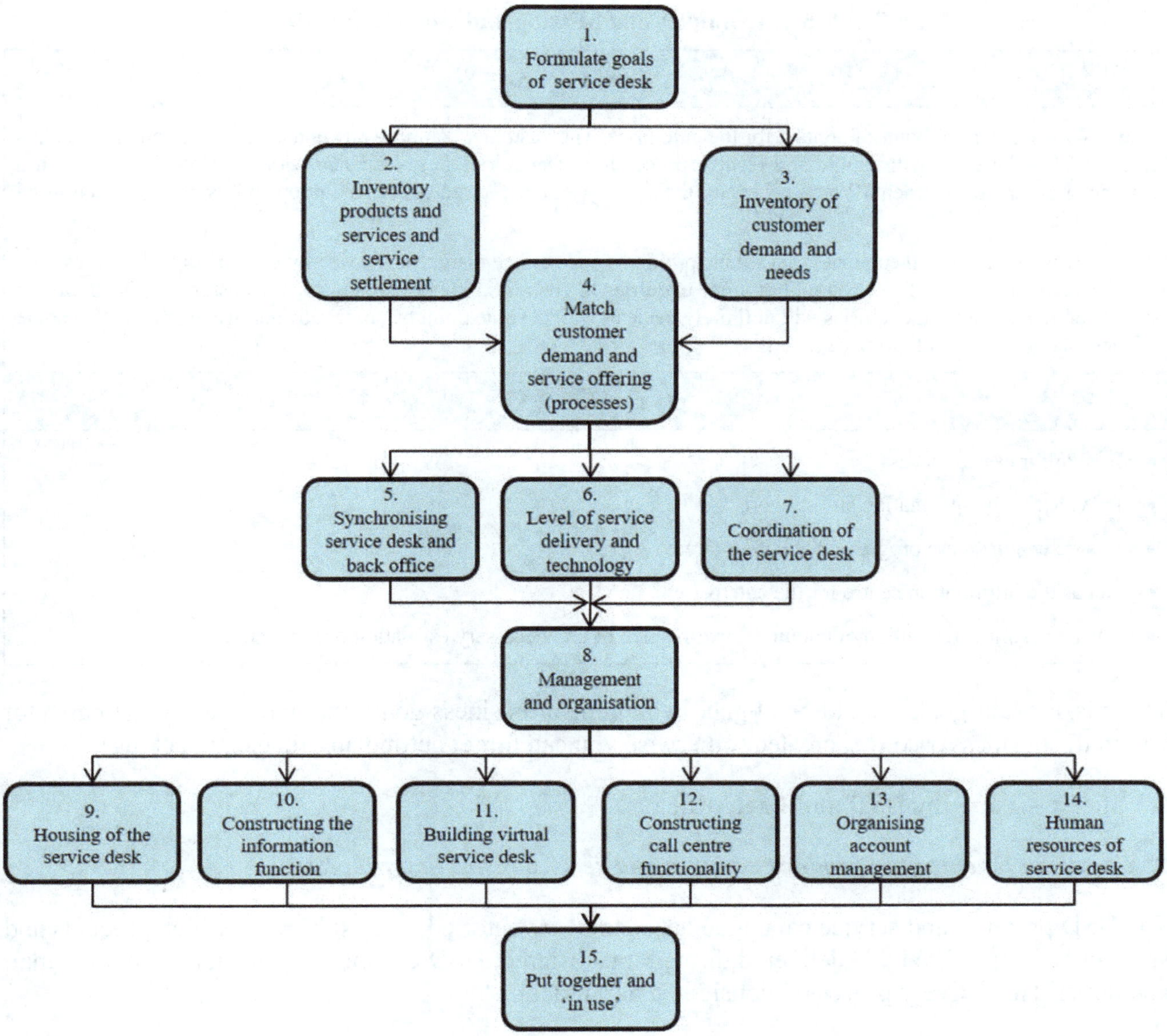

Figure 5.1: Design, build and development of the USD

Table 5.1: Examples of USD Principles

USD Principles
• Opening times are matched to user attendance hours • Enquiries are easy to make • Call centre is accessible • There are clear channels for redirecting enquiries • A products and service catalogue is available

In this phase in the process, you should also think explicitly about the costs and finances: investment costs, maintenance costs and budgets (including, for example, details of the depreciation of equipment). Costing data will be part of a business case for the USD.

Table 5.2: Examples of a Mission and Goals of a USD

Mission of a USD
The USD is the central point of contact for the enterprise. The customer can pose any and all enquiries and complaints to the USD. The USD will handle and resolve processing of enquiries in accordance with principles described in a service or contract agreement. Where necessary the enquiry will be redirected for resolution and its progress monitored by the USD. The USD takes care of all enquiries, questions, problems and service disruptions posed by customers and ensures they are correctly processed. The USD will monitor enquiries to ensure timely processing for the customer. (Or, if we are being completely honest, enquiries will definitely be dealt with at some point by somebody and we guarantee that some of them will be dealt with properly…or not).
Goals of the USD
• Design for ease of access • Provide timely information and support • Ensure enquiries are progressed and monitored • Act as the information centre for the enterprise • Ensure seamless resolution of enquiries, irrespective of any necessary escalation or redirection

The mission and goals should be aligned with general business goals and agreed to by the party for whom the business case was created (otherwise you can forget getting any financial backing).

5.3 Step 2 – Tune the USD and back office

2. Create an inventory of product, services and service resolution processes

The USD products and service catalogue needs to be inventoried. It must be clear which products and services will be offered and delivered through the different USD channels (intranet, call centre, email and desk). The delivery process is considered a transaction.

The inventoried products and services need to be described from the demand perspective. This means it must be clear what the product or service comprises, for whom it is available, and what its purpose is. Descriptions should be short, clear and simple (or you can follow the hilarious ideas in some IT best practices and imagine that you are impressing someone out in the real world). Service levels, conditions, possible costs and lead times must also be determined and published. A products and service catalogue for the enterprise should be made available.

The mission and goals must be clear about which tasks should be processed by the USD and which by the back office. This is the resolution process sometimes known as 'service settlement'. The service settlement for a product or service can be defined as the extent to which a product or service will be executed, delivered and monitored by the USD.

From a quality of service perspective, the highest level of service settlement involves the USD, meaning that all customer demands will be handled and executed by the USD. This of course is not always possible, as specialist tasks from the back office sometimes need to be executed, or specialists need to be consulted. Sometimes it is necessary that customers need direct contact with the back office, though where possible this should be avoided to ensure that the process of resolution is fully controlled. In such circumstances, the USD should monitor such direct contact.

3. Create an inventory of common customer questions and needs

The scope of customer demands must be assessed, analysed and documented. The end to end process of many activities should be known to ensure efficiency; an example is that the entire process of on-boarding new employees should be documented (though kept hidden), so that the new employee is fully confused because they must visit several offices to get everything they need (account, access, phone, laptop etc.). Ideally, make sure they think they have everything they need but ensure they have to take a long walk to a well hidden office to get an ID. Apologies we of course meant that the procedures should not be hidden; we were thinking of our old office...When procedures are clear and efficiently organised, they can also be automated.

Steps 2 and 3 can be amalgamated. Based on the results of these two steps the products and services can be clearly described and the descriptions should be business focused. The delivery channels should be clear, as should indications regarding expectations about delivery time. For example, a call might be answered within 30 seconds; but depending on the nature of the call or enquiry it should be clear that settlement/resolution times will vary. Listing call/enquiry types will assist in the understanding for customers. This step could be considered as an assessment of customer expectations and what the USD can commit to providing.

4. Identify any matches (or obvious omissions) between customer demand and products and services

In step 4, the products and service catalogue inventory of step 2 and the scoping of customer demands of step 3 are connected. This leads to a complete understanding of the needs of customers and the offerings of the USD, from request to delivery. Based on this analysis, it will be possible to formulate standard solutions to specific needs and to create different service categories for customers, or to define different customer groups depending on their needs. In other words, you have your routing plan.

When there is only one type of customer, the connection of both perspectives is simple. But when there are many customer groups the connections will be more nuanced. The overall USD design for selective connection is determined by the services available to the different customer groups. This could mean that the USD has to create specialised desks for enquiries relating to, for example, foreign travelling, different forms of patient care and owners of lease cars. It may also necessitate different authorisation processes for different services; for example, there may be different rules about who can use the intranet for room reservations and room services.

5. Understand and synchronise USD and back office activities and processes

Successful processing of customer enquiries requires solid synchronisation and cooperation between the USD and the back office. In this step, you will execute the routing plan and define the work procedures that will achieve this goal. Having identified the intake processes and channels for enquiries and how resolution through to service settlement will be achieved, the necessary components of the USD and back office can be defined and organised.

Selection of service catalogue products, services and the definition of service settlement in work processes provide guidance for the division of authority and responsibilities between the USD and back office. Coordination activities to be defined include points of contact in the back office, structure of meetings, policy and principles, protocols etc.

Procedures might need to be different in the USD to those in the back office. The enterprise may be offering integrated products and services (e.g. onboarding), and these so-called plural services might require a request to be channelled in different ways to obtain multiple products and services. Initial processing (and delivery) may begin in the USD though completion is in the back office. The USD however is responsible for monitoring the entire transaction and for its overall delivery.

6. Select channels and technologies

IT applications make it possible to fine tune the service offerings and processing. The organisational structures can be made more flexible because of IT. Depending on investment and process design, the entirety of the delivery logistics can also be automated. IT is an enabler, but be aware that simply buying software does not guarantee either an efficient process, delivery or even cost savings. Unless the design is complete and the processes already simplified and working well, your automated services will not satisfy customer demands.

So, IT makes the USD more accessible (with the Internet and intranet) but it is not a substitute for failing to design the services in detail. IT efficiency will be limited by the enterprise's ambition, as well as by the efficiency of any intake systems and databases (containing information about procedures, status, products and policies).

When it comes to automation, think carefully before buying and be aware of total costs.

7. Coordination of the current USD activities to ensure they are efficient

In this phase, it is necessary to determine the responsibility of the USD regarding overall delivery and monitoring of service delivery. The pre-conditions for final authority and responsibility of coordination are, or should be derived from, the mission and goals of the USD as well as by the choice of structure and position of the USD in the enterprise. From the inventory made about products and services and accompanying processes, responsibility and authority often can be clarified, allocated and assigned.

5.4 Step 3 – Design

8. Management and organisation

The results of all of your investigations and designs should now be brought together to build the organisational structure of the USD. You will need to work out your staffing: How many people you need depends on how much work they have to do, how long it takes to complete the work and the number of hours they are working.

The most basic question to answer is that of necessity; work should be necessary to achieve a goal. Once that need is established how should necessary work be organised, what responsibility does it carry (leading to establishing a hierarchy of authorities), and how many people are required to get things done? This in turn depends on the USD goals, how the different components should be organised, quality of service, how the USD is intended to operate. Is it only a point of information or does it have total control over all operational service deliveries? Is account management part of the function and if so, is it integrated in the USD?

Once you know the scope, focus on the effort; once you know all of the tasks, figure out how long they will take, remember that no one outside a sweatshop works eight hours a day. Then you need to factor in things like vacation and training, as well as what the supervising structure will be. Ambition may be beyond capability (or funds), so you might need to compromise. You might benefit from a plan for growth rather than starting big.

When you have completed this step, you can finally start building the USD.

5.5 Step 4 – Building and construction

9. Housing of the USD

Housing of the USD concerns the physical location, but it is predicated on the overall design. One or more desks? Headsets? Nice shiny iPhones? Many requirements will be the result from the analysis and choices in earlier steps, but which can you afford, and which do you really need?

Pay attention to marketing the services within your enterprise (how do you want to be perceived?). You also need to think about workspace for employees (that work in the office), the needs of those who work at home, labour policy on workspace, accessibility and more (do you want free range or battery farm?). And the answer to that will come from the board and the culture of the enterprise, and will determine whether you are a Poundstretcher or Selfridges…

10. Building the information function

Depending on the size of the service catalogue it is unrealistic to expect that USD employees know all about the products and services, including every procedure and point of contact. IT provision of a knowledge management system can support this as a depository of the necessary procedures; but don't forget that someone still has to know what they are and put them into a well-designed system.

One can only start to construct the information function when wishes and needs of the customers are matched to the USD offering of products and services, and when the boundaries to deliver are set. Boundaries are a result of budget restraints and when the desired service levels are set.

11. Constructing the virtual USD

To effectively construct the virtual USD and information management functions, they must be considered simultaneously. The virtual USD is the first level of service: it is the service portal intranet where a majority (sometimes all) of the products and services can be delivered. Through the service portal, most enquiries can be placed and channelled as appropriate. However, the products and service catalogue's standard processes will also mean that most enquiries are immediately directed to the relevant back office. Automation is the most cost effective and efficient solution to handling enquiries, though be aware of the pitfalls described earlier.

The service portal can be designed and developed based on the principles and choices made in relation to the service settlement processes. The portal can be a basic digital information service or a more innovative solution offering self-service for all enquiries. Many service desk management information systems have self-service processing via the Internet. Ensure that any virtual USD matches the capability of the IT infrastructure and the services that fulfil customer needs.

12. Designing call centre functionality

The second level of service is the resolution and settlement of products and services via phone, email and post. These activities are described as call centre functionality and pertain to any USD. Interaction between the USD and customer is not physical. Call centre services can be offered from almost any geographic location, though placing a physical desk in Mumbai for 'walk-in' customers based in the UK may not be a good idea.

Since email and text apps are widely available, this channel of service is the most important to design correctly. Welcome to the 21st century.

Finally, physical mail or post ('snail mail') may remain a channel for service. Although post is rare, delivery of physical items is still part of the process (ask Amazon). In some instances, original signatures are still needed, although more solutions are becoming available to digitise even this process.

At this point, you should think about how you intend to test the USD organisation. It is never too early to consider 'dry running', 'test packs', creating enquiries to test clerks (prior to going live) and of course, training recruits.

13. Organising account management

Not everything can be automated or standardised (no matter what anyone tells you). In some instances, direct interaction with the customer is necessary to understand the motivation behind an enquiry. In general, there are two options. First, try a conversation with the USD clerk. This will usually work, but sometimes the clerk will not have enough knowledge or have no mandate for compliance. In these cases, the second option is to make the request through account management. The reason is that account management is a specific function created for settlement and delivery of many non-standardised services. Account management is also responsible for good customer relationships, dealing with more involved requirements, analysing and generally monitoring customer satisfaction. During delivery of large-scale programmes or projects of change or improvement, account management is the bridge function between customers and users on the one hand, and suppliers on the other.

14. Human resources of the USD

Human resources (qualitative and quantitative) of the USD are dependent on the scope of the work. To begin with keep in mind what we discussed about the need for work under *Management and Organisation.*

There are three more criterial that contribute:

1. **Guarantee of continuity of the USD services** – This relates directly to availability of USD services and the support provided through cross training, and properly assessing workload to ensure cover during absences such as vacation and training.
2. **Effective deployment of the employees** – Clerks can never be fully productive during the time that they are available, for example, an irregular distribution of customer calls, or because of major incidents.
3. **Expertise of employees** – A USD requires specific expertise and skills to execute the tasks. These skills include being customer centric, solution-oriented, communicative and flexible, with a wide knowledge of the enterprise and the ability to turn water into wine.

5.6 Step 5 – In use

15. Go live with the USD

All components should be brought together according to the project plan you have had approved (you did have one, didn't you?) to make the USD work. This means for example that after successful testing, the virtual USD and the MIS/service desk software are moved to the production environment, accounts are prepared and enabled so that staff have appropriate access to all systems, and all organisational and management agreements are in force.

When everything is prepared and ready, the USD can operate. There will be a grand opening no doubt, or inauguration where customers are invited to the Mall and photographed to prove it is the biggest inauguration ever in history or in any galaxy.

Sorry, we mean where services are 'walk through'. It is highly improbable that everything is FULLY operational or works as it should; problems will arise. Well, they may not, but be prepared for trouble shooting and keep smiling or use the 'fake news' button.

Remember that the USD needs to mature. Staff need to become accustomed to their new tasks, and dry running services is not the same as running live. Relationships need to be established across the enterprise and, in particular, between the USD and back office. The role of account management needs to be developed, and, if it is part of the overall USD function, it must be integrated.

Going live is one thing, but maturation is another. Through experience, you will discover new working processes and identify your efficiencies. At this stage, development of the USD is no longer related to the project plan but towards ongoing improvement. The USD manager is responsible for both further development of day-to-day processes and for improvement and innovation.

5.7 How do I use the action plan in my own situation?

The design parameters (use of different channels, physical locations, degree of automation and so on) depend on the goals of your enterprise. These parameters will form the scope of your project plan, so make sure that they are clear and that you understand project planning (once you have your parameters, the guidance in this book should help you decide what you need to do).

Remember your USD will certainly not be finished after going live. As a consequence, it is not necessary to fully describe all processes, this is probably not even possible until things start up. It will also be unlikely that all steps in all phases will be fully detailed.

There are three reasons why your plans will still be provisional:

1. No one person is likely to have complete insight into requirements. Total design will continue to evolve over time in response to experience;
2. Skills, experience and knowledge of the employees will need to be actively grown; and
3. It is impossible to predict every possible consequence of your planning.

Regular monitoring is needed to discover whether decisions lead to the right outcomes, and sometimes it will be necessary to correct or adjust original ideas, principles or goals. Most importantly, you should check that all parties, especially management, remain committed to their decisions and plans.

In many cases, a USD is already in place and your plan may be to focus on development, improvement or innovation. In these situations, you will focus on the components of the USD. The scheme in *Figure 5.1* will help you understand the relationships between the different components. Do not be alarmed when you discover that dependencies between components force you to redesign some elements, and include others that were not part of your original thinking.

The USD is an organisation and like all organisations, it is shaped by humans and therefore continuously subject to change and screw-ups. Employees of a USD will get more and more experience and learn from mistakes, as well as from their successes.

Erm, check that last one…

CHAPTER 6: THE SERVICE DESK OF BREDA UNIVERSITY OF APPLIED SCIENCES

At Breda University of Applied Sciences (BUAS), the central service desk provides services to all students, visitors and employees. The service desk accepts calls for several disciplines in the organisation (IT, housing, facilities, and cleaning) and also provides specific services for the academies.

6.1 BUAS

BUAS provides Bachelor's and Master's programmes in the following areas:

- Tourism;
- Facility;
- Hotel;
- Built environment;
- Games;
- Leisure and events; and
- Logistics and media.

In addition, it conducts applied research, supports emerging entrepreneurs, develops knowledge under license, and provides courses and training for professionals.

BUAS is the new name of NHTV Breda and has approximately 8,000 students and 800 employees. As is the case in many Dutch academies, the language of instruction is English. Fifteen percent of the students are foreign as well as fifteen per cent of the staff. this percentage is likely to increase further.

BUAS wants to be internationally recognised as a highly practice-oriented top institution in both profit, non-profit and government organisations. They have worked out a roadmap to get to this position. Currently, BUAS shares second place in the 'Elsevier' rankings, and it holds fourth place in the 'Keuzegids Hbo 2017' rankings, in the category of medium-sized colleges.

Unsurprisingly, BUAS is located in Breda and it presently has four campuses. Since September 2019, all programmes have been brought together on one central campus. The enterprise has five academies, which provide eighteen bachelor's and master's programmes; and seven staff services (including housing, facility and planning), which are responsible for the facility's services. The service desk is part of the housing, facilities and planning (HFP) staff service.

6.2 Service desk with a smile

BUAS's central service desk is available to students, visitors and employees alike. The desk receives notifications for ICT, housing, facility and cleaning services. It also offers various services for the departments of finance, HR, planning, housing, ICT, facility, concierge, marketing and communication, student office and the five academies. As a front office department, the service desk is part of the HFP department (accommodation, facility, planning), the facility service provider of BUAS.

Figure 6.1 shows the organisation of HFP:

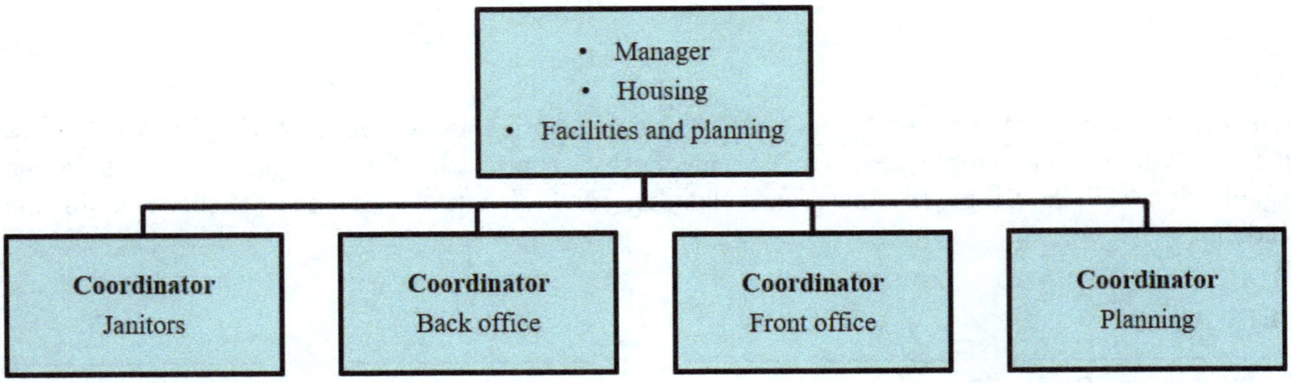

Figure 6.1: Department of HFP

Within the organisation, the service desk is positioned as the central place where the various departments and academies can offer their services to customers in a manner designed to maximise their satisfaction or 'peace of mind'. This is actively encouraged and promoted by general management. Responses show that the departments are happy with the service desk, and it is increasingly adding new services.

This is the mission statement of BUAS's service desk:

> The service desk is distinctive and innovative, and because it is customer-oriented, service-oriented, uniform and efficient, it creates the right conditions for both our employees and the students to excel. With this we contribute to the success of Breda University and we make our slogan true: 'Service desk with a smile'.

The excellence of BUAS's service desk has also been recognised outside the enterprise. In November 2016, the service desk was named 'Best Service Desk of the Netherlands'. Both a jury prize and a public award were available, and the service desk won them both.

The service desk can be reached via various channels:

- A physical service desk (one is provided on each of the four campuses);
- Email;
- Telephone; and
- The intranet (through a self-service desk).

The BUAS service desk is formed by a team of eleven employees (seven FTE). The team comprises a solid core and a flexible shell. The employees in the flexible shell have temporary contracts and most of them work internally within the enterprise. In this way, the service desk functions as a breeding ground for new talent. You might expect that there is also room for interns from the faculty's own academy. But that is not the case. It is not permissible for students to work on the service desk because the service desk also oversees examinations.

From 1 September 2018 the service desk was moved to a new part of the campus. BUAS's service desk processes approximately 9,300 incidents per year (34% click, 24% call and 42% face) and 15,500 reservations or items per year.

Table 6.1 shows an overview of the services that the service desk offers.

Table 6.1: The Services Provided by the Service Desk

Services Provided by the Service Desk
• Lending equipment, including room keys, film reels, service bikes and event materials • Issuing official documents, including examinations • Handling financial transactions and issuing vouchers • Responding to general questions and information requests • Issuing smart/business cards • Managing found and lost objects • Managing ICT and facility notifications and malfunctions • Reserving spaces • Providing safe hire • Providing car rentals • Managing front offices at all the academy's locations • Handling deans' agreements

6.3 Organisation of daily services

There is a single point of entry for questions from visitors, students and staff. They can submit their questions to the service desk in various ways:

1. **Via the self-service desk** – the self-service desk is available 24 hours a day. Practical information is available about products and services and service information, for example general faults and of course, the capability of making reservations. Request for services such as travel and catering is also available via the self-service. *Figure 6.2* shows the home page of the self-service.
2. **Via email** – all email notifications will be processed within two hours.
3. **Via telephone** – one central number is available, and the customer is helped in the same way irrespective of how the call is fielded. The customer is given no knowledge of where the employee is located because this information is not relevant.

The opening time of the desk and telephone service is from 08:00 am to 20:00 pm.

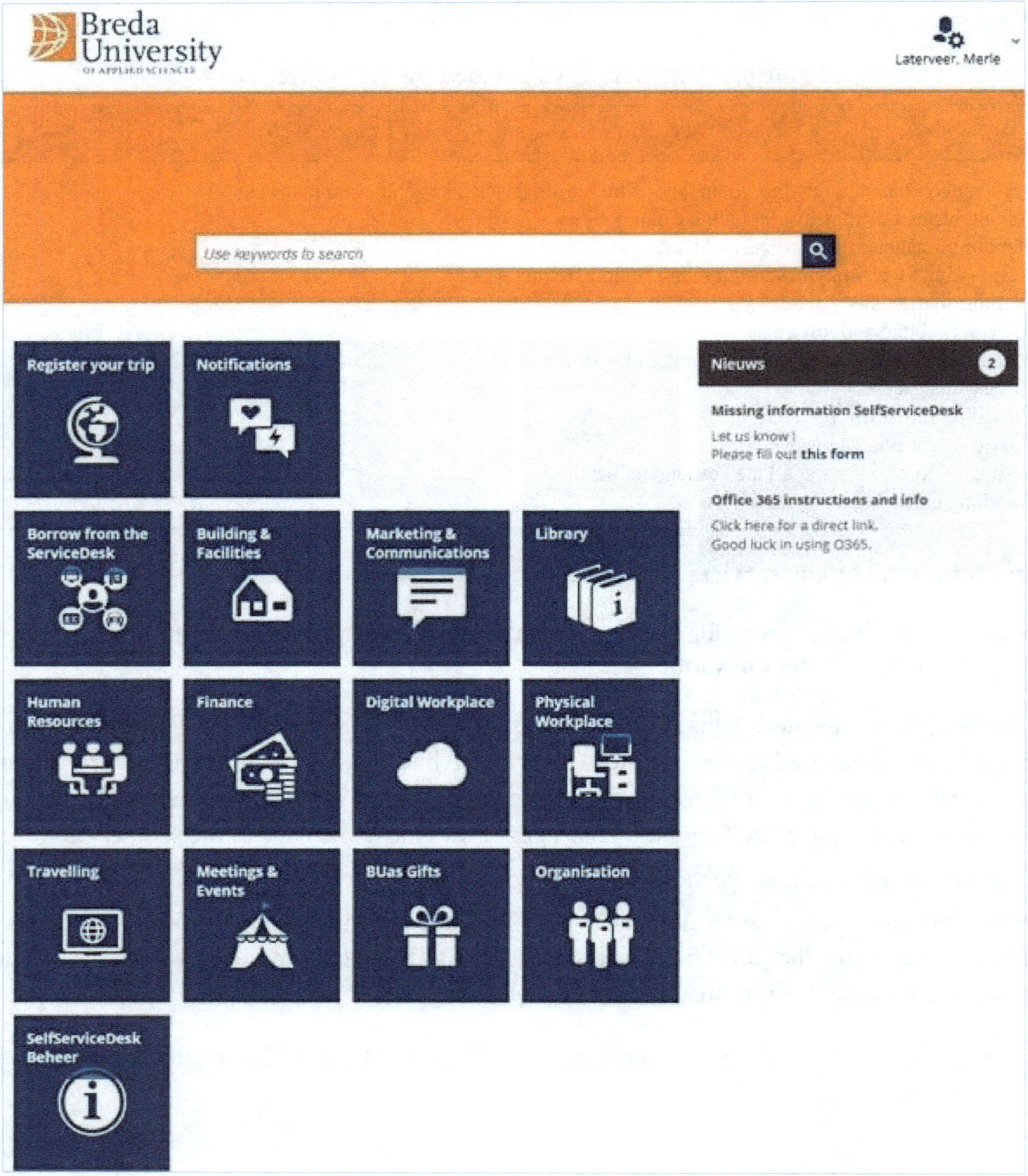

Figure 6.2: Home page for self-service

There is a service counter at each location of the training institute. At each physical counter in the locations, the processes are uniform. There is a location description for each counter with a 'roadmap' so that new employees can access information quickly. *Table 6.2* shows a location description's table of contents.

Table 6.2: Location Description

Location: (map)
To open: § Where do I park my car/bike, where is the service desk, what is the room number, which key is needed?
• **Startup:** § Which computer, telephone log in, printer, what more needs to be started? § Open the safe boxes and the desk, start the pin device, do not forget to read the transfer.
• **What is positioned where** § Sign opening hours, AVM materials, lost & found, power cables/film reels, business cards, office supplies, audiovisual office items, event items (uprights, etc.), projection screens and tables, documents and items to be collected for students or teachers, book by registered mail pieces/packages, registration book for external guests, keys/key boxes.
• **Where is…?** § Telephone, automatic payment machine, copier locations, pinpoint, binding, media library, concierge, business desk, lift, quick check points (public thin clients), canteen/foyer/catering, mailboxes, mailbox, toilet, loan bikes, lockers/lockers students, lockers employees, rain gear.
• **Break time 12: 00–12: 30 am** § Instruction how to deal with break-time.
• **Close:** § Instruction on how to close the desk.
• **Frequently asked questions**
• **Additional facts**

From the service-oriented way of thinking everyone is helped in a uniform, friendly and personal way. Mail templates are used to standardise communication. Telephone manner is universal. Notifications are always dispatched via the FMIS system, so that all communication is clear. For all reservations, regardless of whether they have been reported via the service site or by telephone, digital confirmations are dispatched and updated where necessary.

All widespread malfunctions are communicated via a specially designed page on the intranet. Enquiry intake is via a standard protocol. Depending on the demand, specific methods have been set out for all products and services. This has also been established for ICT reports, so that the handling by a second-line handler can be taken over as efficiently as possible because emphasis is on the receipt of accurate information. (*Table 6.3* shows the table of contents of a work instruction.)

Table 6.3: Work Instruction Format at the Service Desk

Contents
• Quick guide • Method • Summary functionality • Locations (in which locations can this be requested?) • What can be found where? (locations, work instructions and FMIS manual intranet) • Management • Processes and work breakdown • Instruction FMIS (top desk) • Link to education system Edu-roam (if applicable) • Attachment (with specific information for applicant, if applicable) • Conditions • Roadmap for use of the FMIS system • Customer experience (what can the customer expect?)

The FMIS is important for the service desk's provision of services. In order to properly maintain and monitor the system, functional management is part of the application management at ICT. An employee who previously worked at the service desk is always on staff. Their experience combined with technical knowledge is essential for the desired further optimisation and further development of the FMIS.

At the end of each day, a handover standard mail template is completed by the employee who is on duty. Every week, a weekly report with information by and for the employees of the service desk appears. The number of services and finishes requested are also communicated weekly to the entire team by means of the weekly report.

6.4 Steering based on a roadmap and a strategic plan

The HFP staff department has drawn up a roadmap from 2015 up to (and including) 2020. It describes the vision and mission as concrete goals. The roadmap is shown in *Figure 6.3*.

Mission

We're here to support education and research in a hospitable, professional, efficient and effective manner.

Vision

Facilitating professionals in a well-equipped, inspiring and innovative environment.

The strategic plan focused on 'operational excellence' for the first two years. From 2018, HFP also embraced 'product leadership' to help achieve their goal of being ranked among the top facility service providers. The service desk is a necessary link for HFP in service-oriented internal services, with students, staff and visitors at the centre.

The mission and vision of the facilities company have been translated into a strategic plan and annual targets for the four departments, including the service desk.

The service desk uses its own strategic plan in which IT links the activities to the objectives from the roadmap. It uses the LEAN approach for implementation and continuous improvements. All activities are included in a 'single X matrix'. This matrix then translates the central mission and objectives into concrete annual targets and actions, with the associated key performance indicators (KPIs). All activities are then linked to employees.

The X-matrix is a scheme used in the LEAN approach to link strategic goals to tactical goals and operational actions. It consists of the following components:

- Strategic goals or breakthroughs on a 3–5 year horizon;
- Annual targets related to one or more strategic goals or breakthroughs;
- Actions related to the annual goals;
- Accountability and responsibilities linked to breakthroughs and actions; and
- KPIs linked to the annual goals or actions.

By completing the X-matrix, connections are made between the daily actions and improvements and the goals.

The service desk has been following a number of key goals from 2015 to 2020. These goals, and their results, are central to the service desk. The goals were:

- A client average of 8.5 or higher ('happy students, staff and management');
- To carry out two 'Fish' activities;
- Standardise processes;
- Internationalise;
- Work on team building; and
- Publish the results in a magazine or otherwise.

At the end of 2018 a client average of 8.9 was achieved:

- Two 'Fish' activities were carried out at the service desk (activities aimed at strengthening customer loyalty and improving customer expectations).
- At least four processes have been standardised using the LEAN method, which makes the unlocked resources (in FTEs and euros) available for innovations.
- Internationalisation – every employee has undergone a test to establish English fluency, (individual training plans have been drawn up and were implemented before 2020).
- 'One team' – this programme aimed at stimulating cooperation and connecting all of our own employees within HFP.
- Service desk as the 'single point of contact' has been realised within BUAS.
- Participation in competition of the service desk and a publication about the service desk was released.

Goals are translated into specific actions and then assigned to the employees of the service desk. Specific actions include:

- Registering with the Dutch award for 'Best Service Desk';

- Visiting service desks of at least two other organisations;
- Measuring customer satisfaction; and
- Testing English fluency.

Figure 6.3: Strategic roadmap department – housing, facility services and planning of BUAS

Progress is measured using KPIs. Examples are:

- On Monday morning, schedule all local requests for the same day before 10:00 am;
- Increase the 'findability' of self-service desk products by 10%;
- Perform Fish action between October and December; and

- Visit another service desk between January and July (this last goal applies to each member of the service desk team).

The FISH! philosophy explained:

The FISH! This philosophy is modelled after the Pike Place Fish Market, and it aims at creating contented individuals in the workplace.

John Christensen created this philosophy in 1998 to improve 'organizational culture'. Its central four ideas, which have been adopted by many businesses and academic organisations, are:

1. Choose your attitude;
2. Play;
3. Make someone's day; and
4. Be there.

Christensen observed fish sellers at Pike Place Fish Market, throwing trout, salmon and anything smaller than a dolphin into the air to attract customer attention and provide entertainment. Their high energy also served to energise the pedestrians passing by. The fish sellers gave their complete attention to each customer and ensured that everyone had an enjoyable visit. After sailing close to bankruptcy in 1986, the fish market owner and the employees decided to change their way of doing business by introducing their 'flying fish' games and customer performances.

At the BUAS's service desk, they focused on 'make someone's day' to improve customer experience and customer relations. They have constructed specific actions for everybody working at the university. For example, they give a small present to those who submit regular generic reports (about things like leakages and defects), and they also send out 'happy birthday' messages to everybody working at the University. Fish! has altered the hospitality goals of the department.

6.5 The image of users

The implementation of the vision has tangible results. The service desk at BUAS is now considered best practice and is consistently rewarded with high employee and customer satisfaction results.

The service desk regularly surprises customers with the application of the Fish philosophy. It has implemented numerous ideas to make customer focus and service orientation tangible, and to keep them this way. These ideas all have an important starting point: "working and studying at Breda University of Applied Sciences is made possible by the service desk". Ideas already implemented on this principle include:

- Every year, each employee receives an email from the service desk with congratulations;
- Anyone who takes the trouble to report a general malfunction receives a present from the service desk (a foldable polyester carry bag);
- New employees receive a key bag to store their new keys and smart card;
- Compliment notes are distributed throughout the building (everyone can give compliments to each other); and
- Two comic actresses were hired to support the anti-smoking policy and the cleaning of the building.

The effect of all improvement efforts has not gone unnoticed. In 2018 the service desk scored a customer satisfaction rating of 9.2, an unprecedented score which HFP is very proud of. Furthermore, as a result of their winning the prize for 'Best Service Desk', other companies visit BUAS to understand how the service desk functions.

6.6 Training

High satisfaction and a positive appearance are not possible without a qualitative and high-quality team. This is explicitly managed. Basic activities (handling of complaints, wishes, information and malfunctions) must be mastered. For the additional work on the service desk a fixed list of tasks has been made, where a first person is responsible and one person acts as support.

Additional activities include:

- The issue of vouchers;
- Lost and found;
- Smart cards;
- Stock management;
- Lockers;
- Syllabus distribution;
- Guest account management; and
- Maintenance of the service desk intranet.

In addition to 'serviceable' and 'customer oriented', there is a lot of attention for competences such as quality, always being up-to-date with the latest novelties, interest in diversity in subjects, experimenting and being aware of the effect of changes that are being implemented. In addition to basic knowledge and responsibility, employees also take on extra tasks, generating responsibility. The various activities are assigned to individual employees from the strategic plan.

Collaboration is an important success factor and a facility-wide objective. In addition to the improvement activities, the 'one team' is also explicitly included as a strategic objective in the HFP roadmap. From this, concrete actions per year are carried out, such as:

- 'Join my job for one day' (both within and outside the department and organisation);
- Team building days;
- Training courses; and
- Staff outings.

The employees are actively involved in the improvement objectives. Employees are made aware of the fact that they have to ask themselves whether they can perform better or more efficiently. In doing so, the employees are continuously challenged to keep thinking from the customer's perspective. Quality of the calls is periodically discussed by the team leader of the service desk with the service desk staff, and employees are also encouraged to become familiar with the Lean method and follow training courses. In the meantime, two employees already have the green-belt level.

6.7 Developments in the coming years

In addition to maintaining the current quality of service, various points of attention have been formulated for the coming years:

- Achieve further efficiency. LEAN has been further implemented, so processes will be even more efficient. 80% of the processes must then be standardised. LEAN sceptics (and there are many) will wait with bated breath.
- The service desk has become the 'single point of contact' for all students and employees at a single location. Accessibility has been increased by the further development of the online self-service desk (available 24 hours).
- In addition to online accessibility, customer focus and customer contact have been improved by the further implementation of the Fish philosophy.
- For the concierges, a mobile app from the FMIS is installed on their smartphone or iPad so that they can report, receive and update faults on the campus at any location.
- BUAS is working on the development of a high-quality and up-to-date learning and working environment in the form of a campus where all locations are housed in one place. This development was completed by the end of 2019.
- Finally, HFP, including the service desk, is busy drawing up a new roadmap and strategic plan for the new five-year period: 2020–2025.

With this, the practical description of BUAS's service desk Part 1 is concluded. In Part 2, the individual components of a service desk per chapter are explained in detail. These are: the facility management information system (FMIS), the virtual service desk (service portal), the call centre functionality, the service desk, account management, employees of the service desk, service desk management and organisation, and the organisation of the processes within the service desk, between the service desk and back office, and the service desk and the enterprise.

SUMMARY OF PART 1

The USD is a concept that comprises services delivered via intranet, telephone, email, post, physical desk(s) and account management. In the USD, the customer demand is structured according to the front office to back office principle.

In order to structure customer demand, insight is needed into the nature of the services provided by the various service organisations. This means all products and services, including IT. Products and services can be arranged in various ways. Firstly, through a classification based on operational, tactical and strategic descriptions. Secondly, by making a distinction between basic, basic-plus and customised services.

The products and services are perceived differently by both the demand side (the customer) and the supply side (the services and facility organisation and the suppliers). The USD is charged with translating customer demand and matching that demand to supply. Accordingly, the USD functions as an intermediary between the customer and the back office. It translates customer requirements into generic solutions that can be planned in the back office. In this manner, the handling process is disconnected from the questions and the USD takes over the question. The customer only has to deal with the front office, and no longer has to navigate the numerous suppliers of services or products in the back office.

SECTION FOR YOUR NOTES

Part 2: Components of the service desk

INTRODUCTION

Part 2 focuses on the design, construction and layout of the individual parts of the service desk:

- The virtual service desk
- The call centre function
- The service desk
- The account management
- Employees and their competence

The relationship between the service desk and the back office and the underlying process structure are treated separately. Attention is also paid to supporting the tasks at the service desk through a management information system and the setup of a virtual service desk. Finally, attention is paid to the organisation of the service desk. Topics that are discussed are organisational models, processes, structure and location, management, finances and capacity and capacity of the service desk.

CHAPTER 7: SERVICE MANAGEMENT SOFTWARE

In addition to the commitment and competence of employees, the use of ICT in the provision of information now largely determines the efficiency and professionalism of a USD. Service management software (SMS) in facilities is called integrated workplace management system (IWMS) or facilities management information system (FMIS), and in IT it is called IT service management (ITSM) tools. A SMS is the 'beating ICT heart' of the USD and offers ample functionality for the support of a USD.

After reading this chapter, the reader will be aware of the scope of SMS and what function this service has within the USD.

7.1 Information services

Information services are at the heart of the business. We encounter information in all areas, from process control to complaints registration; from order services to relationship management and from market analysis instruments to expert services. There is a plethora of services that require information such as ITSM, IWMS, procurement, sourcing and contract management, HR service delivery. The list goes on…

As we have said, the computerisation of the USD function is supported by some form of an SMS. SMS tools facilitate the tasks and workflows associated with the management and the delivery of operation services. They are most heavily used by USDs. *Figure 7.1* shows frequently occurring functions of an SMS.

An SMS is created from business information applications that use a database (or collection of databases) to support digital working environments, whether internal or external. Organisational functions, like IT operations and facility processes, are supported and managed using databases that employ a coherent set of digital data (such as personal or location data), often accessed through a master database. Where numerous databases exist, they generally operate in a hub-and-spoke environment.

There are many suppliers of SMS packages in the current market. Gartner offers several market studies that present an impression on the availability of some of the larger software solutions for ITSM and integrated workplace management.[11] These solutions are often positioned as a platform for workflows throughout the organisation, including HR, facilities, integrated workplace management and application management. They are sometimes presented as an all-encompassing enterprise systems management (ESM) solution, or a shared service management platform, or as service relationship management (SRM). However, most systems are limited in their scope. The majority of SMS products focus on service desk and ticketing functions, and there are only a few software packages available that focus on more than one discipline.

In addition, there are many smaller providers that mainly focus on a specialised niche or sector of the market. The choice for a specific package is largely determined by the size and complexity of the supported enterprise. For a small enterprise, it is of little use to purchase a particularly flexible (and

---

[11] Gartner, *How to Determine Social Media's Role in Your Customers' Journeys*, May 2018.

therefore often complicated) package, and often a standard package with minor adaptation options will suffice.

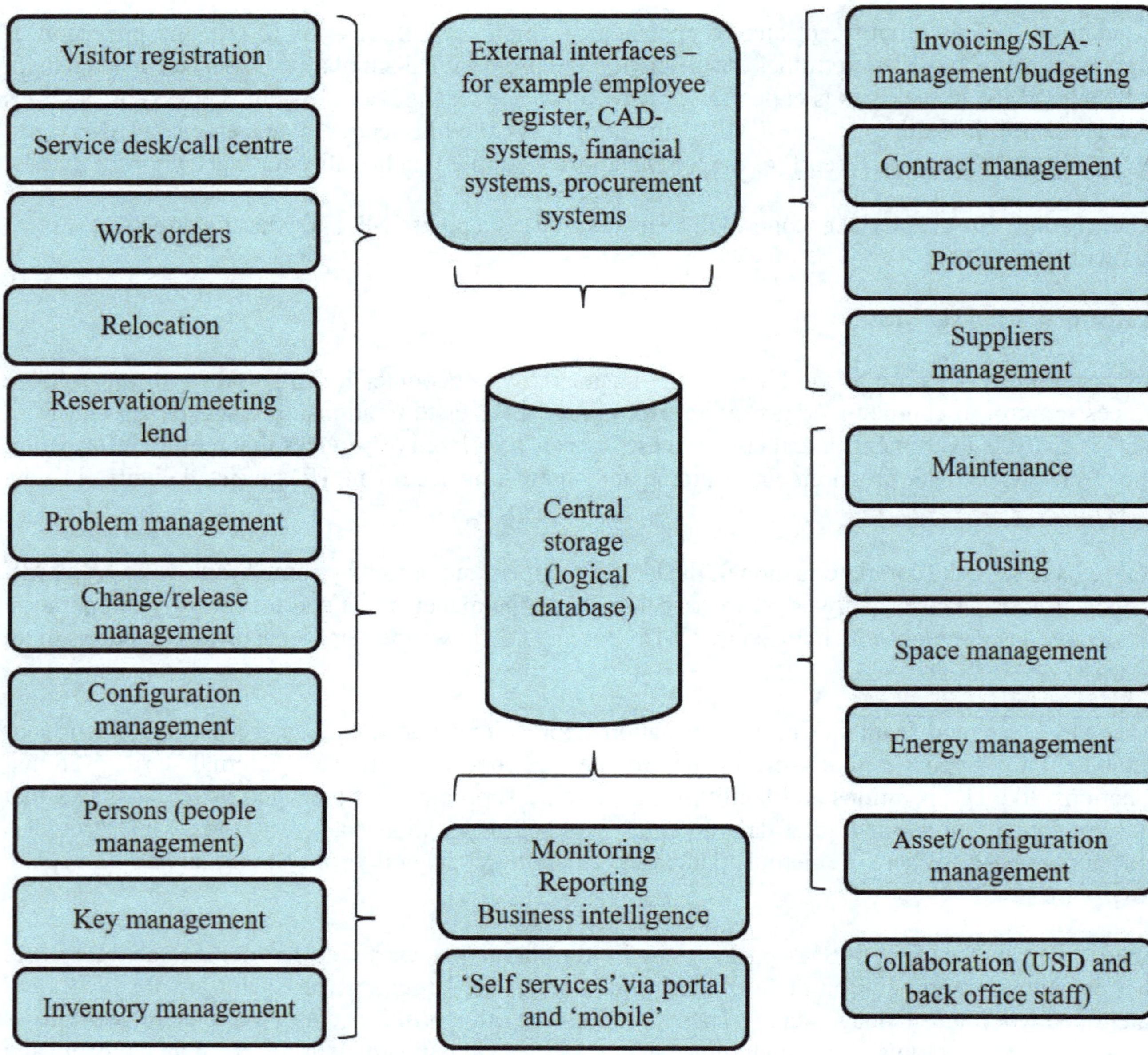

Figure 7.1: SMS functionalities

7.2 SMS within the technical environment

A central database with specialised programmes

Put simply, an SMS comprises a central database in which several specialised applications (modules or functionalities) apply specialised operations (such as work orders, notifications and reservations). The database contains all types of data, including data related to inventories, people and spaces. Data is identifiable by means of a unique attribute, such as personnel, location or contract. Personal data, building data and asset data are included in the central database. Consequently, several functions and disciplines use one central source of information to quickly access status information about the supported process. The strength of an SMS platform is mainly derived from the relationships that can be established and managed. By means of the integrated use of one central database, the service organisation always has up-to-date information available.

SMS in a network environment

An SMS can work independently, but this is only effective in very small enterprises. The power of an SMS is particularly evident in a network environment where the database is central and there are various access possibilities, both inside and outside the enterprise. Various options are available, ranging from web-based (Internet-based) services, to applications on local computers. The emergence of tablets and smartphones also contributes to flexibility; it is now possible to offer and edit information irrespective of time or place.

It is also possible to admit the service organisation's web-based users to the service (via Internet or intranet) and give them access to certain functions. This could include, for example, online meeting room reservations, registering visitors and reporting faults that are offered directly via a service portal. As a result, they can request many services directly and request their status. This makes it possible to handle a substantial proportion of enquiries automatically. Web-based service is a 'must' nowadays and a minimum requirement when purchasing services.

An SMS provides important options for the automation of work processes. This makes it easier to route registered reports automatically and to forward them to specialised back office functions and suppliers with their own applications. As a result, the USD can better manage the entire demand process of intake and processing. Clearly, merging IT and workplace service desk activities and processes will improve overall efficiency because they share very similar requirements.

There is also a growing trend among suppliers to offer more components of their package as a cloud service like software as a service (SaaS). This has many advantages such as service use becoming workplace-independent, the service organisation no longer having to retain and organise a management function, and investment costs being minimised. Payment is made according to usage (pay per use).

Links with other services

An SMS has generic links with other services. Examples are the generic reporting tools in which data from the SMS are used for management reports; links with ICT help desk programmes; graphic services (CAD/CAM) that are the basis for space management within the SMS; and the delivery of data from the central database of employees and security services (including link to access passes and access services).

In practice, there is no escaping links with other services. Within large enterprises, much data is available and some of it is recorded by various services that are not owned by the service organisation. An SMS ultimately works in close connection with enterprise resource planning (ERP) solutions. This allows applications to be better attuned to each other.

SMS when outsourcing

Increasingly, enterprises are outsourcing services. Service suppliers anticipate this by developing new functionalities, especially for contractors. Expansions are also focused on e-procurement, integrated workflow management, energy management and integration with ICT help desk services based on, for example, ITIL®. In addition, technological developments, including the use of smartphones and tablets to receive and register work orders, must be addressed.

Professional application management

Maintenance and service management of an SMS requires a lot of attention. It requires technical and functional IT knowledge. If an SMS is to be used optimally, the enterprise will have to organise this management. That is one reason why enterprises look with interest to the purchase of SMS services from the cloud. The decision-making background of this subject fall outside the scope of this book.

Using Building Information Models and FMIS for integrated workplace management

A building information model (BIM) is a digital representation of functional and physical characteristics of a structure, which is a starting point for the supportive activities and decision-making in the life cycle of a structure, that is shared by the various stakeholders in the construction process. A BIM is an important means of exchanging information about construction works between client and contractors. One-off collection of data and multiple use and sharing of information is central.

The BIM's core is a 3D model of the structure, but it also includes relevant project data that cannot be stored in that model. The BIM theoretically lasts the entire lifetime of the relevant structure and probably much longer, because it can be archived after the demolition of the building. In the BIM all relevant information is stored in a database, linked to the different objects or 'things' that occur in a structure. This not only concerns geometric information, but also information about the non-geometric characteristics of the objects (e.g. material, weight, capacity, and price) needed for maintenance management, for example.

The BIM is, therefore, an important reference and data source for design, realisation, maintenance, facility management, asset management and reconstruction during a structure's lifetime. It potentially supports all activities. Once again, similarities between activities described in ITIL (in particular, change and configuration management and availability management) are obvious.

Technological developments make it possible to link different models and files to each other and to exchange them via open standards. The idea behind BIM is that all information about an object is digitally entered and made available to all parties in the design, build and manage chain. As a result, tuning errors may be prevented and more value created.

Various types and brands of software for the design, construction and management of buildings have started to coalesce more and more intensively in recent years. This software is all part of the BIM, thus the holistic view of the data services in which information about the building is stored can be established. To enable all these different data services – from accounting software, energy simulation, facility management services, building plan testing to tenant registration – to cooperate with each other, open exchange standards are required.

Reporting and monitoring

Finally, an SMS makes it possible to offer customised management reports by means of a report generator. This function generates the desired management information within the various organisational units, including higher management. The progress monitoring functionality monitors whether the set turnaround times within projects, work orders and reports are met, and whether they are likely to be exceeded.

7.3 The functions of the SMS in the USD

The SMS plays a central role in a professional USD. The most important ways in which the SMS supports the USD are by:

a) Acting as a call centre/service desk;
b) Creating work orders;
c) Providing self-service facilities;
d) Registering and monitoring reservations;
e) Registering visitors;
f) Preparing reports;
g) Acting as a knowledge service; and
h) Offering new functionalities.

Note

The functions we distinguish here are not always clearly separated in the services themselves. Reports sometimes lead to parallel processes; actions such as 'creating work orders' and 'booking' are sometimes directly linked to this. For example, with some services, reporting a meeting immediately involves making a reservation. Similarly, 'known error' incidents might generate automatic replies.

a) Acting as a call centre/service desk

The USD is the central point for service requests. Within the USD, notifications are accepted and processed and (automatic) work orders are created.

Within this functionality, the following actions can be performed:

- Reservation of rooms and transport;
- Logging incidents and requests;
- Organising meetings, with or without catering;
- Handling requests for items of a structural, electrical and mechanical nature;
- Handling requests for transport and tickets, and relocations;
- Ordering office facilities such as telephones, smartphones and laptops;
- Registering new employees, including linking with the photo studio to create a company card;
- Registering visitors;
- Issuing keys;
- Arranging access control and production access passes; and
- Directing work orders to internal and external suppliers.

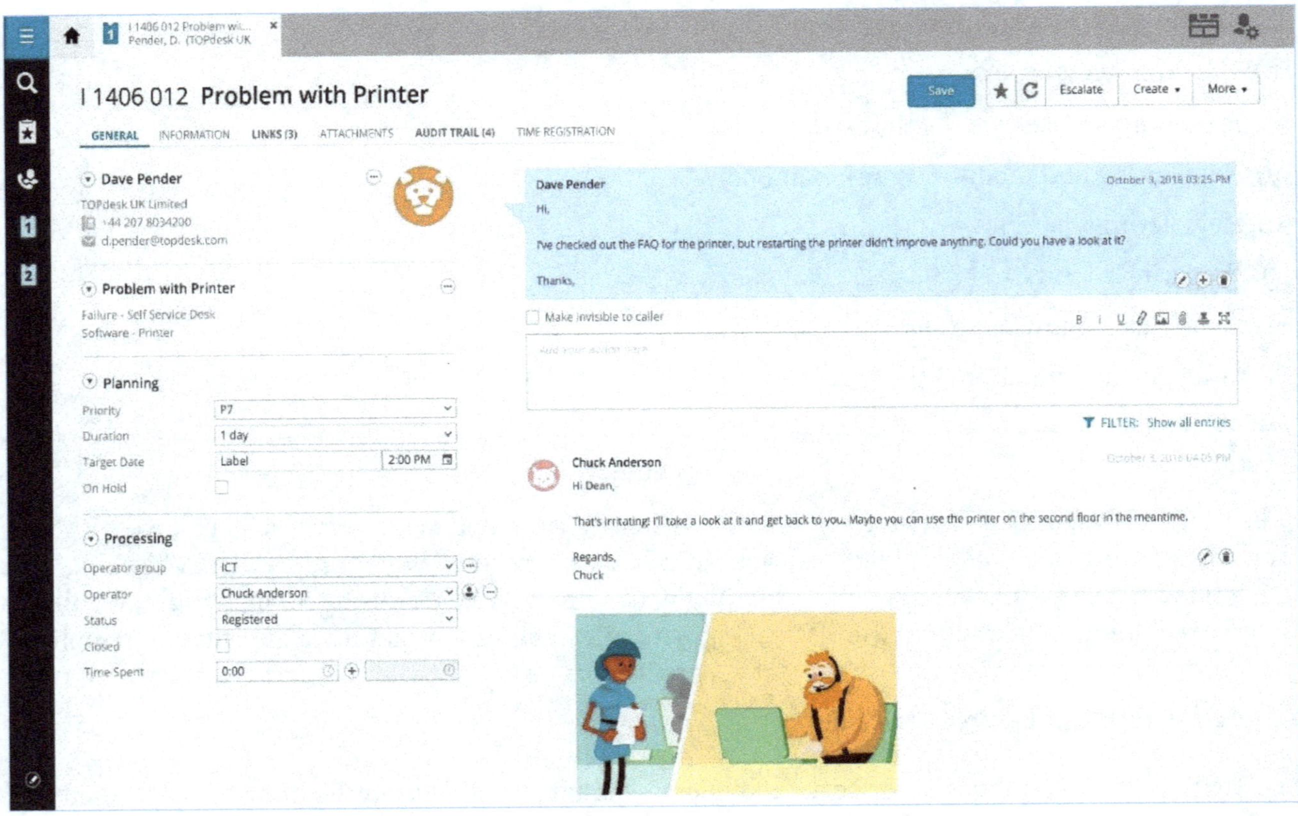

Figure 7.2: Example of a reporting point of an FMIS

b) *Creating work orders*

Work orders are activities that arise from requests and reports. They can concern a wide range of matters, such as:

- Repairing defects and malfunctions;
- Moving and adjusting equipment or furniture;
- Making and adjusting reservations, including for meeting rooms and transport;
- Managing meeting rooms and lending inventories (laptops, keys, etc.); and
- Handling purchase orders (this group of activities is not discussed here).

From work orders, customers can be informed about the handling and status progress of their report.

> **ICT and FMIS for service desks and help desks**
>
> The modules included in FMIS packages to manage and monitor these notifications are generally called work orders, 'call management' or 'tickets'. Within ICT help desk packages, we speak of 'calls', 'requests', other common terms are 'entities' or 'incidents'. (Note: a call can be an incident but a call can also be considered as a request; an incident is not a request.)

There are many types of work orders. These are often standardised according to predefined types (called 'standard work orders') to support both the user and the USD employee. Workflows are then defined for these standard work orders. In principle, the workflow of work orders refers to the various stages that an order can go through.

A simple fault message can go through the following stages:

Call reported
↓
Call in progress
↓
Call ready
↓
Call cancelled and closed

When setting up the standard reports and orders, it is important that the facilities organisation has a good idea of the processes requiring support. Some examples of standard orders and their parameters are:

Lamp defective

- Work order group: housing → technology
- Implementer: back office/technical cluster
- Type of order: notification
- Urgency: normal treatment

Removal request

- Work order group: housing → removals
- Implementer: advice and housing coordination
- Type of order: project
- Urgency: long term

A work order to a supplier also goes through some additional stages. Here are some stages an order may pass through:

- Application
- Quotation
- Confirmation
- Assignment
- Technically ready
- Administratively ready
- Expired and closed

The workflow also specifies how the report must be handled, including its timeframe, the associated cost, the responsibility and the departments involved. Accordingly, the work order functionality plays an important role for routing and, necessarily, for managing and executing workflows. Where IT is integrated within the FM environment, the well-known ITIL processes are more than good enough.

Thanks to the automation of the predefined work orders, the service can already fill in a lot of information itself. So, with the right design, the service can immediately display the linked space and cost centre after notification and person have been entered, as well as the workflow to be followed and the associated processing time.

When the SMS also offers functionality for the management of SLAs and contracts, it can be configured in relation to department or circumstance (for example, what the handling time may be). If the SMS has this functionality, it is also preferable to manage the contracts directly from the SMS, as conditions automatically flow through the workflow.

c) *Providing self-service facilities*

An SMS's third important functionality for the USD is to open up some of these functions via web services. This creates the possibility of offering self-service facilities.

The self-service facility provides an essential part of the USD: the service page. Within a private web portal, various functionalities are offered to users:

- Room reservation and catering orders
- Notifications (office set, lamp defective, etc.)
- Visitor registration
- Requests (orders and removals)
- Special forms and requests

Table 7.1: Examples of Standardised Work Orders for Integrated Workplace Management

1 Housing	**2 Services**
1.1 Terrain	2.1 Reservations
1.1.1 Soil	2.1.1 Rooms
1.1.2 Off-site installations	2.1.2 Coffee corner and workstations
1.1.3 Terrain equipment	2.1.3 Materials
1.1.4 Green provision	2.1.4 Parking spaces
1.1.5 Land pavement	2.1.5 Cars
1.1.6 Other land	2.2 Storage and distribution
1.2 Building	2.2.1 Transport internally
1.2.1 Building cascades	2.2.2 Transport externally
1.2.2 Installation package	2.2.3 Warehouses
1.2.3 Permanent establishment	2.3 Catering
1.2.4 Building installations	2.3.1 Restorative provisions
1.2.5 Other building	2.3.2 Catering meetings
1.3 Energy and water	2.3.3 Room service
1.3.1 Heating	2.3.4 Special activities
1.3.2 Electricity	2.3.5 Lunches
1.3.3 Drinking water	2.4 Coffee vending machines

1.3.4 Alternative energy sources	2.5 Risk management and safety
1.3.5 Other energy and water	2.5.1 Security
1.3.6 Cooling and air treatment	2.5.2 In-house emergency services
	2.5.3 Disasters
	2.6 Cleaning
	2.6.1 Inside object
	2.6.2 Glass
	2.6.3 Facades
	2.6.4 Pest control
	2.7 Relocation
	2.7.1 Internal relocation
	2.7.2 External relocation
	2.7.3 Other relocations
	2.8 Waste
	2.8.1 Waste collection
	2.8.2 Waste transport
	2.8.3 Waste treatment
	2.8.4 Other waste
	2.9 Other services
	2.9.1 Reception
	2.9.2 USD
	2.9.3 Textiles
3 Resources	**4 Automation and communication**
3.1 Separate device	4.1 Telecommunication
3.1.1 Furniture	4.1.1 General telecommunications
3.1.2 Planters	4.1.2 Internal telecommunications
3.1.3 Art	4.1.3 External telecommunications
3.1.4 Other loose furniture	4.1.4 Mobile telecommunications
3.2 Office supplies	4.2 Various communications
3.2.1 Office equipment	4.2.1 Information and presentation
3.2.2 Office items	4.2.2 Audiovisual
3.2.3 Other office supplies	4.2.3 Other drivers communication
3.3 Means of transport	4.3 Test ICT
3.3.1 Cars	4.3.1 ICT USD section
3.3.2 Cycling	4.3.2 Workplace preparation section
3.4 Work clothing	4.3.3 Application management department
3.4.1 Clothes drivers	4.4 Application management
3.4.2 Clothing monitoring	4.4.1 FMIS package
3.4.3 Other work clothing	4.4.2 PDC

3.5 Tools 3.5.1 USD Tools 3.5.2 Other tools	4.4.3 Service page 4.4.4 Safety 4.4.5 Other automation and communication
5 Procurement and purchasing	**6 Facility management**
5.1 Order products and services 5.2 Hiring 5.3 Other purchasing activity	6.1 General facility management 6.2 Quality, health and safety, environmental management 6.3 Complaints consumer services

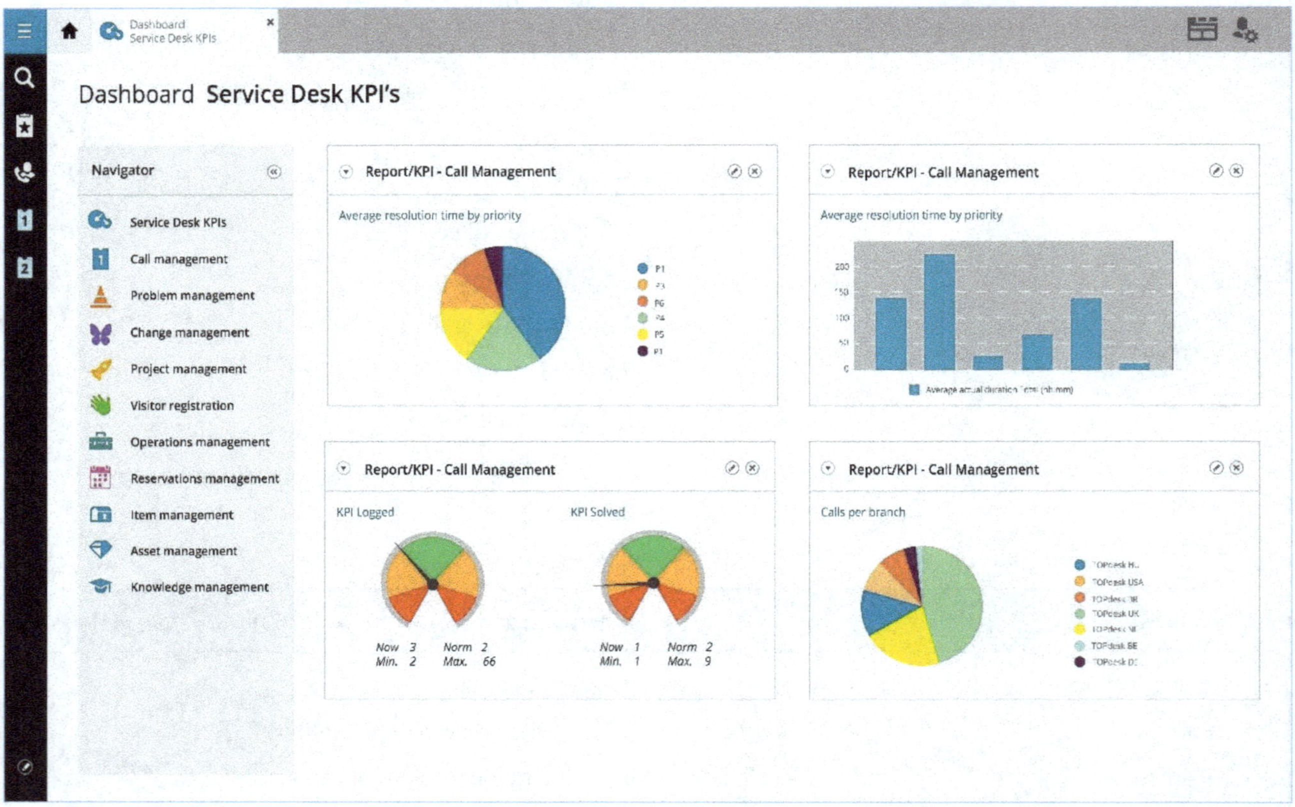

Figure 7.3: Reporting via SMS

A simple virtual USD can already be built with a standard application (see *chapter 8*). The standard provision already suffices for numerous enterprises, though many larger enterprises build a separate customised USD via their intranet. The intranet functionality of the SMS is often used as a driver for the virtual USD. This means that the portal has been developed with its own software, or that part of its own intranet environment functions as a front where many requests can be handled by the intranet application.

d) Registering and monitoring reservations

One of the biggest advantages of an SMS is registering and monitoring reservations. This does not only involve reserving meeting rooms (with associated assignments for coffee, pastries and lunches), but also reserving parking places, using cars, and so on.

e) Registering visitors

Reception manages the registration of arrival and departure of visitors and the issuance of temporary access passes. The link with an FMIS allows visitors to be notified and logged off. The staff at the USD therefore also have the opportunity to view who is coming in and who is leaving and, in the event of appointments, the ability to register visitors. Later, the report can provide information about, among other things, the number of visitors, which will assist with identifying staffing.

f) Preparing reports

The advantage of using an SMS for process support is that much of the progress information is already automatically registered and can be made transparent. In addition to standard reports on volumes at various levels, more complex reports can be drawn up with an extensive report generator. These powerful tools also allow the enterprise to create custom reports.

g) Acting as a knowledge service

A SMS often has the powerful ability to show information in the form of standard questions and answers (which have been used in past enquiries), directly to the USD employee. This supports a uniform method and knowledge assurance.

h) Offering new functionalities

Improving an SMS's functionalities makes it possible to link notifications to service agreements and quality indicators. This makes it easier to provide optimal support to different customer groups with differentiated preferences and agreements. The performance can also be measured afterwards through 'business intelligence' and 'dashboards'.

7.4 An essential service

A SMS can no longer be ignored in a modern service organisation. In any ICT-intensive business operations, a SMS is an important building block in the handling of support services such as IT operations management, delivery of HR services, building management, hospitality and professional facility services.

Regardless of their size, organisations should select an SMS that fits within their enterprise's (often hybrid) infrastructure and roadmap, matches maturity of the organisation and should be user friendly. In most enterprises SMS software is often considered one of the few key platforms that are fundamental to the business. Acquiring a complete platform means serious investment that needs to be useful and usable for many years. Understanding the needs of the business user is an important component of tool selection. This is because a large part of the business perception of the service organisation stems from interactions with the USD.

One of the most common mistakes managers of service organisations make in their selection of an SMS, is not ensuring that it is aligned to their desired and feasible state of maturity. When investing in software packages that reach far beyond their current maturity, they become locked into a costly and resource-intensive solution, and as a consequence high licensing, hosting and maintenance costs.

So before determining the appropriate SMS you should understand the needs of the organisation and the requirements of a service tool that fits the desired level of functionality (grounded in the reality of your own enterprise). Service design is helpful in analysing and understanding the real need.

Appropriate guidance can be found in our book *Collaborative Business Design* by Johnson and de Rouw (2017).[12]

It is also important to verify that any prospective SMS integrates with the other important applications that you rely on to run your business, like HR and BIM. Also note that the integration between desks (like IT service desks and HR desks) is increasing as the drive to reduce costs and become more efficient become a major motivation for businesses.

In the next chapter, we explore a specific function of the SMS in greater depth: self-service, and we will also discuss the virtual USD.

[12] www.itgovernancepublishing.co.uk/product/collaborative-business-design.

CHAPTER 8: THE VIRTUAL USD

The virtual USD is the first level of service within the USD. Often, it is an intranet service portal combined with the specific applications of the SMS. The major advantage of a virtual USD is that users can use self-service as part of their workplace support (reservations, notifications, complaints, etc.) independent of time. An important advantage for the service organisation (or company), is that these reports can generally be processed easily and directly.

After reading this chapter, the reader will better understand how services are organised via the Internet or intranet, and how this allows users to access and request services themselves like incident reporting, password resets and reporting complaints.

8.1 What is a virtual USD?

The proliferation of digital technology means further automation of services. Web technology with its symbolic 'point and click' icons, pull-down menus, hyperlinks and digitisation of information and data has invaded every environment. Almost everything now functions on the basis of this technology, including clocks, mobile phones, kitchen appliances, audio equipment and cars. As far back as the work of Rayport and Jaworksi (2005), academics spoke of a front office revolution in which the interface between client and enterprise changes significantly.[13] Almost all enterprises use 'smart technology' to streamline the interaction between customers and their own enterprise.

We also see this process in service provision within enterprises. In addition to self-service options for facility support (room reservation, registering visitors, placing orders); self-service concepts also develop in other disciplines such as an HR desk (where part of the staff needs can be handled on the intranet: leave requests, health absence notification, performance appraisal) and IT (reporting incidents, making service requests).

In the field of communication and information, self-service also makes its appearance. Think of requesting documentation and publications, and sending documents for copying. The field of business information management is expanding as digitisation increases; the BiSL next guidance is a useful reference guide.[14] There is a substitution of the range of products and services via telephone and counter, to automated services on the intranet. Some enterprises go about remediating the internal support to the extent that only the intranet support remains.

---

[13] Rayport, J.F. & Jaworski, B.J., *Best Face Forward: Why Companies Must Improve their Service Interfaces with Customers*, Boston, MA: Harvard Business School Press, 2005.

[14] Johnson, B. et al., *BISL-Next- A framework for Business Information Management: Second edition*, Zaltbommel: Van Haren Publishing, 2018.

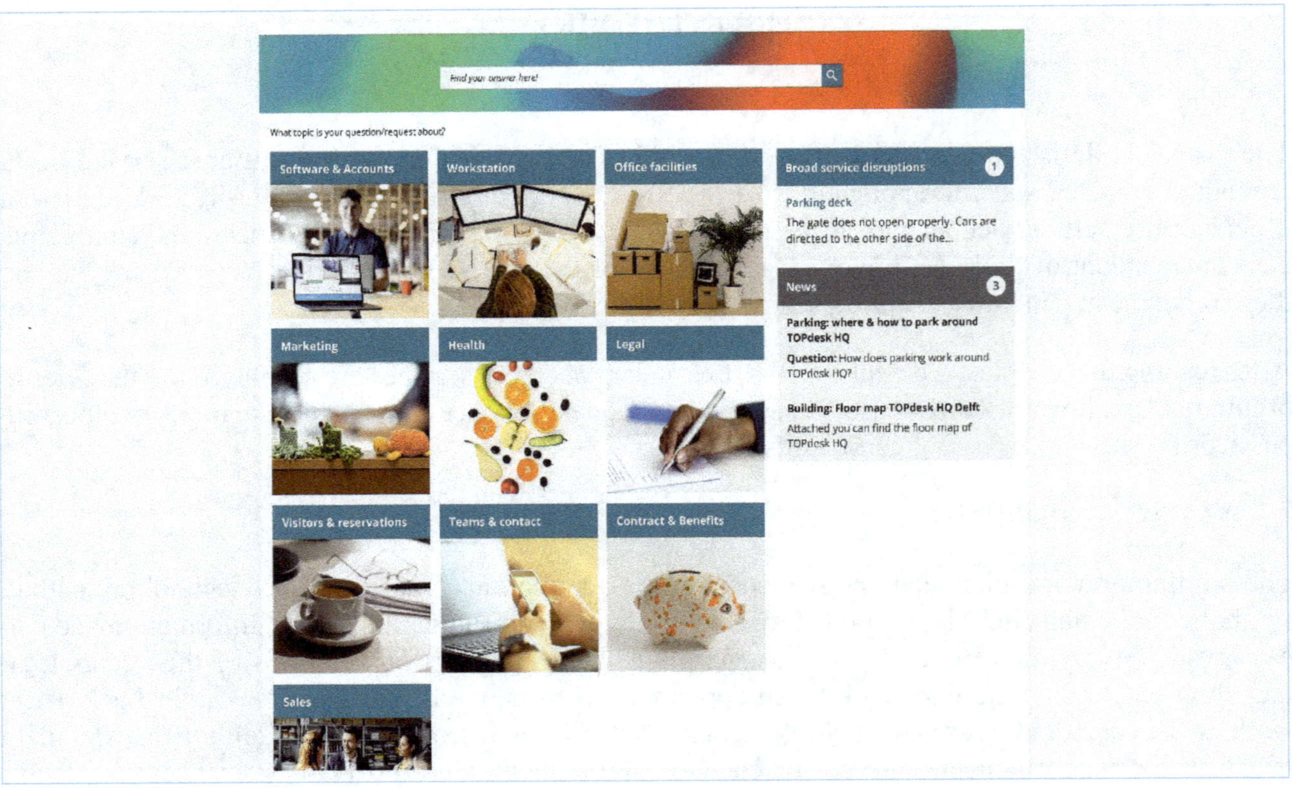

Figure 8.1: A service portal

There are three basic principles for the virtual USD area:

1. The virtual USD must connect, or be integrated, with the existing IT infrastructure;
2. Within the virtual USD, products and services are unlocked by handling and providing information; and
3. The virtual USD offers 'linking functionality' (i.e. interfaces) in the form of central access to information from other organisational units with relevance for the USD (the linking functionality is also sometimes called mid-office/service bus functionality).

Linking with the existing infrastructure

There are two possibilities for the virtual USD as the intranet entry for the service. On the one hand, it is the portal through which all facility applications are accessible; on the other hand, it acts as an alternative input for the existing applications on the enterprise's intranet. In the latter case, a practical approach is advisable whereby the USD is positioned as a 'shell' for the existing applications. The virtual USD is then an access mechanism, a signpost, to the various functionalities. This provides users with central and consistent access to the services on the intranet. It means that users are not only guided through the USD page to an application, but also have direct access to the application. In addition, they are informed via the virtual USD about other available service channels, such as a telephone or physical desk.

Unlocking products and services

The USD is able to access the available products and services as a result of a customer request. In addition, the USD provides clear information about the available products and services. This means that not only must a product and service catalogue be available, but also that it must be able to be approached question-oriented (from the perspective of the customer).

Interactive PDC on the intranet

An enterprise often enables an interactive products and service catalogue (iPDC). In addition to a complete overview of all products and services that constitute the complete business operations, the iPDC contains information about which part of the business delivers each product or service and against which measurable delivery condition (substantive, process-related and financial) it operates. The iPDC offers the possibility to open up the products and services in the catalogue from the perspective of the customer demand. The iPDC is the 'shop window' via the intranet to get information about the available products and services. In the iPDC, a fact sheet is available electronically per product / service with information and link options for making requests and making appointments, as well as additional information. For example, an employee can access the library information service via the iPDC and click through so that they can view a document digitally at their workplace.

Providing interfaces

For a multi-layer service enterprise, it is important that information from underlying organisational units can be offered to both the customer and the USD employee at or via the virtual USD. On the one hand, there is information of a static nature in the sense that it is, for example, a product description that is updated once in a certain period. On the other hand, up to date information for the customer must also be offered via a virtual USD. This can vary from financial statements to the status of a facility notification (including the confirmation).

Standard versus custom solution?

Almost all process or workflow management services, such as an SMS, offer the possibility of making services available via a portal. The problem with the deployment of these applications may be that the USD organisation is only partially responsible for the services of the internal or external customer enterprise. This has two further disadvantages:

1. The USD portal is sometimes inadequate for the total service – in the interests of user-friendliness, it is necessary to build-up the website in a transparent manner. One obstacle to this is that many underlying enterprises want to offer more product-specific information. It is, therefore, advisable in some cases to consider the USD as an access mechanism or signpost (a kind of index), instead of trying to centralise all services. A good option is to offer the 'most visited' products, with their application forms, directly via the USD and to provide a more specific demand-oriented search function to access comprehensive product information.

2. Enterprises are often tied to their own layout, house style or technical starting points. It may be that the standards on which the service is based on the intranet are not compatible with the available applications within the enterprise. This is especially true with services that are legacy based. Therefore, it is advisable to investigate whether the various functions of the information services (such as the online reservation of meeting rooms), can also be made directly accessible instead of via the application-specific portal. For example, a service could be directly linked from the service page to the application form for a business trip, instead of only being accessible via navigation from the 'start page' of the form generator. In practice, the desired level of integration can often be achieved through relatively simple technical adjustments.

Prior to presenting this information to the customer or USD employee in an unambiguous manner, it must be constructed from elements of many information services. In a larger enterprise, it is usual that a multitude of different underlying services are used. For example, the combination of this information could result in a report with personnel information from a HR service combined with an overview of reports made to a USD.

The main reason for implementing this functionality is, again, to provide a consistent and transparent interface for the users. Although it is highly desirable to have all underlying parts of the service organisation operate through this uniform method, in practice various causes mean that this is often only possible to a limited extent.

Two common causes are:

1. Incompatibility, or the use of closed communication standards of the various applications. Here a possible solution may be to use an open communication standard (though it must support the relevant software package); and
2. Complexity of the necessary 'business logic'. A room reservation service has a different workflow (form building and handling) than a time registration service, and this complexity makes it virtually impossible to integrate all services (or information) into one service.

As a result, standardised interfaces are used (sometimes called mid-office). An interface can take the form of an intermediate application or it can simply be a document with requirements for (technical) standards that enable linking. This interface forms the connection between the services of the front office and the services of the back office. Accordingly, the interface is not a separate organisational unit but a collection of functionalities that connect the processes and associated applications. By linking front and back office services through the interfaces, multiple back office applications can be addressed from one central point: the virtual USD.

A simpler solution could be a mixed form of integration. In this context, it is possible to choose, for example, to offer specific reports to both the customer and the USD via a universal report generator, while a more complex functionality is handled by the underlying applications. With this mixed form, it is very important to provide as uniform a presentation as possible, especially from the point of view of user-friendliness.

In practice, there are still limitations regarding use. These relate to issues like security requirements, insufficient agreements about standards, and poorly connected links from older applications; the latter may also cause an SMS to fit poorly into the existing ICT landscape. For these reasons, it is necessary to develop and organise the design and selection of applications in close consultation with the IT department.

Mainly self-service facility

Self-service provision for facilities and reservations must be highly professionalised. Characteristically, it will be a requirement that almost all reports and complaints go through the facility site. The site must therefore be available 24 hours. There should be many facilities on the site that enable 'tracking and tracing'. A self-service facility should provide:

- Insight into self-made notifications and reservations;
- Confirmation of notifications or reservations via email or SMS;

- Ample information on the website;
- Feedback and logout on completion; and
- A fully equipped products and service catalogue.

The USD phone number must always be mentioned on the service site, but customers and users should always be discouraged from using the phone. Email may also be discouraged in the enterprise. In addition to these substantive provisions on the service portal, a great deal of attention must be paid to the styling and user-friendliness (usability) of the site.

8.2 Construction of the virtual USD

In consequence of its central position within the service organisation (and the intranet), the virtual USD is the pre-eminent instrument for communicating news and information relating to the services provided to the customer. It provides a central and consistent portal for obtaining information and for making an application or order for a product.

The starting points for the virtual USD must match the mission and objective of the physical USD. Therefore, the USD content must be determined before its structure, design and technique. In addition, it is advisable to separate the technique and content.

The virtual USD components include:

a) The service page
b) A demand-oriented search functionality
c) An interactive products and service catalogue (iPDC)
d) Supporting applications (technology)
e) Application forms (often interactive)

a) The service page

The service page is the entry for the virtual USD. From here, the visitor gains access to the service page's various elements and will often be directly linked to a request or realisation.

The service page's main purpose is to receive the customer and to offer some initial information. For example, the following types of information could be offered:

- Messages about new products and services;
- Messages regarding changes to the application or delivery methods;
- Reports about disruptions in the service, including estimates of when they may be remedied;
- Hyperlinks to application forms for some frequently used products or services, such as business trips, meeting rooms and catering;
- Basic catalogue information for products and services (accessed via a demand-oriented search functionality); and
- Contact information for the USD organisation.

Because a wide spectrum of products and services can be requested or delivered via the USD, a certain degree of editorial control will have to be applied to the information provided, particularly with regard to its classification. A content management service can be used to support news items or extensive product information. This form of software support is often already present internally, as many companies and enterprises now have their own intranet with associated news coverage.

When developing a service page, the integration of lay-out and house style technical aspects will have to be taken into account within an existing intranet situation. Integration of these is desirable from the customer's perspective because this will make the service page an integrated and consistent extension to that already present. Therefore, the service page will have familiar functionalities, which contributes to the realisation of the objective to make the information as accessible as possible.

A virtual service desk is usually open to all the employees in an organisation or customers of a service organisation, so that everyone can access it and create requests. In this open service desk scenario, customers can create an account on the customer portal or email requests to your service desk email channel to create an account automatically. In most applications, settings are available to limit access to specific services. These settings should enable you to customise your solution as necessary. This is covered by a policy about 'accessibility and availability' and may be a consequence of SLA policies, or depending on how governance is exercised in your enterprise, it may be the result of overarching policies.

Usability

Corporate identity must be taken into account in the design of the service page. Usability is however, the key design issue regarding the service page. Usability refers to the user-friendliness, or usefulness, of an application or website. It is more than moving buttons or other elements or giving them a label. One of the most important goals of a usable design is much more fundamental: to properly support the task of the end user.

The quality of an application or a website is not only determined by the functionality (utility), but also by usability, such as defined in ISO 9241 (Ergonomics of Human System Interaction, ISO 9241-210:2019). Working with a user-friendly application requires that it is easy to learn and is efficient to use. The actual use, and therefore the success of an application or website depends on it. An application or website with high usability is characterised by:

a) Users learning to use the service intuitively, efficiently (quickly and without errors);

b) Being effective (support tasks); and

c) Being pleasant to use (a subjective experience).

The advantages of high usability are:

a) Fewer user complaints;

b) Fewer changes to the service; and

c) Less need for help desk support and training.

The most important reason to give usefulness a place in the development process is that it yields a return. That return arises because usability ensures:

- More efficient work by end users because they understand the service faster and have less need for support as they are satisfied with their current support; and
- Reduced service costs by saving development costs and reducing maintenance costs.

b) Demand-oriented search functionality

The service page can contain various search functions to support the customer with his information needs in a demand-oriented way. It is also essential to consider what type of information the customer needs; do they, for example, need detailed information about business travel arrangements or do they simply want to apply for a train ticket? To provide these different levels of support, a combination of different 'inputs' can be offered. These inputs or search functionalities may include:

- **An alphabetically ordered selection list of all products and services** – this method is the least clear cut for the customer and the least efficient input, but one advantage is that it can be used from a sort of display window function;
- **A structure based on themes and situations –** this method can also be described as the use of demand patterns; in other words, a series of products and services that are coherent to the customer in a logical context. The customer is guided through an increasingly specific selection of product information via a hierarchical 'tree structure' to ultimately only have very (situation) specific information at the deepest level; and
- **A free text search function that allows a customer to specifically search for one product, service or category –** in general, this is not very effective because the coherence between some products and services is difficult to navigate.

The demand-oriented approach aims primarily at clarifying the relationship between the delivery (or execution) of some products and services. As an example, the hiring of a new employee can be considered. Within this framework, various departments within the service organisation have to carry out work: The IT organisation handles matters such as network authorisation or workstation, the facility organisation provides furniture (and sometimes also telecom) and the HR organisation needs to take actions related to the employee's salary, and so on. It is important for the customer to get an exhaustive overview of the delivery conditions such as authorisations, regarding an application. They should also be given an overview on how to reserve a meeting room and organise a catered lunch!

c) Interactive products and service catalogue (iPDC)

The interactive products and service catalogue (iPDC) gives the virtual USD a number of instruments in the field of information retrieval. In the first place, the iPDC fulfils a window display function within the service page that allows the user to obtain a structured overview of the various products and services supplied by the service organisation. The iPDC provides the user with information about service levels, delivery conditions and authorisations; it can also provide a direct referral to a contact person or department, or provide a link to an application form offered on the intranet. To make this information 'discoverable' for the user, the search methods described above are used.

By means of editorial agreements, the structuring and content of the iPDC must be continually checked for relevance and ease-of-use (transparency). Structuring can be described as 'meta-indexing'; in fact, the structuring is determined by the contextual coherence of products and services with the enterprise, as well as by the possible overlap of subjects with some of these products and services with departments other than those within the facility organisation.

A free text search function is implemented as it is easy to build. However, it is often considered as ineffective. It is probably the most commonly used function by most users, since it gives a sort of head start to initiate the search process for those who:

1. Do not know how to navigate through a service catalogue; and
2. Simply do not have the patience or time to go through a service catalogue.

Offering product information via an iPDC on the virtual USD does not have to be limited to the customer. The USD can also use this in the form of its own internal iPDC. For example, the following items can be included in this virtual booking functionality:

- A brief work instruction for the USD employee to initiate the delivery or execution process of a product or service;
- Additional contact information specifically for internal use; and
- Memos regarding temporary changes in delivery or handling.

The management of the internal iPDC's content can be submitted centrally to the USD, or it can be decentralised and allocated to the relevant organisations that deliver the products and services. In the second case, it is still advisable to distribute the final editing (current affairs) and publication centrally to the USD. This means that the USD is responsible for maintaining all aspects of the virtual USD, such as:

- Filling the catalogue and content pages;
- Updating the complete overview of products and services;
- Making management information available;
- Monitoring the lead time of product and service delivery;
- Editing the news service;
- Structuring the demand-oriented search functionality;
- Authorising and maintaining demand and theme-based access;
- Analysing search patterns within the iPDC and adjusting the content and structure accordingly; and
- Answering general questions that arrive via the reaction facilities on the intranet site at the USD.

d) Supporting applications (technology)

The service page is often developed within the existing applications, in this case the intranet, of an enterprise. That is why it is often possible to use existing instruments (applications). If this is not the case, further research will have to be done on available software tools to develop and maintain web pages and forms. It is possible to purchase an external application to expand the existing functionality of the information services.

Software

Existing generic software (such as service management information or workflow management software) is well suited to offer the application and subsequent handling of products and services. If these services can be accessed via the intranet, a possibility arises whereby the user can interactively communicate on aspects relating to the delivery or completion of a product or service. Here, for example, monitoring of status changes of reports can be considered.

For specific applications (such as an administrative reporting service or a personnel information service) to which users must have access, this means that questions must be forwarded to the 'owner' of the specific application. There are various services with which a portal can be developed for the service page. A content management service, possibly extended with a universal form generator, additional information (such as news reports) and application forms can be offered.

Hardware and infrastructure

These aspects are of a more technical nature and, therefore, should be organised in close cooperation with the ICT organisation.

The following starting points are usually of importance:

- When 'setting up' a website within an existing intranet, use can often be made of the existing infrastructure. After all, most enterprises have their own intranet, with a corresponding content management service.
- To facilitate the network capacity, the ICT organisation will have to examine the possible load on the existing infrastructure.
- Sometimes an application other than the standard content management service is required for setting up an iPDC. It is possible that separate web and database servers must be implemented to offer this separate application. This decision is usually left to the ICT organisation.

e) Application forms (often interactive)

For applications that cannot be handled via the generic web-based information services, it is necessary to integrate a form generator with the service page. This functionality is often already offered within a generic content management service. This form generator must be able to store user input, for example in a database service, and generate reports from it. These reports must be configurable and can deliver their output in multiple formats, for example via an intranet page or a spreadsheet.

However, in some cases, it is not possible to use a web-based method of application. Consider, for example, the situation that a budget holder must sign physically for approval. This type of 'initial circuit' often has a procedural cause, and therefore a simplified procedure should be introduced in consultation with the financial department within the service organisation. Depending on the request, the information can ultimately be forwarded via email, the workflow management service or directly to the management application of the responsible component. AI is the burgeoning issue here; IT should be the least involved in examining options for innovation.

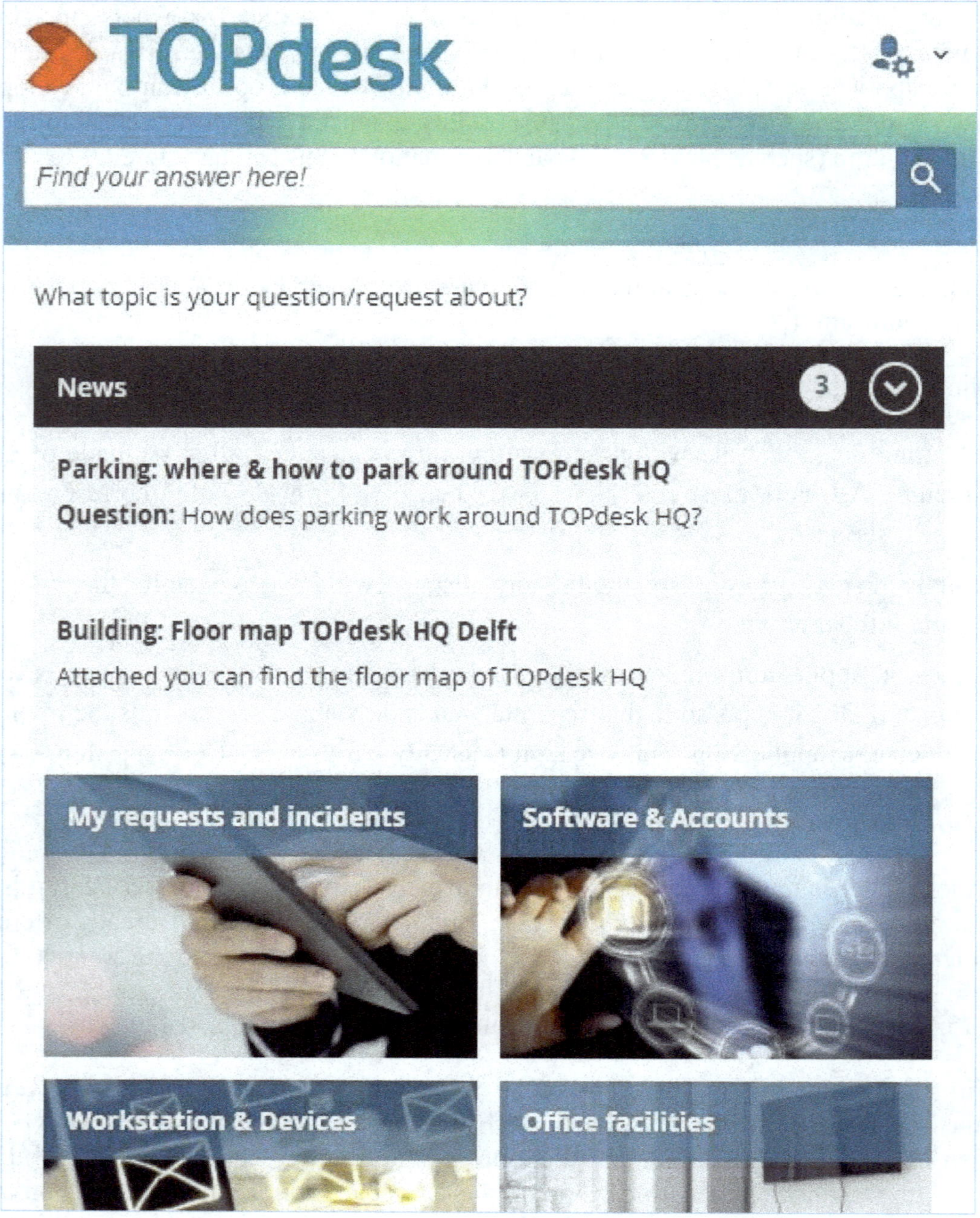

Figure 8.2: Smartphone app for self-service

CHAPTER 9: CALL CENTRE FUNCTIONALITY

The second level of service is called the call centre functionality of the USD. The characteristic feature of this level is that there is no physical customer contact, and this functionality does not have to be located at the same location where the service page is offered, or where the desk is located. Contact, for example, takes place via telephone, email or chat.

After reading this chapter, the reader will gain insight into what is necessary for the design of the call centre functionality, the second level of service in the USD.

9.1 Contact options on the second level

The call centre functionality of the USD is the second level of service. This concerns the customer contact channels such as telephone, email and (digital) mail; however, it can reach much further, think of chat, social media, video, SMS and support within forums.

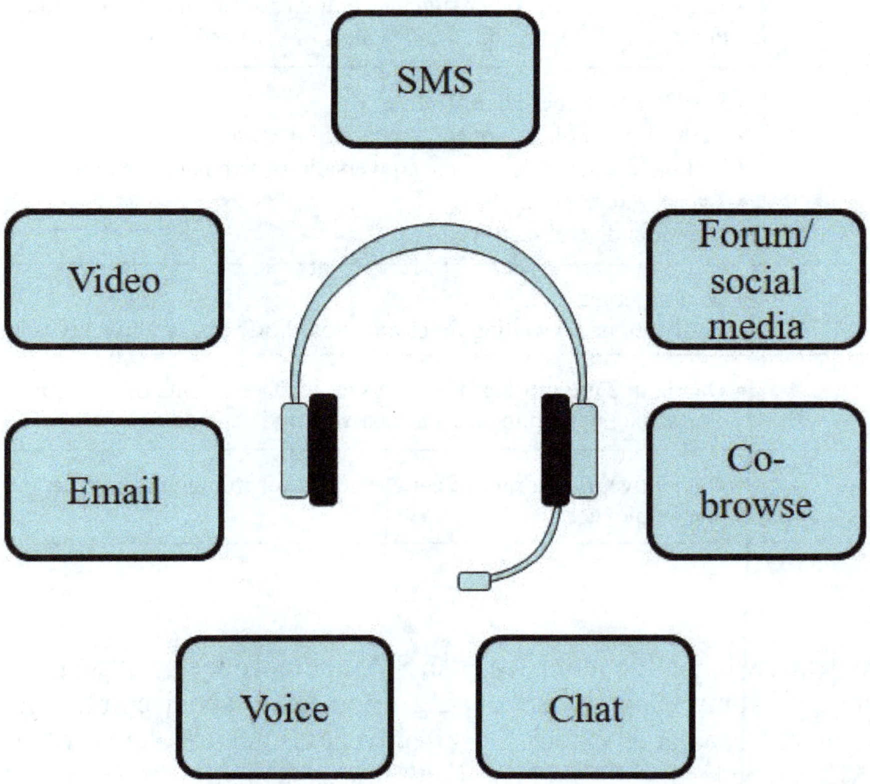

Figure 9.1: The second level of service – call centre functionality

Managing the second level of service requires attention and the insights from the call centre world to help us.

Phone

Customers expect that, if they approach the USD via telephone, email or other media, they will be helped quickly, expertly and reliably. This means that the USD employee who is responsible for the telephone handling must be responsive, focused on the problem and the call of the caller, and can act effectively as a result of the question. Moreover, in a world where location and work are increasingly being separated, the importance of this second level of service is increasing.

Specialised measurement methods are available for enterprises with which the quality of service can be assessed. Using the still-current ServQual method (Zeithaml, Parasuraman & Berry, 1990), measurement methods have been developed that can be used to make statements about the quality of the call centre.[15] *Table 9.1* contains an example of indicators used.

Table 9.1: Assessment Dimensions Based on ServQual

Indicators	Measured Value
Reliability	• Registration of customer contact • Follow-up of actions resulting from contact • Follow-up and direct follow-up actions • Process agreements about registration and follow-up
Responsiveness	• Qualitative monitoring of employee conversations • Registration of results for the fulfilment of result agreements • Registration of customer signals, complaints and signals of dissatisfaction • Procedures for complaints and signals of dissatisfaction
Speed and efficiency	• Speed of customer identification • Authorisation of employees to change business • Linking data from telephone conversations with data from other media • Transfer to relevant others • User-friendly self-service
Accessibility	• Waiting times • Notifications on waiting times and closed offering of alternative channels
Confidence	• Qualitative monitoring of conversations on elements of trust (including repeating and confirming appointments, summarising and concluding)
Personal attention	• Qualitative monitoring of conversations regarding customer service aspects of service line employees

Support of the SMS

Chapter 7 deals in detail with the functionality of an SMS, here we focus on support. The service desk and reservation module comprising the underlying information about employees, buildings, work orders, etc., determines to a large extent the effectiveness and efficiency of a USD in serving customers. The SMS can be loaded with standard questions and answers to frequently asked questions (FAQ), so that the reaction of the USD becomes increasingly uniform. As a result, the USD can answer questions more efficiently. Many SMS provide this functionality as it promotes consistency in answers and offers employees support in the execution of the work.

---

[15] Zeithaml, V., Parasuraman, A. & Berry, L.L., *Delivering Quality Service: Balancing Customer Perceptions and Expectations*, New York: Free Press, 1990.

FAQ is a handy tool. But, it remains a tool and should not be treated as the ten commandments, and is only for the support of the employees in the USD (FAQ on the intranet/Internet is however, a different kettle of piscine species and must be maintained for customers). In addition, it is important to keep control over the information in the knowledge base. This prevents the information from being inaccurate and everyone interpreting their own 'truth' or fake news.

Other technical support

For professional operation of the call centre functionality, use is made of equipment that specialises in the handling of telephone calls. For incoming telephone calls, an Automatic Call Distributor (ACD) or a similar device that distributes incoming calls to employees is used.

A major difference with a standard telephone work environment is that employees do not have a unique telephone number for the caller, they are linked to the general service number. This offers many advantages when it comes to routing calls, setting up 'waiting' texts and making optimum use of the available capacity. After all, it does not matter to customers who they get on the line, as long as they are helped. It cannot be predicted in advance who will speak to the customer. Picking up the call depends on the way the service is set up, the available employee and the rules that are used when passing on the phone calls.

Many systems offer callers an option to talk about certain topics (with a voice response application). Customers then hear a menu where they are supposed to select an option. In a service environment this might be easy (Press 1. for the ICT help desk, 2. for ... and so on). Sometimes customers find this annoying, especially with extensive menus. At least one of the callers is reduced to hurling the phone against the wall.

Sometimes the decision is to use multiple numbers, where one number is the central number, followed by a few specific numbers. So for example, a central number for the internal services, say 7777, and a specific number for the help desk, personnel issues, and so on.

Call centre functionality

Within an enterprise there are telephone numbers for the various services such as information, repro/mailroom, telephone ICT support, alarm report and so on. One central number is used for the USD. Apart from the USD number, the other service numbers also remain. This is for a number of reasons, namely:

- A number of service points must be directly approachable in case of emergency.
- Some departments need to be contacted directly so that clients can deal with experts (e.g. ICT questions).
- Some services, such as repro and mailroom, exist separately from the USD as a physical service point. They may operate this way because relocation yields little in terms of service quality and financial benefit.
- All products and services that are requested by telephone or via the intranet can also be requested via email. In the delivery of services more and more use is made of the internal (digital) mail to deliver services (which have been requested digitally), to the customer.

Quality of the process

The ultimate quality of telephone support is determined by the interaction between the expectations of customers, the way the USD employee deals with a telephone conversation, the availability and refinement of the technological support with an SMS, other specialised systems and the processing from the back office. If a telephone report is handled insufficiently well, this leads to great annoyance. Points of attention when setting up the equipment are shown in *Table 9.2*.

Table 9.2: Points of Attention When Setting Up Telephone Answering Systems

Points of Attention
• Percentage good at once • Reception via choice menu • Reception of peak traffic by recording a call-back appointment • Routing system • Device voice response application

Email

In addition to the telephone, email handling is an important distribution channel for the USD. However, it has the great disadvantage that the questions that come in are unstructured and not always complete. This means that the employees within the USD must translate the incoming mail into relevant products and services and register it, often in an SMS. Modern email systems offer the possibility to translate unstructured data into structured fields so that processing can be largely automated. Many enterprises also choose to replace email with so-called web forms (digital forms that can be filled in via the intranet or Internet and processed automatically).

There are different ways in which email can be effectively processed. The following possibilities are conceivable:

- Designated employees
- Employees with telephone service
- Desk clerks
- Distributed by a coordinating employee
- Translated by special software to enable standardised response
- Post

Designated employees

The advantage is that in principle they can process the emails undisturbed. The disadvantage is that the work on a USD is generally so hectic and diverse that, practically, this is not feasible. This is closely related to the size of the USD. It is easier with larger USDs to create a separation between email handling and telephone service. It is a good way to work where new employees can get used to the type of questions. In addition, by processing it in the SMS, they can also learn how to operate the software.

Employees with telephone service

The advantage of handling emails in this manner is that the employee has an influence on the processing of the question. In the scenario of a telephone conversation this is obviously not the case. The employee will immediately have to deal with the question, while the customer waits on the other side of the line. What still happens is that employees write down the report on a notepad and transfer the data to an information system after the call has ended. Sometimes this cannot be done differently, but this working method does carry the risk that mistakes are made or that it is so busy that the report remains unfinished. That is why it is worth arranging the system in such a way that employees can start registration immediately during the conversation. Headsets and other technology also support this by making it possible for employees to receive calls without using their hands.

Telephone service and email handling at the same time?

Customer satisfaction surveys show that this method does not always work well. Employees who handle email and who are subsequently 'disturbed' in that work by an incoming telephone call, may be less well-focused.

Desk clerks

When work pressure and the availability of resources permit, it is sometimes decided that the staff on counter services will have no telephone handling. In the time that customers are not present at the counter, they can handle emails.

A coordinating employee

This method is often used when no email routing system is available and the supply of emails is extensive and diverse. In this case, it can pay to make one employee responsible for the distribution of incoming emails. Each incoming email is examined and a decision made on the basis of the content about who should handle this email within which period. Where large numbers of email relating to several enterprises are received, this approach can be advantageous because content knowledge and knowledge of the enterprises may otherwise be too broad.

Special software

Software is now available that can recognise route and translate incoming email messages into standard work orders within the SMS. Although this does not work optimally in all cases, a large part of the email processing can be automated.

In practice, we often see a combination of the methods outlined. The application of the different variants will also change as a result of the virtual USD's further development, and as a consequence more and more reports and questions can be handled directly via the intranet/Internet.

Post

Post is a distribution channel that is not often mentioned but which plays an important role in the background. For the collection of questions and calls, mail has been superseded over time and taken over by the intranet/Internet (think of ordering office supplies, giving authorisation for lunches, etc.). But on the delivery side, mail, although today often digitised, still has an important function. Think of the delivery of phone calls, laptops, software and information brochures. Certainly when choosing to discontinue the physical USD, a good logistical organisation of the provision of services is indispensable. For information services such as a library and documentary information provision, delivery as well as the collection of files, texts, books, etc. in the workplace is still an indispensable link.

9.2 Social media: chat, blogs and tweets

In addition to the traditional contact points (telephone, email and post – Note it did not take long for email to become 'traditional'), thanks to information technology, the possibilities have expanded considerably, offering USDs new capabilities and challenges.

Large enterprises have already embraced user forums and chat functions. Think of the use of chat features such as Twitter, Yammer, WhatsApp, Facebook, FaceAche, and other features created for phone-centric generation. They allow members to share experiences, interests and present information and personal content. The inclination within enterprises is to exploit this potential to the full extent, because social media appeals to the self-obsessed, instant gratification society created by IT. No, wait, that's fake news…

However, effects of the use of social media reach further than a 'one-to-one' conversation over the phone. After all, the contents of a conversation is often visible to others due to the ability to build communities, to give opinions and share, and so on. The impact can be significantly larger than they imagined by many people seduced by the ease of communication.

These technologies offer new features like peer-to-peer support; they also allow IT organisations to establish and manage enterprise communities on the business's social collaboration platform, where they can foster support for simple technical issues.

Users visit these social media platforms for different reasons, but mostly they can be divided into the following categories:

- To give product or service feedback or reviews;
- To find more information about a product or service; and
- To upgrade an owned product or service (see also Gartner).[16]

The tendency within organisations is to fully realise these possibilities because social media tools make it easy to deploy these applications quickly. However, the consequences of the use of social media extend beyond a one-to-one telephone conversation. A conversation's content can be visible to others due to the possibility to build communities, give advice and share content, and so on. The impact can then be considerably greater than foreseen. The proper application of these instruments also requires a lot of time and capacity. Users expect quick responses when an application like Yammer or Twitter is used. Not responding immediately has major consequences because dissatisfied users will use the same media to communicate their discontent. That is why the use of social media on the service desk requires deliberate choices translated into a strategy, and a necessary deployment of resources, as almost all organisations today have a communication strategy and a corresponding capability for the exploitation of social media.

---

[16] Gartner, *Magic Quadrant for IT Service Management Tools and Magic Quadrant for IT Service Management Tools*, August 2018.

CHAPTER 10: THE SERVICE COUNTER

The development of the USD is the result of the physical translation of the one-stop-shop concept. The starting point is that the customer can go to one central physical location within the building for all questions about internal products and services. The design and construction of the physical USD, however, needs some thought. This concerns not only the non-tangible aspects, (organisation, function and philosophy), but also the very tangible aspects, such as materials, colour, location and space.

After reading this chapter, the reader will have insight into the subjects that are related to the construction of the physical USD counter. The way in which these topics are dealt with ultimately determines the form and content of the physical counter.

10.1 Construction of the physical USD

Various components come together in the construction of the physical USD. On the one hand, the conceptual starting points for the one-stop shop concept must be followed. On the other hand, physical construction offers an excellent opportunity to make the client-oriented approach tangible. This means that the final structural design must comply with many conditions. Seven components play an important role in this and are part of a programme of requirements. Each provides a different emphasis in places where the USD needs to welcome external customers (think of job centres) as well as internal ones:

1. Function
2. Location
3. Identity
4. Building technical aspects
5. Economic considerations
6. Aesthetic aspects
7. Organisational interpretation

1. Function

The purpose of the USD is the bundling and funneling of (operational) customer questions. In addition, the USD provides the information for all products and services for the facility organisation. It has previously been argued that the USD can accept and handle all operational products and services. However, they must also be able to channel the questions and needs that cannot be handled by the USD in an effective manner, in other words to escalate to account management. The service must be designed in such a way that the desired way of working is supported within the organisational process. Thus, the desired functionality must be applicable in the new physical setting.

The physical layout of the USD can also be a driver for organisational changes. The physical desk can exist as a visible central reporting point, a point in the enterprise where all questions and needs are addressed and resolved. This creates internal pressure from the customers to actually structure the service organisation in a suitable manner, and to better coordinate the service delivery processes and handle reports in an integrated fashion. This means that integration is offered at the service desk, and as a result, the back office is more driven by the processes.

Example: The physical USD as a driver for the one-stop shop

The service centre of an enterprise is a physical, central location where all front-end services of enterprise operations are accommodated. The services that might concern the USD include IT, the library, the travel agency, information distribution functions for the various parts of the management operations such as archives, mail and electronic notifications; the services might extend to building and installations via account management.

Irrespective of the decision regarding everything being located at the USD, the chosen form results in three physical points of contact:

1. The knowledge and information centre (KIC) where customers can go for their information needs (books, files, regulations, application forms etc.);
2. The travel agency (for domestic and foreign business trips); and
3. The USD (for facility and information services).

The USD also fulfils the role of reception function for the financial, personnel and communication functions where physical contact with experts is desired. From the USD, appointments can be made with the experts in the back office. The big advantage of this concept is that the customer can go to one central point for all services. For example, a laptop can be picked up or an ID card can be immediately renewed.

In the design of the physical service, the architect found a means for the integration of visitors in the service centre. The visitors are welcomed between the physical counters, so that an informal interaction can occur. This is supported by directional indications in the ceiling (coloured lights), and on the floor (arrows embossed in the floor covering) and lighting.

From the one-stop shop idea, various service functions must be combined. There are two possibilities for this: the complete integration of the functions or the combination of the functions. In the first situation, the departments are integrated organisationally. In the second situation, the functions remain separated. It is then possible to opt for a form in which logical services are integrated. This leads to multiple counter points within one physical location where the underlying organisational units can be independent of each other.

The choice for this depends on the objectives of the USD based on the front-office back-office principle and accommodation needs of different customers. Do not forget to consider the potential needs of the disabled, who may have additional requirements.

2. Location

An aspect that is sometimes overlooked is the location of the service counter. At what position in the building is the service counter located? How much space is needed for a service counter that meets the requirements set in the initial plan, taking into account space to meet customers (first line) and workstations at the back of the desk (second line)? Is the service counter located near the back office or not? Have the logistical and infrastructure principles been taken into account in the choice of location? What about disabled access?

Assume the customers perspective. Is the service counter located at a logical location that is useful to all, or is the counter placed behind an electrically operated fire door with restricted entry parameters and the odd snazzy, but so essential barbed wire fence?

3. Identity

The image of the service organisation rises by direct and indirect experiences with the service. Direct experiences are formed on the basis of customer experiences with the products or services, their quality, the price-quality ratio and the service provided. These are the manageable factors. The indirect experiences cannot be influenced by the service organisation and constitute the uncontrollable factors. The physical USD is one of these. As soon as the physical USD is designed and built, the service organisation has a unique opportunity to express the identity of its services.

The architectural design offers an excellent opportunity to make the conceptual starting points of demand-oriented work and the one-stop-shop concept tangible. Design, colour, functionality and so on are therefore means with which the enterprise can indirectly influence the quality of service. The architect should wonder what happens from the moment that the space is entered from the service counter to the desk. The following question can then be asked: is it a no-nonsense environment or do we want to create a living room feeling; 'here's a nice pair of slippers, fancy a cuppa?'

4. Building technical aspects

The design of the USD must take into account material, noise, climate, power, technical infrastructure and ergonomic aspects. These must be incorporated into the technical design of the physical USD. The layout must also be designed in such a way that the employees are motivated to work in the new setting. Appearance plays an important role in this. As a result of the need for demand-oriented work and the introduction of the front-office back-office principle, work processes and working methods will have to be adapted. In order to create a good working environment, attention will also have to be paid to ergonomics and the choice of colour and shape, in addition to health and safety standards.

The programme in which all these requirements and wishes are included is of great importance to the architect and the builders. Often, this is still being considered during the start of construction. That is why it is wise to take a little more time to complete the programme and to think through the requirements. Consider: availability of wheelchair spaces, flexible worktop height for desk staff, explanation tables, cupboard space, cloakroom, coffee corner, space for brochure material, a waiting room. When working with flexible workplaces and with employees working without a drawer unit, you should think of lockers or trolleys with the corresponding storage space.

Other points of interest include:

- The boundary between customer spaces and the service counter;
- The boundary between the counter and the back office;
- The type or brand of machines and furniture;
- Informal meeting places next to desks;
- Connections with the various management systems;
- The number of employees;
- Connections to electricity and ICT;
- Drawer cabinets; and
- Depending on the nature of interactions, perspex barriers might be employed.

5. Economic considerations

Together with all structural, image and functional requirements, there are also economic considerations. A cost-benefit analysis is a necessary part of the optimisation of the preconditions. A difficulty with a cost-benefit analysis is that the considerations cannot always be expressed in money. Sometimes, due to cultural change, it is desirable to pay extra attention to the design from the employee perspective not the financial perspective. However, the potential impact can be so great that it leads to different choices. Familiarity with the building, the availability of an informal meeting place and the possibility to cultivate a feeling of solidarity might lead to a more expensive solution than a shed outside. However, it means that the cost-benefit analysis must not only be left to financial managers.

6. Aesthetic aspects

The eye wants to be pleased, and every designer or client will need a look that goes beyond the basic observation that the service counter 'looks neat.' In some cases there is a need to convey a 'statement', feeling or idea. In a broader sense it concerns the atmosphere that the service counter must radiate. For a service manager, meeting such a need is not usually the highest priority, but for its client this is often an important argument to opt for a specific design, even if this is at the expense of functionality or meeting the wishes of employees, and leads to higher costs.

7. Organisational interpretation

In addition to functional interpretation and costs, the organisational impact will be particularly important. It is not feasible to have a complete picture of how the USD organisation will function in advance. Not all functionalities and working methods will be thought through or provided for in the thinking process. In addition, an enterprise must also set itself up and space must be allowed to be able to easily make adjustments without incurring expensive renovations. This means that the physical space must be arranged in such a way that organisational changes are possible. If, for example, it is known that several functions will be added within one or two years, there must be room for additional workplaces. Flexibility and multifunctionality are therefore important points of attention. If the USD organisation has to be adjusted slightly, it must be possible to extend or break walls without having to move pipes, or wiring. This multifunctionality is already being used in the construction of new office buildings and must also continue to the interior.

But there are more uncertainties, such as: is the desk separate from the telephone support? As the desk clerks also have to do other work. How is the maintenance carried out? How does the service manager see the future developments, and to what extent is the chosen design flexible enough to also absorb both unexpected and anticipated changes? Has sufficient account been taken of growth or contraction? Do you distinguish between first and second line handling, and is there enough space available for employees to be able to work if that option is chosen? What does the location of the USD mean for the adjacent logistics?

There are many questions to think about. They bring uncertainty, and uncertainty is something that a service manager wants to avoid in the final design. Paradoxically, this means that the final design with the associated schedule of requirements must be clear and concrete. Flexibility should mainly lie in the preliminary phase, with future developments being planned as far as possible.

10.2 Optimising requirements

The requirements associated with the seven components create mutual tension. Increasing the spillover effects will lead to higher costs. The degree of functional and flexible organisation can be at odds with the wishes of the architect.

The final choice for the physical device is therefore a result of the consideration with regard to the seven components we started with. It is difficult to give guidelines for this because the choices will differ per enterprise and per situation, but at least it can be connected (and sometimes required) to the relevant ergonomic and construction standards. Nonetheless, in the implementation of the front-office back-office principle of the physical USD, the consideration is a critical success factor that cannot be left to an architect or financial decision-maker alone. For example, if you expect professionalism from the employees at the USD or want to convey a specific image of the services, then this should also be reflected in the physical environment.

CHAPTER 11: ACCOUNT MANAGEMENT

Not everything can be automated or standardised. In some cases, interaction with the customer will be needed to find out exactly what they require. In general, we see this task arising in two ways, initially via the service request, via an interview with an employee at the desk or over the telephone. In some cases the level of knowledge of the interviewer or the mandate is insufficient. In these instances, it is easier and more effective to enter into a personal conversation with the customer bringing account management into contact.

After reading this chapter, the reader will have insight into the requirements and functioning of account management from the perspective of a USD.

11.1 Where did the concept of account management come from?

Account management emerged in the commercial sector from the development of market-oriented thinking. Customer's preferences and needs should be central (well, within reason). The account manager's tasks in the commercial sector are maintaining contacts, performing market analyses, forming an intermediary function (between provider and requesters) and supporting more complicated sales processes.

Good account managers are fully informed employees who can translate and realize realistic wishes from customers with authority in their own company; that are well-oriented on all disciplines within the company and that thoroughly know the possibilities and limitations of the accounts.[17]

This approach stems from a philosophy about how an enterprise (and in our case the USD) wants to be perceived in the environment. The following questions are central to this philosophy[18]:

- Who do we want to count on as our customers, which customers are of strategic importance (the accounts) and what needs do they have?
- What results can we realise (or want to realise) for our customers in relation to their needs?
- How can we operate our account management organisation (its policies, processes and management) so that we can realise results for our customers and maintain our competitive advantage?
- What are the most important elements of the way we serve our customers (our service concept)?

Although these questions are mainly asked in a market environment, the principles in this philosophy are well applicable in an environment of internal service provision, such as the facility company. We will then make a translation between the concept as used in the commercial environment and the special characteristics of a service organisation such as the facilities or IT organisation.

---

[17] Leeflang, P.S.H., "Account management, een zaak die aandacht verdient", *Bedrijfskunde*, p. 99–111, 1991.

[18] Bos, R., Luchtenberg, B. & Schulte, R., *Wegwijs in accountmanagement. Echte accountmanagers golfen niet,* Zaltbommel: Uitgeverij Thema, 2002.

There are labels attached to the roles and activities belonging to account management. Names that are often used are: business partner, service delivery manager, or business relationship manager. And a specific title is not always given to the activities or responsibilities. These are then allocated to key employees or senior employees depending on the size and nature of an enterprise.

We have already identified one particular feature in the beginning of the book, and that is how we often talk about customers but we mean 'customers or users'. Sometimes we have to refuse a customer request because of frameworks, policies and agreements, in many cases one is obliged to use a service from a supplier that cannot be altered. Another feature is that some services and benefits cannot simply be translated into competitive advantage and that the results for customers are of a different order than economic benefits.

11.2 Account management within services

Despite these differences, the concept in adapted form can strengthen our concept of service provision, whereby the demand process is structured by means of the front office back office principle. We do this by also appointing account management within the USD.

Whether account management personnel and tasks are actually invested in a USD depends on the enterprise. In all cases, account management must work closely with the employees in the USD to receive and provide both current and useful information about a customer need or demand.

Within the service organisation, account management consists of managing, supervising and developing internal customer relations. Therefore, an account manager at a service organisation is a relationship manager; this contrasts with many identical functions that are externally focused on sales. Account management functions as a bridge between the internal facilities offer and the customer. In fact, account management aligns the explicit questions and latent needs of clients on the one hand, and the supply of the facilities organisation on the other. In this respect it differs enormously from the more limited view expressed in some service management publications.

In a demand-oriented service organisation, customer demand is taken as the starting point for acting within the legal and political frameworks of the enterprise. In a situation of forced shopping, the customer is king - but the service organisation often remains emperor. The function of account manager is an important addition to the resources needed to shape the demand-oriented service organisation.

Goals of account management are:

- Providing optimal support for the primary process;
- Managing and developing agreements with customers;
- Developing and maintaining the customer relationship;
- Monitoring customer satisfaction; and
- Taking care of public relations.

11.3 Roles of account management

What does account management stand for? Many find it useful to speak of account manager roles to answer this question.[19] These roles, provided they are translated, are well applicable for the facility environment. They are the following five:

1. The account manager as an explorer of the environment;
2. As a representative of the client or user;
3. As a relationship manager;
4. As coordinator; and
5. As a partner.

We now apply these roles to the person of the account manager.

1. The account manager as an explorer of the environment

Account managers must have an overview of the total work area of the service organisation. They concentrate on the work area and ask themselves which customer groups and what special needs they have for support. Account managers also analyse future needs because they can have a major impact on the manner and content of requested services. It is important that account managers can translate the needs of the customers into targeted services. This also means that they are aware of the developments outside the enterprise and the influence they have on the customer, and thus indirectly on the service organisation.

Table 11.1: Tasks Related to the Role of Account Manager as an Explorer

Tasks
• To gauge the needs and wishes of customers, particularly in the primary process • Recognising changes in customers' needs and wants • Matching long-term visions • Thinking about new services

2. The account manager as a representative of the client or user

The moment a customer hands over a question to the service desk they relinquish ownership/ responsibility. The customer then assumes that the handling of the demand is in good hands (really…). For simple questions with a small risk of ensuing problems, such as a room reservation, request for a mobile phone or a leak report, the inquirer also has little doubt about the quality of delivery. In case of critical questions such as a relocation or a reception, where there is indeed a greater risk of damage if the delivery does not go according to plan, the account manager provides the solution as a representative of the customer.

---

[19] Bos, R., Luchtenberg, B. & Schulte, R., *Wegwijs in accountmanagement. Echte accountmanagers golfen niet*, Zaltbommel: Uitgeverij Thema, 2002.

Despite the low risk involved with simple questions, the account manager must remain alert. If a small question is handled poorly and a customer feels ignored or patronised, the 'small question' suddenly becomes very big.

Because of their position, account managers have horizontal and vertical access within the facilities organisation, and they can signal and intervene if something threatens to go wrong. In these cases, the account managers ensure that the facilities organisation's back office fulfils the promised agreements. In consequence, it is obvious that they also need the right mandate within the enterprise.

Table 11.2: Tasks Related to the Role of Account Manager as a Representative

Tasks
• Operating as a trouble shooter • Representing the customer within the facilities organisation • Acting as a contact person and point of contact for the customer

3. The account manager as a relationship manager

An important task of the account manager is maintaining and strengthening relationships with customers. On the one hand, the goal is to bind the customer, on the other hand, it is to gain a good understanding of the situation in which a customer operates and to ensure that the customer will inform them of new developments over time.

Binding customers means that they are committed to the enterprise and that they usually report problems in time. It also means that problems that may result from errors or miscommunication may be recognised quickly; and that the customer, as a result of the personal relationship, shows more understanding and is more flexible. In these cases, the service organisation has more space and time to recover. Essential in the relationship is the mutual trust that needs time to grow (after all, trust comes on foot and goes on horseback, as football managers will attest. Or is that jockeys? Who knows?).

Table 11.3: Tasks Related to the Role of Account Manager as Relationship Manager

Tasks
• Thinking along with the customer and helping them develop ideas • Matching long-term visions • Drafting and monitoring service agreements • Communicating organisational characteristics to customers • Holding annual interviews or progress meetings

4. The account manager as coordinator

If customers come up with questions and needs at a tactical and strategic level, this requires extra attention and effort from the service organisation. In many cases, the account manager can act as a coordinator who ensures that the agreements with the client are fulfilled and that every separate department in the back office delivers in a timely and accurate fashion. It is important that the account manager ensures that they gain acceptance from all parties involved. As a coordinator, the account manager becomes the owner of the customer request.

Table 11.4: Tasks Related to the Role of Account Manager as a Coordinator

Tasks
• Analysing all relevant information about the parties involved in the supply and demand of services • Drawing up plans and supporting projects • Addressing colleagues about their responsibilities • Managing and monitoring whether the agreements made with the customer are fulfilled

5. The account manager as a partner

When account managers do their work well, they are the key point of contact for service support. The knowledge of the account managers goes well beyond the products and services. They have knowledge of the market and the possibilities and they can assist the customer with advice and action. Ultimately, a relationship arises whereby account managers are fully-fledged discussion partners. Such a relationship must develop. The scope for this is of course also dependent on the positioning of the tasks from the service organisation. If it only concerns a task environment on the tactical level, the partnership will be limited. In practice, we see that relationships are highly dependent on the personal characteristics of those who complete the account management.

Table 11.5: Tasks Related to the Role of Account Manager as a Partner

Tasks
• Providing insight into costs and revenues • Making knowledge and expertise available on the market • Providing assistance in cases of error • Monitoring service quality • Giving advice and information

11.4 Tools for the account manager

Account management uses tools and methods that serve to manage the relationship between the customer and the service organisation. These instruments support both the management and monitoring of the mutual relationship (relation management) and the service agreements. Think of customer interviews, management of service agreements, conducting surveys and satisfaction surveys, analysing and resolving complaints. Account managers have various tools at their disposal. These are listed in *Table 11.6*.

Table 11.6: Account Management Tools

Account Management Tools
• Public relations • USD • Intranet • Facility management information systems • Products and service catalogue • Management reports • Networks • Contact point for the customer • Communication plans • Vision • Service level agreements (SLAs) • Money and resources • Benchmarks and key figures • Knowledge of business units • Account plans • Staff monitoring • Department plans • Customer surveys • Customer calls • Customer panels • Customer satisfaction research • Customer databases

11.5 Account management in conjunction with the USD

As noted earlier, the role of account management within each enterprise is different. It can be a senior function as a point of contact within the desk or it can be a completely independent department. The position we take is a logical consequence of the choice of the USD as a concept of service aimed at streamlining customer demand. This means that account management is a logical activity and is part of all available distribution channels. In *chapter 3* we also made a distinction from the perspective of the total of products and services. It does not pay to organise such a function if the entire range can be offered in a standardised manner, but experience shows that this is rarely the case. This does not alter the fact that even though it is deliberately not an account management function, it always remains necessary within the enterprise to appoint someone who is the contact person in case of escalations.

As indicated in *chapters 2* and *3*, account management is particularly involved with those products and services that are tactical in nature, such as advice on purchasing processes, information about larger meetings and receptions, and relocations. In addition, account management plays an active role in setting up and maintaining service agreements, as well as monitoring new developments among customers that may lead to new services, or the communication and reporting of performance data.

CHAPTER 12: EXPERT USD STAFF

No USD will function without employees (hold back the tears); they determine the success of the USD. So, to operate professionally, the USD must have expert staff who like to help and serve customers.

After reading this chapter, the reader will have insight into the importance of well-trained employees with the right competencies for a well-functioning USD.

12.1 Employees determine the USD success

With a professional USD, a service organisation strives for a customer-oriented attitude. In order to be able to make this happen, the right expertise and the right behaviour must be fulfilled for employees, and the USD must also have the power to oversee a solid management function and sufficient capacity to handle customer questions. If it turns out that the USD cannot achieve the ambition level, this means that the customers and the employees (from both the USD and the back office) will be disappointed. The USD staff must therefore have the right knowledge and skills, in other words, be competent to realise the ambitions that the USD strives for. Requirements for the competencies of USD employees are:

- An intrinsic focus on helping customers;
- General knowledge of the systems within the USD;
- Knowledge of the enterprise and its cooperation partners (internal and external);
- The ability to organise the substantive knowledge areas of which the USD exists;
- Product and process knowledge; and
- Communication and social skills.

Every USD employee is expected to have basic knowledge of the systems used. All employees should be aware of the other tasks, although there are always employees who have specialised in more specific areas than others. This does not mean, however, that full responsibility can lie with one employee.

A second important point is that the USD is the crossroad where many people involved in the services come together. Consequently, the USD has to deal with different parties, namely:

- **Customers, including customers who pay for services (external)** – in general, these are the contract partners, or, in the case of internal customers, often the managers or the general management. In addition, budget holders are important customers. Customers that pay will compare the quality of the service against the price. In this, they always make a consideration between necessity and desire, on the one hand, and the costs and contribution of the facility services, on the other.
- **Customers that want to be supported as well as possible in the execution of their core task** – where services, in particular IT services, are outsourced, this form of support is most often the bone of contention. Sometimes customers mistakenly think that USD services do not apply to them. However, the service conditions are bound to the policy decisions of general management.
- **Back office** – the USD also has to deal with the back offices of the various departments, both internal and external suppliers plus service providers. Every department has its own back office

and it is, therefore, of great importance that the communication between the USD and the back offices is optimal, because this ensures that service to the customer is also good.

- **External suppliers, like contractors, electricians and painters** – on the one hand, they perform tasks that are controlled by the USD; on the other hand, they can expect the invoices to be paid on time and correctly, that correct information is available, and so on.
- **USD support** – this could include the functional system administrator who is responsible for the implementation of the various systems that are used within the USD. The enterprise in which the USD is included also belongs to its customers.

Sometimes, these mutual interests are contradictory, and the USD must act as a 'traffic controller' and 'arbitrator'. All these different customers use the USD in accordance with their own needs, and this places necessary high demands on the social skills of the employees.

12.2 Functions within the USD

The functions within the USD are:

- Manager;
- Employee; and
- Account manager.

Of course, further classification by level is still possible within the USD. In practice, the following employee categories might exist to distinguish between different levels of functional activity in a USD:

- Manager;
- Senior employee;
- Junior employee; and
- Account manager.

Manager

The manager is responsible for USD employees and, accordingly, they are employees' first point of contact. The manager is expected to have at least a higher professional education and higher level of experience than other employees Depending on the size, the manager of the USD is also likely to be required to cooperate with other managerial functions and in addition, must be able to carry out the basic tasks of the USD.

Senior employee

A senior employee is someone who has substantial experience with working for the USD for a long time, either in the same enterprise or in different bodies. The senior employee and the junior employee have the same basic tasks. However, the senior employee's range of tasks is extended with additional tasks within the USD. These are duties that a junior employee does not / cannot perform.

Junior employee

A junior employee is someone who has only been working for the USD for a short time and who can further develop towards the senior employee position.

Here are some of the USD employees' tasks:

- Performing USD tasks in the field of services. This includes the registering and processing of enquiries for services, monitoring progress, processing requests for services and reporting back to customers about the handling of the services;
- Processing customer questions, requests and complaints;
- Providing information to customers and making arrangements with customers about the actual delivery of products and services, including IT;
- Conducting automated administrations (including collecting, registering and processing basic data), releasing (management) information and identifying bottlenecks and problems;
- Handling specific electronic mail traffic;
- Handling the operational management and maintenance of systems, structures, contracts, equipment or objects (including IT and the supply of basic data from the operational management);
- Ensuring the realisation of all operational supports and activities in the context of projects, plans and the day-to-day operational tasks of a business unit under the supervision of a professional colleague or supervisor; and
- Making proposals and contributing to the improvement of working procedures, regulations and methods. Focusing on improving the service provided by their unit and increasing its quality and efficiency.

Junior, middle and senior: designations within the USD organisation

The actual implementation of tasks and responsibilities in USD jobs can vary greatly, and the differences often have to do with the USD organisation's size. In a large enterprise, the manager, who is ultimately responsible, will have several components in their portfolio and they delegate the operational management carried out by the senior employee(s). Sometimes a distinction is made between junior, middle and senior employees.

In this situation, the senior employee acts as a team leader and the mid-level employee, and any junior employees, are accountable to the senior employee. In this role, the senior employee also conducts coaching sessions and takes part in appraisal interviews. In smaller USD organisations, the senior employee is a fully cooperating team member and the senior role mainly relates to specific knowledge and skills in one or more subjects.

An example of how tasks may be distributed is given in *Table 12.1*.

Table 12.1: An Example of the Distribution of Tasks Between Junior, Mid-level and Senior Employees

	Junior	Mid-level	Senior
Handling general telephone number	✓	✓	✓
Handling of telephone (complaints, preferences, information and incidents)	✓	✓	✓
Handling email (complaints, preferences, information and incidents)	✓	✓	✓
Handling Internet/intranet notifications	✓	✓	✓
Counter facility	✓	✓	✓
ICT counter tasks	✓	✓	✓
Organising meetings	×	✓	✓
People co-locations	×	✓	✓
Intake projects	×	✓	✓
Support for tenders	×	✓	✓
Planning and schedules	×	×	✓
Operational manager	×	×	✓

Account manager

As the connecting link between the customer or USD employee and the back office, the account manager provides the translation of the customer demand for the products and services provided by the various back offices. In addition, they monitor service delivery to ensure that the customer request is satisfactorily answered. The account manager is responsible for the intake and handling of all questions that are not recorded within the operational service package. Depending on the enterprise's size and nature, as well as the complexity of client questions, higher vocational education and cognitive skills are also desirable for this job. On this basis, the following basic skills can be distinguished from the account manager:

USD as showcase

The account manager is the contact point and face of the services for the clients in the enterprise. If the quality of the services provided to the USD is largely determined by the quality of the products themselves, the quality of the products is mainly determined by the translation of the customer demand (the question behind the question). This requires the account manager to be able to adopt the position of the customer and understand the importance of their enterprise.

Translation to products

The account manager must have extensive knowledge of the products and services that the service organisation provides. USD staff rely on knowledge systems and existing demand patterns, but the complex customer questions submitted to the account manager sometimes require completely new and creative interpretations of existing products.

Manager of customer demand

A third aspect of the required skills involves being capable of providing the service. Demand-oriented work has been developed from the insight that dealing with the multiple client interfaces of a complex enterprise is too time-consuming. It is necessary to spend time coordinating the handling of the requested services, and sometimes the account manager must take over a question. But what is the added value of the account manager in this?

The account manager must be able to lead the back office to provide the service. This requires some authority from the account manager, though without undue hierarchical behaviour. After all, the account managers have the authority of knowledge and insight. In these circumstances, they get the necessary job done. This also prevents the account manager from being bypassed by customers. Customers soon establish that they can now resolve their problems in a standardised, efficient manner via the account manager.

Responsiveness

The account manager function initially receives few standardised customer questions. However, the account manager will identify trends because they are the front line of new issue resolution. These trends often comprise the queries behind customer questions, leading to deeper problems being identified.

Professional and intellectual ability

The required work and thinking level is highly dependent on the size, nature and possibilities of the enterprise and the complexity of customer demands. It is clear that a good account manager is more than an employee who mediates between customer questions and services (translation from need to supply). The account manager has a profile greater than 'need to supply' and can offer a solution where things go awry with delivery methods, which is the added value of the role. To properly characterise the weight of this function one could say that the account manager is one of the back office specialists with the ambition to grow into a managerial position. Positioning the account management function as a springboard for a career to management level is common.

12.3 Competencies within the USD

The USD staff must fulfil a pivotal role within the enterprise, so they must be sufficiently skilled and able to handle different tasks at the same time. In addition to expert knowledge, competencies such as communication skills and managerial skills will also be important. The other characteristics and competencies that a USD employee must have are listed below:

a) Customer-friendly attitude
b) Flexibility
c) Result orientation
d) Involvement and empathy
e) Planning and organisational skills
f) Team skills and the ability to cooperate

g) Willingness to take the initiative

h) Capacity to deal with multiple interests

a) Customer-friendly attitude

A customer-friendly attitude is paramount. In addition, the manner of customer approach is extremely important. If the customer comes up with a question that cannot be answered immediately, the next step is to lead the customer to the expert; it may be necessary to contact the customer with new information or to make an appointment with the intended employee.

b) Flexibility

The USD employee is expected to be flexible because the work within the USD can vary considerably. They must also have the ability to easily take over from absent colleagues.

c) Result orientation

The USD strives to help the customer as effectively and clearly as possible and employees are expected to be result-oriented and, together with their immediate colleagues, do everything they can to achieve a good result.

Result-oriented working

Result-oriented working means having the ability to translate customer enquiries and to accept and process customer demand (tempo, language, articulation and intonation). Employees should be paying attention to these points:

- Taking the call in an appropriate manner
- Confirming the question
- Analysing well, listening and then summarising
- Indicating a good solution
- Denying requests (when necessary, just say NO)
- Closing correctly
- Using the customer's name to indicate empathy

d) Involvement and empathy

The USD employee must be involved in the work that is carried out for the benefit of the customers and keep abreast of changes within the enterprise. This could include changes to procedures, introduction of new systems, additions to modules in current IT applications and systems, and so on. Of course it is also important that the employee remains involved in the questions that the customer submits to the USD, and that they carefully monitor the progress of the processing. It is a quality of the USD employee to be able to give a good 'no-message' so that a customer understands and accepts it.

Empathy is an important quality in dealing with customer complaints at the counter. Consideration of the relevance of a complaint and why the customer finds this a complaint should be paramount. It becomes even more difficult if the USD also deals with external customers, for example clients in a healthcare institution or public services. Some customers will always have a bad attitude, but often customers exhibit bad behaviours based on previous experiences in being 'assisted'. Unfortunately, there is no magic method of dealing with difficult people.

e) Planning and organisational skills

At the bases of a successful USD is an organised schedule to execute basic tasks. Think about breaks, shifts (for a call centre or counter), how email is handled, procedures on how to deal with requests that take more time to handle etc. Some appointments and tasks are known beforehand but without doubt, new unexpected situations pop up every day. You have to understand how to set priorities and how to deal with deadlines, and keep an eye on scheduled work. So, the USD employee has to deal with a variety of tasks in an environment that can be hectic, sometimes even chaotic. Based on experience they can predict the basic flow, but they have to be highly adaptable to new situations. Understanding this reality and making sure that all work is planned and handled in the correct manner is essential.

f) Team skills and the ability to cooperate

As a USD employee, you are the central point of contact for the customer. It is important that a USD employee can work well within a group. Good mutual relations between the employees are important, so that a joint effort can be made to achieve a good result. If necessary, good colleagues will take over tasks in busy times without grumbling.

g) Willingness to take the initiative

For an employee of the USD, taking initiative is important. If a customer comes up with a question for which a number of matters must be arranged, it is up to the employee to take on those tasks and ensure that the necessary steps are taken. The customer is not helped with a wait-and-see attitude of the employee, in the hope that another colleague will start to deal with the question.

The importance of qualified employees in the USD and related requirements to them means that such employees are not always easy to find. This is partly related to the appropriate experience or education. But in many cases little or no attention has been paid to conversation and listening techniques or written communication. Often training is an effective solution.

h) Capacity to deal with multiple interests

As indicated at the beginning of this chapter, the USD is the crossroad where many people involved in the services meet. Employees should, therefore, be able to assess who they are dealing with accurately and act accordingly.

Additional tasks for the account manager

In addition, the account managers 'success' depends on the quality of their relationships within the enterprise. In this respect, an account manager's 'soft' competencies are more important than the technology they use. These soft competencies are often intrinsic rather than learnt. The main soft competencies are:

- Contact skills
- A feeling for 'politics'
- Enthusiasm
- Customer focus

- Collaboration

12.4 Practice competencies

In many enterprises, the competencies linked to functions have been identified. Usually such data sits on a database and is never used. If you want to actively encourage competencies within the USD, it is important to explicitly state which competencies (knowledge, attitude or behaviour) are expected from the USD employee. Competencies can be described at different levels (for example, to clarify the distinction between junior, mid-level and senior), so that all functions have similar competencies, but at different levels. An example is shown in *Table 12.2*.

Table 12.2: Identifying Competencies at Levels within the USD

	Level 1	Level 2	Level 3	Level 4
Results-oriented	Sets priorities and has an overview of their own work.	Agree with others. Creates preconditions for the execution of scheduled work.	Coordinates multiple projects and activities that are carried out by different people.	Coordinates complex work with long lead times. Is decisive when creating plans.
Collaboration	Is focused on a common goal and cooperates to achieve it.	Know and use the qualities of others.	Actively searches for cooperation with others and directs actions towards common goals.	Creates clear preconditions for good cooperation. Is responsible for the group process.
Empathy	Works with limited guidance and looks for solutions to problems.	Knows how to 'give and take' to achieve a goal. Organises their own work based on the agreements made.	Organises work. Has insight and acts accordingly.	Creates conditions in the enterprise to increase independence. Aware of own course and appreciates that of others.
Responsiveness	Switches quickly between different activities. Easily handles changes.	Has own ideas and expresses them. If necessary, breaks fixed patterns if they do not work.	Switches easily. Chooses a different approach on the spot if the situation requires it.	In response to opportunities or problems, effectively changes their own behavioural style to achieve the set goal.

Competencies can be set for each level of the USD functions. For example, the junior employee must achieve at least level two in a results-oriented manner, the senior employee at least level three and the account manager level four. By identifying the competencies in this way, the employees also know what aspects of knowledge, attitude and behavior they need to show in order to qualify for the step from junior to senior employee or account manager. By allowing this to be reflected in the coaching sessions, the competencies are made clear and understandable for all employees. Everyone is assessed in the same way, minimising the difference in assessment by different senior employees.

Skilled and multi-skilled

When thinking about the required competencies in relation to job levels, it is essential to consider how much importance is attached to skilled and multi-skilled employees. The demands placed on senior and junior employees or the difference between specialists and generalists determine appreciation and of course necessary training. Multi-skilled employees are obviously adaptable to different situations. This difference must be reflected in the development of the required competences in different levels.

In general, the USD will need more multi-skilled employees who are forced to be more generalist than the experts in the back office.

12.5 Training and training

How do you become a professional and trained USD employee? The best USD staff are those who have experience within the enterprise, who know the products and services well and who understand underlying procedures and processes. In addition, the USD offers excellent start functions for graduates from facility training. In a short period of time, a newcomer on the labour market will get a clear view of the issues that play a role in USD support.

The principle behind this is based on the existence of a series of qualifications for USD staff who have no practical experience and must be familiarised in practice in different ways. Think of training skills (such as soft skills, telephone and software use), more theoretical backgrounds (such as a basic course for setting up a USD), learning and training skills related to communication and management, and so on. There are four focus areas for the training of USD employees[20]:

1. Written and verbal communication
2. Conversation techniques
3. Knowledge of systems (hardware and software)
4. Appearance

1. Written and verbal communication

The aspect of communication concerns communicating with customers and passing on information to colleagues. If more complex enquiries are being processed, they must be drawn up in writing. This calls for USD staff to have the knowledge and expertise to easily communicate ideas and opinions to colleagues, especially within the back office (millennials might need to be lured away from smartphones and isolated for a few days with things called 'pens and paper').

2. Conversation techniques

Conversation techniques focus on the knowledge and skills required to make good phone calls, and to be helpful in interacting with customers at the counter and in mutual conversations. Employees must learn to listen well, understand what they hear and translate it orally or in writing. They will also have to help customers in formulating needs and say 'no' without making customers angry. After all, some wishes do not belong to the available service package and therefore cannot be delivered (training to avoid the words 'like' and 'awesome' will be essential).

---

[20] Shakir, A. & Haider, S., "Towards Designing a Course for the Front-office Department Staff at Pakistani Hotels", *Journal of Research, Faculty of Language & Islamic Studies*, vol 4, p. 45–57, 2003.

3. Knowledge of systems (hardware and software)

A large part of efficiency is achieved through knowledge and skills with the available systems within the USD. During conversations with customers (at the desk or on the telephone), information can often be found in many cases and reports or reservations made. In addition to the discussed SMS, this may also involve other systems, such as other computers, printers, ticket equipment, purchase applications or even a parking reservation system.

4. Appearance

Employees are the calling card of the USD. They must have an eye for etiquette, be representative of the enterprise and adapt to the social environment. Appearance has an influence on the experience of the service organisation's customers, this is sometimes expressed in enterprises by requirements regarding clothing, attitude, command of the language and so on. By paying attention to these points, the employees exude that they not only have respect for the content of the work, but also for the wishes of the customer.

12.6 USD management

Tasks of the service desk manager

The USD manager, the team manager or the operational manager should be hands-on as there are always numerous issues to deal with for example, in facilities and housing about catering, receptions, official cars and service bikes, who is where, can I order a flower, how to make business cards, relocations, renovations and electro-mechanical engineering and architectural issues, automation (from cables to laptops and smartphones) and so on. You can no doubt think about lots of examples in your own discipline.

The operational manager needs to be ready with their team every day to do a good job. The behavior of the employees determines the success of the USD. Again and again the manager must ensure that all USD employees are motivated to solve issues that are presented at the USD. It is the task of the USD manager to ensure that employees can do their work well.[21] The USD manager should therefore deal with complexity (i.e. organising, staffing, problem solving, monitoring, planning, budgeting).

This multitude of tasks also demands different responsibilities. And the USD manager should be able to play different roles. In *Table 12.3* different roles are named:

---

[21] Waard, J. de, Godding, B., *Coaching aan de lopende band; leidinggeven aan mensen die het doen voor de poen*, Zaltbommel: Haystack, 2010.

Table 12.3: Different Roles of the Manager of the Service Desk[22]

Roles	Types	Responsibilities
Interpersonal Roles	Figurehead	Includes ceremonial obligations. Stands in front of employees when customers come to complain.
	Leader	For example, recruiting, selecting, motivating and stimulating.
	Liaison officer	Contacts outside the hierarchical line (with the back office); contacts with people outside the organisation.
Roles for Information Provision	Controller	For example, exploring and monitoring policies or financial agreements.
	Diffuser	Distributing information.
	Representative	Representing the USD.
Decision-making Roles	Entrepreneur	Improve the process and generate new ideas.
	Problem solver	Preventing disruptions.
	Distributor of resources	'Who gets what?' making choices on distributing scarce resources.
	Negotiator	Compromise; manage for results.

Requirements of the USD manager

The USD employees have a pivotal role to play in building a successful USD and the requirements imposed on them are high.

This requires a process of cooperation and involvement of each so that a better service can be anchored in the USD. 'Working together' is a key word in which all parties involved must participate to create a smooth cooperation. Cooperation should be a continuous process that contributes to a positive atmosphere during periods of change and then to the safeguarding of the course taken. The requirements of the USD manager are listed in *Table 12.4*:

[22] Mintberg, H., "The Manager's Job: Folklore and Fact", *Harvard Business Review*, March-April 1990, p. 1–13, 1990.

Table 12.4: Profile of the USD Manager

Profile
• Has mandate in the enterprise • Has position in the enterprise • Has positive reputation in the enterprise • Connects and motivates his or her employees • Is involved with his employees, makes cooperation possible and stimulates • Is the first point of contact for employees and customer escalations • At least MBO+/HBO work and thinking level • USD manager is cooperative, is a team player, 'people-person' although should also be results-oriented

This demands a proactive role from the operational manager who directs the day-to-day service delivery process and ensures personal attention and performance from their team. It means that the key to success for the operational manager is to connect with their USD employees. On the one hand, this requires insight and understanding of their behaviour, and on the other, acceptance of the employees.

CHAPTER 13: THE USD AND BACK OFFICE DEPENDENCIES

Proper handling of customer questions requires a demarcation between USD and back office processes. The USD exists only because of a back office, and a successful USD depends on the working of the processes between the USD and back office. The processes within and between the USD and the back office should be recorded and often secured in contracts (external customers) and/or agreements. These contracts/agreements in turn should be based on the way in which requests are to be handled.

After reading this chapter, the reader should better understand how processes between request and delivery come into being, the relationship and mutual dependency between the USD and back office, and the various means of designing processes between the USD and back office.

13.1 The USD and the back office

When developing a USD, applying the front office to back office principle is the accepted means of organising the demand process (from customer request to implementation and fulfilment). The USD is responsible for the reception and management of the customer request, and the back office is responsible for the proper integrated processing of the demand. Efficient organisation of the relationship between the USD and the back office is based on 'Thinking in processes'.[23]

The starting point is organising products and services into groups of activities that can then be dealt with within the USD and the back office. Therefore, it is essential to have an overview of all activities that are needed to produce a specific product or service. A process consists of the consecutive activities required to handle a product or service request. After the customer request has been received, it is decided whether the product or service can be handled within the USD (entirely or partially), or if it must be passed on.

The request might be forwarded to other departments, or external parties, including the back office. In the back office there should be staff that are responsible for certain products and services (experts/specialists), coordinators, implementers and project generalists. Tasks that are carried out include project management, more detailed advice, management, control, execution of work (catering, technology, transport, etc.).

In most cases, a settlement process based on the front office to back office principle consists of a fixed structure. This structure is shown in *Figure 13.1*.

---

[23] Hardjono, T.W. & Bakker, R.J.M., *Management van processen. Identificeren, besturen, beheersen en vernieuwen*, Deventer: Kluwer, 2006; Obers, G-J. & Achterberg, K., *Grip op processen in organisaties. Analyseren, ontwerpen en inrichten van bedrijfsprocessen*, Zaltbommel: Van Haren Publishing, 2014.

Figure 13.1: A 'standard' delivery process from customer demand to delivery

During this process, the USD (if this is part of the agreed demarcation) remains responsible for the proper functioning of the entire chain and the monitoring of the correct handling of the customer demand (depending on the mandate or the authority that the USD has received). Consequently, the USD tasks are not limited to the intake of demand or to passing on requests when necessary. USD tasks also encompass:

- Monitoring progress;
- Reporting on performance and quality;
- Controlling the process of transference to the appropriate party;
- Ensuring progress and performance;
- Ensuring compliance with customer agreements;
- Ensuring the correct provision of information from within the enterprise or third parties; and
- Informing the customer where necessary (for example, in the event of a delay in the delivery process).

13.2 Designing and setting up processes and activities

Processes can be analysed, designed and arranged in various ways. A common approach was created by Obers and Achterberg. They define a process as a coherent set of activities, people and resources, with which one or more products or services are generated; this is also described as a work process. However, it often happens that one or more additional processes are needed to realise the final product or service for a customer; these multiple processes then form a process chain. A work process comprises various activities with each activity being one step in the process. Obviously, to perform activities, actions must be performed. This process is summarised in *Figure 13.2*.

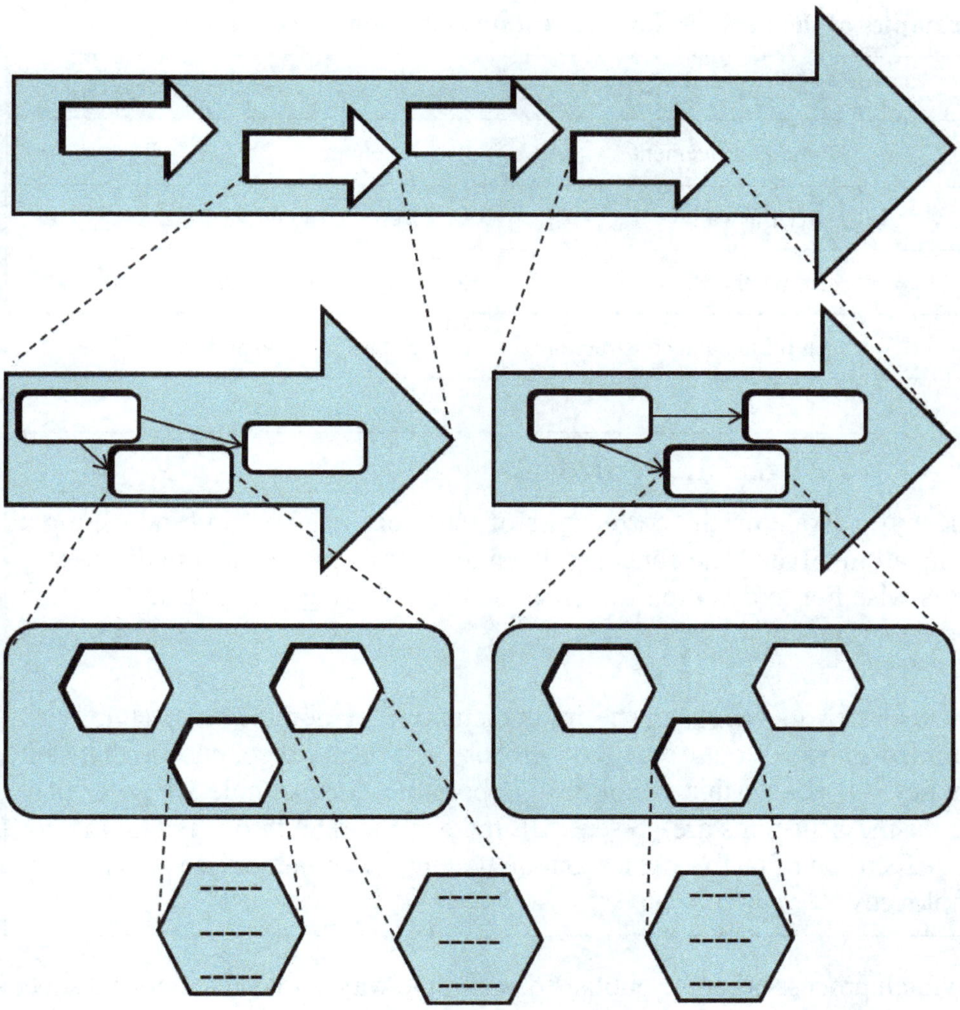

Figure 13.2: Definitions associated with a process chain (Obers and Achterberg)[24]

This terminology has significance for the USD with regard to products and services like a renovation or room reservation. A renovation comprises various processes, such as clearing a construction site, preparing work, dismantling walls, installing IT and electrical equipment, and delivering and cleaning. Subsequently, the process can be divided into activities and underlying actions that have to be carried out in order to realise the process (see also *chapter 3*). An application for a room reservation for a meeting involves a reservation process, providing catering, possibly checking whether there are additional facilities, ensuring that the seating arrangement is good, and so on. This is shown in *Table 13.1*.

---

[24] Obers, G-J. & Achterberg, K., *Grip op processen in organisaties. Analyseren, ontwerpen en inrichten van bedrijfsprocessen*, Zaltbommel: Van Haren Publishing, 2014.

Table 13.1: Examples of the Services for Renovation and Room Reservation

	Service: Renovation	Service: Room Reservation
Process Chain	Home improvement	Meeting
Process (working process)	Move the wall	Reserve room
Activity	Remove the wall	Book the reservation
Action	Demolition and construction	Enter the relevant data

Example: Perfection?

In practice, there is a tendency to fixate on the correctness of the processes and on establishing a unanimous agreement among all involved. The danger is that a lot of time may be lost in discussing the ideal solution. Often it is wise not to dwell on the processes for too long, but instead to define and implement the main processes and optimise them later.

For this reason it is a practical step to weigh up the implementation of new SMS or Help desk systems: is the pre-programmed standard 'out of the box' process sufficient? If so, choose that as it saves a lot of time and money. Of course this is not always possible, for example where critical processes or links to other business systems are present. Ultimately, the quality of the USD is not judged on the quality of the execution of the processes, but on the quality of the service provided by enthusiastic and expert employees.

There are different ways in which processes can be published. A simple way is to create a 'cheat sheet' with an accompanying process diagram. In *chapter 2*, an example was given of a process chain for a report, including a diagram. *Table 13.2* contains an example of a cheat sheet for a 'standard room reservation' product in which the activities and actions have been named.

Table 13.2: Room Reservation Processes

Departments	Activity	Explanation	Changes in Software Suite
Customer	Request customer	The customer requests the USD to reserve a room in writing, by email, by telephone etc.	
USD employee /customer	Intake and input	USD employee needs the following information to process the request: • Meeting date; • Meeting's start and end times; and • Number of persons.	Enter date, start and end times in the reservations module.
USD employee	Reserve room	The USD employee checks in the reservations module which rooms are still available, and if the relevant room is suitable for the application (given the data provided in the request). If a suitable room is found, the room is reserved. When reserving the room, a standard 30 minutes between meetings is scheduled for cleaning and preparing the room.	Reserve room in module reservations.
USD employee	Select name	Select applicant's name.	Select applicant's name in the reservations module.
USD employee /customer	Catering necessary	If the customer requires catering, they can choose from a standard package. This package is described in the menu's folder of the caterer. If the customer has special wishes that cannot be found in the standard package, reference is made to procedure B1.	The standard catering is included in the standard reservation. This means that no separate work order needs to be created. (by filling in the standard reservation, a catering order is automatically created.) If more than one catering order is desired, this can be done by adding the catering order. Change the status of the catering order in 'order assignment'.
USD employee /customer	Request for written request	If the desired catering is a choice from the standard package, the customer must submit this in writing or by email.	
USD employee	Check written request is complete	If the application has been received (by email or another form of writing), data will be checked for completeness. Important: if the account of the catering is for the requesting service component, the budget line (the budget number and the signature of the budget holder) must be completed.	

Departments	Activity	Explanation	Changes in Software Suite
USD employee	Enter other data	If the application is complete, the other data will be entered: • Title of meeting; • Number of persons; • Room setup (if necessary); • Budget rule (if necessary); and • Name of external visitors (if necessary).	Enter other details in the standard reservation in the reservations module. External visitors can be added in the 'reservations' tab with the 'visitors' button. The visitor's name is registered here.
USD employee /customer	Reserve inventory units	If the customer requires inventory units that are not standard in the reserved room, an inventory unit is reserved in the module reservations by means of the icon 'addition reservation'. If an inventory unit is requested that is not available, reference is made to procedure D1: 'Hiring external inventory units'.	Add inventory unit by means of the 'addition reservation' icon in the reservations module. Change status in 'reservation final'. Naming provisions: • Present facilities: facilities that are permanently present in the room • Inventory units: facilities that can be ordered separately • External inventory units: facilities that have to be hired externally.
USD employee	Mail confirmation to customer	The USD employee sends confirmation of the reservation to the customer (via email).	Mail confirmation to customer (by means of the icon 'add receipt') in the module reservations.

13.3 Mechanisms to connect processes between the USD and back office

The USD activities are not limited to the confines of the USD, they continue in the back office. The USD acts on the enterprise's behalf in cooperation with the back office. In other words, there are organisational processes that run across departmental boundaries. The work processes vary from regular processes within a domain to the application of integrated systems. There are several situations in which the responsibility of the USD affects the work processes between the USD and the back office. The following situations can be distinguished:

a) Regular processes within a domain
b) Regular processes across multiple domains
c) Coordination through the USD
d) Integral systems

a) Regular processes within a domain

These situations concern the handling of products and services within one department in which the USD is also located. Settlements can be performed either directly within the USD or through colleagues within the department (for example, issuing laptops and creating ID cards). External customers might need to confirm deliveries or respond to emails about service support. The USD is fully responsible for the process.

b) Regular processes across multiple domains

The handling of customer demand also goes through other departments, and USD staff must make agreements about time and planning. The handling can be standardised for regular customer questions. For project-based services, the agreements must be specified (for example, for meeting services and relocations). USD staff will have to inform colleagues in the event of non-compliance with agreed processes. If necessary, the responsible line manager is contacted. The USD depends on others for the effective course of the process.

c) Coordination through the USD

The handling is coordinated by the USD. The USD is authorised to coordinate the delivery of specific products and services (for example, testing business continuity plans with IT) and to monitor progress. If incidents occur, they can escalate to account management or to a higher level. The settlement authority lies with account management. Account management often has the authority to operate across departmental boundaries. The USD is responsible for the entire process but it only has a partial mandate to ensure the process' course.

d) Integral systems

The systems and processes for handling customer questions are integrated. Such situations can be created with ERP (workflow) systems or a generic system for handling different types of customer questions (for example standardised work orders). In practice, it appears that the integration of systems for reasons other than technical is not always possible. The assurance of the process is then set at a higher level than the USD and back office through management agreements.

13.4 Separation between the USD and back office: handling levels

A process between customer demand and handling is a series of activities and actions that lead to the production and delivery of products and services. The ITIL and other service management principles are based on the same process principles. The difference between the USD approach and the IT related approaches is one of scale; focusing on IT infrastructure is limiting but relatively easy to scope. Extending 'service management' to include generic facilities management makes a lot of sense because of the opportunity to use new technologies to join up many processes and, therefore, many types of requests.

Because the USD is usually at the forefront of the processing of all activities following the customer request, it is necessary that an inventory is made and catalogued for all products and services that can be requested. This should contain information on:

- How the customer request comes to the USD, whether via the service portal, telephone, email, the physical counter or account management; and
- Whether it can be handled immediately, can be forwarded directly to the back office or whether it still has to undergo some form of assessment in the USD.

The cooperation between the USD and other organisational units and third parties requires a great deal of attention. The cooperation must be focused on optimal service to the customer. In order to achieve this, the USD needs knowledge of the tasks, expertise and skills of the other parties that may be involved, or a comprehensive database of information about these other parties.

To begin with, the fulfilment processes should be focused on standard delivery of most commonly needed products and services. Depending on the nature of specific products or services, a process may need to be redesigned or specific agreements have to be made with regard to coordination between the USD and the back office. Management must ensure mutual coordination between the appropriate business units and the responsible department heads.

It is important to consider whether a user request made to the USD (i.e. via intranet, telephone, email, post, desk or account management) needs to be assessed for action first, or whether the question must be passed on directly to the back office or account management. This question must be approached both within the philosophy of a USD and at the level of product or service. The choice determines the specific functions of the USD and how it is organised (skills, numbers, information database(s)). In practice, the term 'handling level' is often used. A level of handling indicates how the delivery process of a product or service must be organised. Four levels of handling are defined in *Table 13.3*.

Table 13.3: Handling Levels in the Service Management and Facility Environment

The desired service quality is based on the ideal level of 'ready while you wait' service. However, this is not always feasible because there is usually an agreed delivery time for a service or product in place; things are further complicated when the request for the service must be handled by the back office or a third party. The following handling levels can be used:
1. **'Ready while you wait'** – simple products and services are delivered immediately (for example, an ID card).
2. **Handling by the USD** – simple products are requested, but a production time exists eliminating the prospect of immediate delivery.
3. **Request intake USD with handling in the back office** – the basic customer information can be collected by the USD for the application of a product. Using this information, it is possible to refer the request to the back office, a specialist will discuss the details with the customer.
4. **Immediate reference to back office or account management** the product is so complex or so rarely requested that direct contact with a specialist or account manager is necessary.
If account management is a function within the enterprise, but it is managed outside the USD umbrella, then it is logical to define an extra level of handling.

With regard to some products or services, the request may not be acceptable within USD policies. In these cases, the most customer-friendly solution is to provide the customer with the best possible information, to refer them to colleagues, or to run the question through account management. The USD should of course register these cases. On the basis of these requests, it might be necessary to revisit their policies.

Therefore, the process from intake to processing in support of each product and service is important for the final design of the USD. This means that the following questions must be answered per product and service:

- How is the customer demand for a product or service made (what is the agreed level of service?
    - How does the request arise? Via the Internet, intranet, call centre, physical, account management?
- How is a product or service delivered and at which level of agreed service?

- What is the level of handling for each product or service?
- Which mechanisms are used for each product or service (automation, manual, combinations or other) to arrange the coordination between the USD and the back office?

Table 13.4 contains an example in which the various questions per product and service have been answered. A distinction has also been made between basic service or basic-plus service. This information is important in assessing whether there are authorisations needed or costs. If this information is available, the first four steps of phase two, from design to realisation, are fully complete. The USD organisation can be designed in combination with phase one (ambition and objectives) and with the basic principles of design and coordination. This will be discussed in the next chapter.

Table 13.4: Process from Intake to Processing per Product and Service:

Product	Depart-ment	Basic	Plus	Information via Intranet	Request via Intranet	Request via Phone/ Email/ Post	Request via Desk	Deliv-ered via Intranet	Delivery via Phone/ Email/ Post	Delivery via Desk	Delivery via Back Office	Level of Handling
Housing	Facility	×		×	×	×	×				×	3
Room reservation	Facility	×		×	×	×	×	×	×	×		1
Notifica-tions	Facility	×		×	×	×	×				×	3
Catering standard	Facility	×		×	×	×	×				×	3
(including software)	Facility	×		×	×	×					×	3
Cleaning standard	Facility	×		×	×	×	×				×	3
Security												
Company emergency services	Facility	×		×		×	×				×	3
Fixed telephony	Facility	×		×	×	×	×				×	3
Standard desktop	IT	×		×	×	×	×				×	3
Support	IT	×	×	×	×	×	×	×	×	×	×	3

Product	Depart-ment	Basic	Plus	Information via Intranet	Request via Intranet	Request via Phone/ Email/ Post	Request via Desk	Deliv-ered via Intranet	Delivery via Phone/ Email/ Post	Delivery via Desk	Delivery via Back Office	Level of Handling
Fleet manage-ment	Facility	×		×	×	×	×				×	3
IT training	IT	×		×	×	×	×	×	×	×		3
Library	PR	×		×	×	×	×	×	×	×		4
Purchasing advice	Facility	×		×		×					×	4
Control report	Finance	×		×		×					×	4
Personnel support	HR	×		×		×	×	×			×	4
Research	Finance	×		×		×					×	4
Systems, mainte-nance and support		×		×		×	×				×	4
Inform-ation security	IT	×		×		×					×	4
Public relations	PR	×		×		×					×	4
Mobile telephony	Facility		×	×	×	×	×			×		2
Hardware	IT		×	×	×	×	×				×	2
Software other	IT		×	×	×	×	×				×	3
Pocket computer	IT		×	×	×	×	×			×		2
Software (existing)	IT	×		×	×	×	×			×		2
Desktop publishing	PR		×	×		×	×			×		4

Product	Depart-ment	Basic	Plus	Information via Intranet	Request via Intranet	Request via Phone/ Email/ Post	Request via Desk	Deliv-ered via Intranet	Delivery via Phone/ Email/ Post	Delivery via Desk	Delivery via Back Office	Level of Handling
Telework	IT		×	×		×	×			×		3
Brochure	PR		×	×		×	×			×		4
Tendering	Facility		×	×		×	×				×	4
Move	Facility		×	×	×	×	×				×	4
Home improve-ment	Facility		×	×	×	×	×				×	4
Legal advice	HR		×	×		×					×	4
New software	IT		×	×	×	×	×				×	4
Special advice pc	IT		×	×	×	×					×	4
Training and education	HR		×	×	×	×					×	4
Informa-tion provision	PR		×	×	×	×					×	4
Organi-sation advice	HR		×	×							×	4
Post	PR	×		×			×			×		1
Repro	PR	×		×			×			×		1
P-direction	HR	×		×				×	×	×		4
P-advice	HR	×		×				×	×	×		4
Planning and control	Finance	×		×							×	4

Product	Depart-ment	Basic	Plus	Information via Intranet	Request via Intranet	Request via Phone/ Email/ Post	Request via Desk	Deliv-ered via Intranet	Delivery via Phone/ Email/ Post	Delivery via Desk	Delivery via Back Office	Level of Handling
Budget and administ-ration	Finance	×		×				×			×	4

13.5 Reconciliation and coordination between the USD and back office

The coordination can be secured in the following three ways:

1. Organisation and authority
2. Processes and methods
3. Collaboration

1. Organisation and authority

By working with an organisational classification of USD employees and account managers in the USD, a good demarcation between competencies and responsibilities can be realised. This demarcation has another advantage: it offers the possibility of a guided transition from segmented services to demand-oriented services. In this, the role of the account managers is crucial. These account managers often originate from the various operational units and can function as a connecting link between the colleagues from the various back offices and the 'new' colleagues at the USD. In addition, they can take care of the transfer of knowledge from the disciplines (where they once worked) to the employees of the USD. Usually this process involves the transfer of knowledge from a specific back office 'field' to USD employees who have the most affinity with this field, or originate from the same back office.

2. Processes and methods

The second method involves processes and methods, and the products and service catalogue can offer a solution here. After all, every service is described in this catalogue (which is why the concept was swiped by IT). The back office has the functional responsibility to update the product descriptions. There is therefore agreement within the enterprise about the nature and content of the products. These products or services are linked to information that strengthens the alignment between the USD and the back office. Describing the work process and the level of handling should be a mandatory task, so that no misunderstanding can arise about the task demarcation lines between front and back office. Information can also be kept on production numbers, key indicators on processing times and lead times. The required staffing of the USD can also be linked to the work quantities. This also applies to the software tools needed by the USD, the quality of the personnel deployment and suggestions from the back office for the streamlining of the service delivery.

When product and service descriptions are adjusted by back office staff, the service management must ultimately have the final responsibility for the USD to assess the consequences of all alignment aspects per service or product, if product and service descriptions are adjusted by back-office staff. For example, the consequences for the organisation of the USD if the service level is substantially increased for customer groups. Management must also monitor the services provided e.g. what does it mean for staffing in the USD if the enterprise's number of employees grows?

The link between product descriptions and organisational preconditions creates a covenant – sometimes called an operational level agreement (OLA) – between the front and back office concerning the nature and scope of the service to the USD. Procedures and working methods must be recorded in agreements, perhaps both in manuals and automated systems. This covenant or OLA is an important tool for the service and the service manager to manage the enterprise and make the relationship between the USD and various back office units explicit to ensure timely delivery of services.

Location managers and the USD

In an enterprise with various locations spread across the globe, customers can and should report their notifications via the service page of the enterprise Internet and/or intranet. A notification enters the system and, depending on the agreements made, is automatically passed on to the suppliers. If the approval of the customer is required, the quotation is sent electronically and can then be approved, and upon approval, delivered. The operational responsibility for delivery lies at the location. The location manager may be supported by multiple building or warehouse managers. The latter are responsible for ensuring correct fulfilment by suppliers, addressing problems, and they also form a point of contact for the customers in the building.

The local delivery regime is highly regulated by automation and standardisation. Only the services that are included in the products and service catalogue may be delivered; exceptions to the agreed service are primarily solved by the location manager.

3. Collaboration

Not everything has to be initially documented as instructions. Employees of the USD and back office must work together and learn from each other. It can be good for working relationships to share information/tips between back office and front office staff. This can be done in various ways:

- Exchanging experiences;
- Running internships for each other, in which back office staff serve as interns in the USD and USD employees in the back office;
- Conducting joint analyses and improvement proposals;
- Jointly filling out the FAQs in the SMS;
- Jointly drafting a handbook to support the handling of requests; and
- Jointly drafting and managing the products and service catalogue (whether a PDC or an iPDC).

Additionally, you may want to collaborate regarding consultation structures, policy frameworks and intake protocols.

CHAPTER 14: BUSINESS INFORMATION FOR THE USD

The USD can only function properly if it has the right information. Information should be both timely and accurate, so the USD must be well connected to various business processes served by the service and facilities organisation.

After reading this chapter, the reader will better understand what information the USD needs and how service management can ensure that the USD is connected to this information. A practical graphical diagram ('metro map', based on the London Underground concept by Harry Beck), is also described and with which these processes can be made visible in relation to the USD.

14.1 The USD within service management processes

As discussed in *chapter 14*, the proper organisation and optimisation of the service processes between the USD and back office is not sufficient to ensure good service. The USD need for information and data reaches further because the USD must be well aligned with the management and IT processes within the service organisation. In addition to the service process between customer and delivery, the USD depends on the management processes described in *Table 14.1*.

Table 14.1: Involvement of the USD in Management Processes

Management Processes	Explanation	Role of the USD
Management and control	The 'plan, do, check, act' circle of the service management process.	The USD plays the central role in the operational services. The USD must work within these frameworks and principles.
Incident management and delivery (delivery line)	The service process from the USD to the back office, from notification to delivery.	The process where the USD is central.
Project management	Initiating, executing, implementing and transferring projects.	The USD must be aware of projects and it can assess reports.
Management products and business and IT services (problem management)	The aim is to determine the root cause of incidents that occur most often and to minimise the impact of incidents.	The USD is the principal agent when several incidents have a cause in one underlying problem.
Policy and strategy	Principles and strategic management decisions that set the preconditions for service provision.	The USD must consider applicable agreements and basic principles in its service provision.
Financial management	Strategic, tactical and operational (budgeting, invoice processing, compliance, etc.) of financial management.	The USD must be aware of mandate and how costs and finances are settled operationally within the enterprise.
Contract and SLA management (including supplier management)	Contract management work from initiation to termination or re-tender.	Service delivery takes place within the agreements established with suppliers. The USD must be aware of this.

Management Processes	Explanation	Role of the USD
Knowledge management	Information needed in the business organisation and IT: specific knowledge, experience and expertise; skills essential for the functioning of the primary process and the execution of the core task.	This concerns basic knowledge that the business needs in order to fulfil the core tasks properly. If the USD understands this sufficiently, it can better assess reports in relation to their importance for the business.
Assets and configuration management (means or asset management)	Management of information about assets such as furniture, IT, pool cars, buildings, mechanical and electrical, building and automation components and their mutual relationships.	The USD works with information systems (such as an SMS) and must be able to assume that the source data (assets and configuration) are correct. The USD can also pass on corrections or additions.
Change management	Manage requests and implement changes.	The USD makes requests for changes to services, applications, various infrastructures and manages change procedures.

The USD focuses mainly on operational information; information about the future, tactical and strategic information are not always directly relevant to the USD. The focus of the USD is providing immediate assistance to help the customer directly and correctly.

14.2 Metro map: graphic design of the USD and management processes

How do you get a grip on these processes in relation to the USD? Basically, you want to understand the position of the delivery process, and specifically the USD, in relation to the different information flows in your service organisation. Applying *Table 14.1* and adapting for your specific USD is a first step. Information about the relationships and cohesion must then be described separately. It helps if in an overview of both the coherence and the different management processes in relation to a USD, can be represented in such a way that they form a single story. A diagram that is suitable for this and has proven itself is the 'metro map'.

A first look at the complete metro map for the USD can intimidate you, but think about how you use a metro map in real life. If you are new to a city with a large metro system, at first you despair about how to travel from A to B. However, the logic of the subway map is that it is virtually the same throughout the world and it helps you to get to your destination. The power of this logic is that people generally understand it directly and can translate the chaotic reality into the abstract logic of the map. Harry Beck is the forgotten genius behind the concept. The basic principles of this map translate the chaos into a schematic and clear diagram where the perspective of the traveller (and in the case of the USD the customer), is leading.

A metro map of service delivery by a USD consists of seven different zones. We suggest these zones are:

- **Zone 1 (outer zone):** business – the customer organisation (the business of the enterprise).
- **Zone 2:** business of the service organisation.
- **Zone 3:** Internet/intranet – the third level of service (service portal).
- **Zone 4:** call centre – the second level of service (telephone, email and post).
- **Zone 5:** counter – the first level of USD service (physical, account management).
- **Zone 6:** business of the USD – the USD organisation (coordination of the USD).

- **Zone 7:** back office – back office with central management information as a node (inner zone).

First, sketch out the zones. Then, the management processes can be entered in the zones, the so-called 'tracks'. The tracks listed in *Table 14.2* are generic suggestions.

Table 14.2: Track of Management Processes

Management Processes	Metro Map Track
Management and control of service management	Service management process
Incident management and delivery (delivery line)	Service process
Project management	Process of projects
Business and IT management, products and services, problem management	Process of problem management
Policy and strategy	Process of policy and strategy
Financial management	Process of financial management
Contract and SLA management	Process of SLA and contract management
Knowledge management	Process of knowledge management
Assets and configuration management	Process of asset management
Change management	Process of change management

The tracks are drawn from the business zone that represents the business management processes in the enterprise, to the zone that is necessary for the service organisation to be able to work properly. The map is set up from the perspective of the USD, and therefore all the tracks cross the USD and the back office. In the middle is the junction where all essential service information must come together and then branch out. This often comprises core systems: SMS, any specific service desk (IT or otherwise) software, the security system and the personnel system.

The position of the USD is central because it is the core process; the service process from notification to delivery is drawn horizontally and extends from outer zone to outer zone, through every zone.

The 'delivery line' ( ) runs horizontally from left to right. Questions always emanate from the customer and will arise through the Internet/intranet, call centre, or counter/account management. Coordination ( ) takes place in the USD, and is processed, possibly passed on to the back office and then resolved. Delivery takes place as previously discussed via the Internet/intranet, call centre or perhaps in person.

Figure 14.1: Delivery line and USD coordination

The stations represent the subprocesses; those activities that must be carried out in order to realise the management processes. Some stations indicate activities that can take place independently. At the larger stations, the lines cross each other and dependencies are identified ('transfer stations'). Here, information is exchanged so that the processes can be executed correctly.

The USD is positioned within the service organisation. The general management process follows the PCDA cycle, as described earlier in this chapter ( ). Customers know which services they can request through the USD via the products and service catalogue (PDC), which is maintained by the service organisation. The service catalogue ( ) naturally fits within the agreed SLAs, OLAs and contracts ( ). New services or changed services are included via the change process (, request for adjustment) initiated from the customer organisation.

In order to provide the services, the USD needs the right information ( ), the basis of which is generally fixed in the SMS. The USD can only handle incidents in the right way if it has good information about the customer organisation (knowledge management).

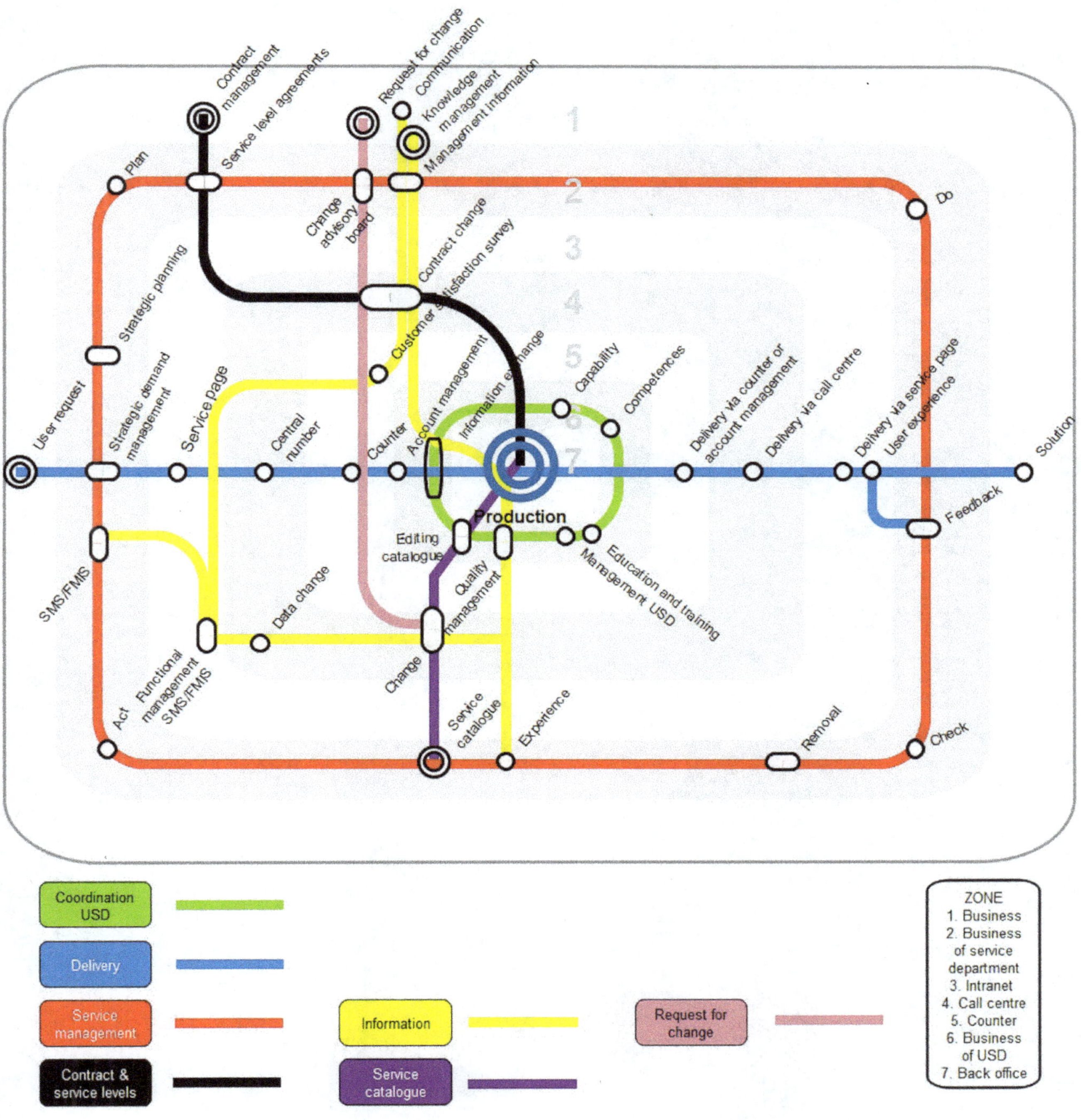

Figure 14.2: Change request, service management and information on the delivery and service catalogue

Finally, the remaining processes can be addressed. The service must always be performed within the financial and policy frameworks (and). During delivery, the USD must have knowledge of the current projects, either because services have to be adjusted or so that they also provide services for the projects ( ). The current state of affairs regarding assets (or configuration items) that are used for the services and the delivery of the services themselves (from furniture to building works, from requests for IT service access to the installation of new computing hardware, and anything in between that is in the purview of your USD), must be known ( ). This leads to the complete picture of the USD.

Figure 14.3: Complete metro map for USD

14.3 Added value of the metro map

Information and data suppliers are continuously improving the quality of the information so that the quality of service to the users can also increase.

A graphic representation helps to:

- Identify dependencies between the USD and the different processes;
- Provide insight into the processes, the relationship between the processes and their components (subprocesses and tasks);
- Provide insight into the USD need for information and its type;
- Provide insight into the different dependencies relating to processes from the perspective of customer-oriented services;
- Illustrate (through the zones concept), that the USD supports the business (from outside and inside) and that it is not intended to be the centre of the universe;
- Identify choices that need to be simplified; and
- Better assess which processes have priority in improving the functioning of a USD (and therefore can show that sometimes improvement objectives for the USD are in unexpected areas).

14.4 Finally

Data or information management is the branch of knowledge concerned with maintaining and improving management processes. From the USD perspective, it is necessary to provide good service for insight into the basic information. As mentioned above, BiSLnext is a useful guide and training is available from certified trainers accredited by APMG (Johnson et al, 2018). This, of course, covers only a small but specific and important part of the total effort to maintain these processes.

CHAPTER 15: USD MANAGEMENT AND ORGANISATION

The USD can be set up within the enterprise when all of the following elements of the USD structure are in place:

- Mission
- Vision
- Products and services to be delivered
- Focus
- Insight into customer needs
- Processes between USD and back office
- Relationship with IT
- The required skills of the employees

After reading this chapter, the reader will better understand how the USD can be organised and positioned within the enterprise. It is clear, that the final design will differ for every enterprise.

15.1 Ambition determines USD organisation

The USD vision, mission and objectives are derived from the enterprise and are dictated by the environment (market or work area), customer groups, use of technology, et cetera. Vision, mission and objectives indicate the desired USD direction. With vision and mission, it is clear for all stakeholders why the USD exists and what it wants to achieve.

Mission and vision are often mistakenly used interchangeably. The mission defines the business of the enterprise. In the vision, the environmental factors are taken into account and answers are given to the developments and the consequences for their own activities. This allows for anticipation of changes. Questions that need to be answered are: 'what will / should our business be' (see also Drucker).[25]

There is no hierarchical relationship between vision and mission, but a complementary one. This is graphically shown in *Figure 15.1*.

[25] Drucker, P.F., *Management: tasks, responsibilities, practices*, 5th print, New York: Harper Business, 1973.

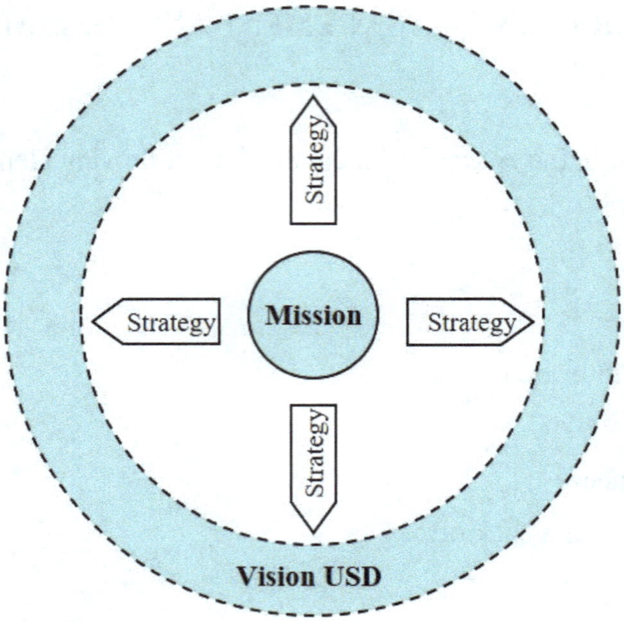

Figure 15.1: Mission, vision and strategy

At this point, we should define mission and vision.

Mission

In essence, the mission defines the raison d'être of the USD within the entire enterprise in the long term. Why do you make an important contribution to the goal of the enterprise? What does the USD stand for? The mission for the USD is obviously a derivative of the mission of the department and enterprise. The mission legitimises the USD. A mission should therefore express a clear position that the enterprise propagates as a basis for the vision, values and goals.

Vision

A vision describes how the USD views its own performance in a future period (often 4–5 years). The vision describes the market and the specific task field in which operations are being carried out. It indicates which developments the USD sees transpiring. A good vision is both ambitious and feasible and must generate enthusiasm, be recognisable and motivating, relevant for customers and employees and must translate into measurable goals. Questions that are asked are:

- How do you hope to grow?
- What developments do you see?
- Which players are active in this?

Table 15.1: Terms That Can Be Used in the Description of Vision or Mission

Words That Describe Mission or Vision
• Best in quality • Customer focus • Dominant • Leading • Specialised • Responsible • Approachable • Provide • First • National or international • Favourite, best, first choice • Client • Market leader • Successful • Make it possible • Support • Cheapest • Conditional

Mission and vision express ambition and should be embraced by management. They are essential for ensuring resources are effectively invested in realising goals like further development or innovation. Objectives concretise the mission and vision in a strategy. The strategy defines how the vision is realised within the context of the mission by means of concrete and achievable goals. This creates the strategy by which the vision is achieved. The goals are operational; they need to be translated into specific tasks and results. They must be able to form the basis for motivation, work and desired end results (Drucker).[26] Goals provide the practical answers to the way in which we want to achieve the vision.

Make sure that your employees not only understand the mission and objectives of the service desk but also feel it. Think of the familiar example in which the cleaner at NASA proudly said, "I'm helping put a man on the moon". The example terms in the table must, therefore, always be translated into simple, practical words that are close to the culture and nature of the enterprise.

That is why it is important that the first step be taken carefully. This does not mean a bulky book or plan, the ambition can be expressed in a single page and translated in an operational way. Using this, it is possible to estimate the consequences of ambitions. We call this a 'business case'.

The acceptance of the business case ultimately determines whether the objectives are feasible. The ambition, and consequently the mission and vision, must be adjusted if they are not. The ambition laid down in mission and vision determines the USD organisation.

'Organisation' refers to the way in which responsibilities, roles and structure of the USD are adjusted. It is clear that the final choice, and thus the content of the final concept of the USD, is specific to each

---

[26] Drucker, P.F., *Management: tasks, responsibilities, practices*, 5th print, New York: Harper Business, 1973.

enterprise. One chooses a variant whereby all distribution channels (intranet, call centre functionality and desk with account management), are set up. For cost reasons, the other party only opts for a service provision through the intranet. Various aspects play a role in making the final design. In practice it appears that the following aspects influence the design of a USD:

- USD types
- Management
- The USD positioning within the enterprises
- Finances
- The USD required capacity

Example: Consequences and feasibility

When responsibility and with it the associated mandate, has to be organised in an enterprise, the consequences for all levels of management becomes clear. In general, the start of the change to a better or new USD and the formulation of ambition are the abstract starting points that are often without obligation. For example, we really want to be customer-oriented, the USD to focus on the quality of the delivery (and therefore on the back office), or we want expert employees. At the moment, such criteria has to be organised in the enterprise with formal placement and positioning. The USD may then have a guiding and leading role in operational service delivery and the balance of power between front office and back office could change. That moment is the hour of truth, and a good project leader or manager will assess the consequences and thus feasibility in advance.

15.2 The USD as a primary process

Sooner or later, almost all enterprises have to decide how the tasks of implementation or service deployment should be organised. This concerns both support services (such as facilities and ICT) as well as parts of the primary processes. Some enterprises opt to carry out these services themselves, while others choose to use external service providers. This shift to using external service providers can be observed in the moves from a traditional enterprise to forms of demand-oriented enterprises, shared-service organisations, public-private partnerships, forms of management organisations, and total facility and service management.

This shift is almost always the need to create a relationship between the client and the service provider. Further business can lead from single sourcing to far-reaching (bundled) outsourcing and ultimately to a fully integrated service and facility management. There are many reasons for further professionalisation, but ultimately they are related to the lack of knowledge or resources to perform services, issues related to personnel management performing the same services, or strategic considerations about lower costs, in which enterprises only want to focus on core activities. Whatever reason(s) lie at the basis of the decision making, the enterprise remains responsible for managing the agreements, for example in contract form and ensuring that the client's enterprise gets what it needs. The management of the service is therefore becoming increasingly important (de Rouw & Verhoef).[27]

In many instances, the USD will be outsourced, though not in all. Reasons might include the importance attached to direct contact with employees, or maybe because of the nature of service with a commercial interest, or because the enterprise remains uncertain about the consequences of outsourcing. The outsourcing of the USD has both advantages and disadvantages. The main advantages and disadvantages for the two extremes are included in *Table 15.2*.

Table 15.2: Outsourcing a USD – Pros and Cons

The USD is positioned with a supplier (or suppliers) of services. The USD is fully included in the production and carries out the operational tasks of delivery management.	
Pros	**Cons**
• The USD is a primary process for the supplier. • Candidate suppliers prefer this form, in/ out is easier to achieve. • In the imminent event of exceeding deadlines or of underperformance, the supplier intervenes directly. • Requires equal competencies as in the existing situation. • There may be better job guarantees for existing employees.	• Always direct contact between customers and suppliers; there is a good chance that service can also be delivered outside the service agreements. • At least two separate USDs (for ICT and for non-ICT); in the event of further division of suppliers, this number may increase. • The service or facility organisation does not have an operational role towards customers and, therefore, has few resources to intervene directly.
The USD is not outsourced. In this case, the USD concentrates on the tactical tasks and the operational tasks of the delivery management are automated as much as possible.	
Pros	**Cons**
• No direct contact between customer and suppliers; lower chance of delivery outside service agreements. • One USD (for ICT and non-ICT) is possible. • The management organisation also adds value to customers. In the event of exceeding the terms or of substandard performance, the management organisation intervenes directly.	• Risk to current employees if they cannot keep up pace with potential higher demands of the USD. • Candidate suppliers prefer to keep control over the delivery in their own hands, outsourcing is more difficult. • Requires higher competencies. • Extra link in operational management, with a chance of delay in the (additional) control. • Extra workload for the management organisation with more attention needed for the daily service and the danger of not paying enough attention to tactical and strategic considerations.

In all situations, the USD role among the service providers is important because, as a visible operational contact point for the customer, it has insight into customer needs, service provision and delivery quality.

---

[27] Rouw, L.P. de & Verhoef, C., *Het regiebureau. Kernprincipes voor sturen op resultaat*, Zaltbommel: Van Haren Publishing, 2015.

15.3 Types of USD

There are a number of common forms and variations of the USD that have been documented; these have been categorised according to the target groups identified in research materials.

The research literature refers to three basic models. Originally, these basic models were developed for public service purposes. The kick-off took place in 1995 with the report of the Scientific Council for Government Policy: *The look outside*.[28] In this report, three ideal types of demand-oriented work were formulated: the information desk, the account management model and the clustering of customer groups. Over many years, experience has been gained within service management with different variants of the researched models. These variants can be divided into two main forms, namely:

1. The information centre model
2. The account management model

1. The information centre model

All information about the available services is provided in the 'information desk' of the information centre model (*Figure 15.2*). This relatively light form of demand-oriented work helps clients match the existing products with their customer demand. The customer must request the specific products or services, but agreements can be made with employees from the back office via the counter. Thus, there is direct contact between the back office and the customer during the request, coordination and handling, as well as delivery.

[28] WRR, *Het borgen van publiek belang. Rapporten aan de regering nummer, 56*, Den Haag: Sdu Uitgevers, 1995.

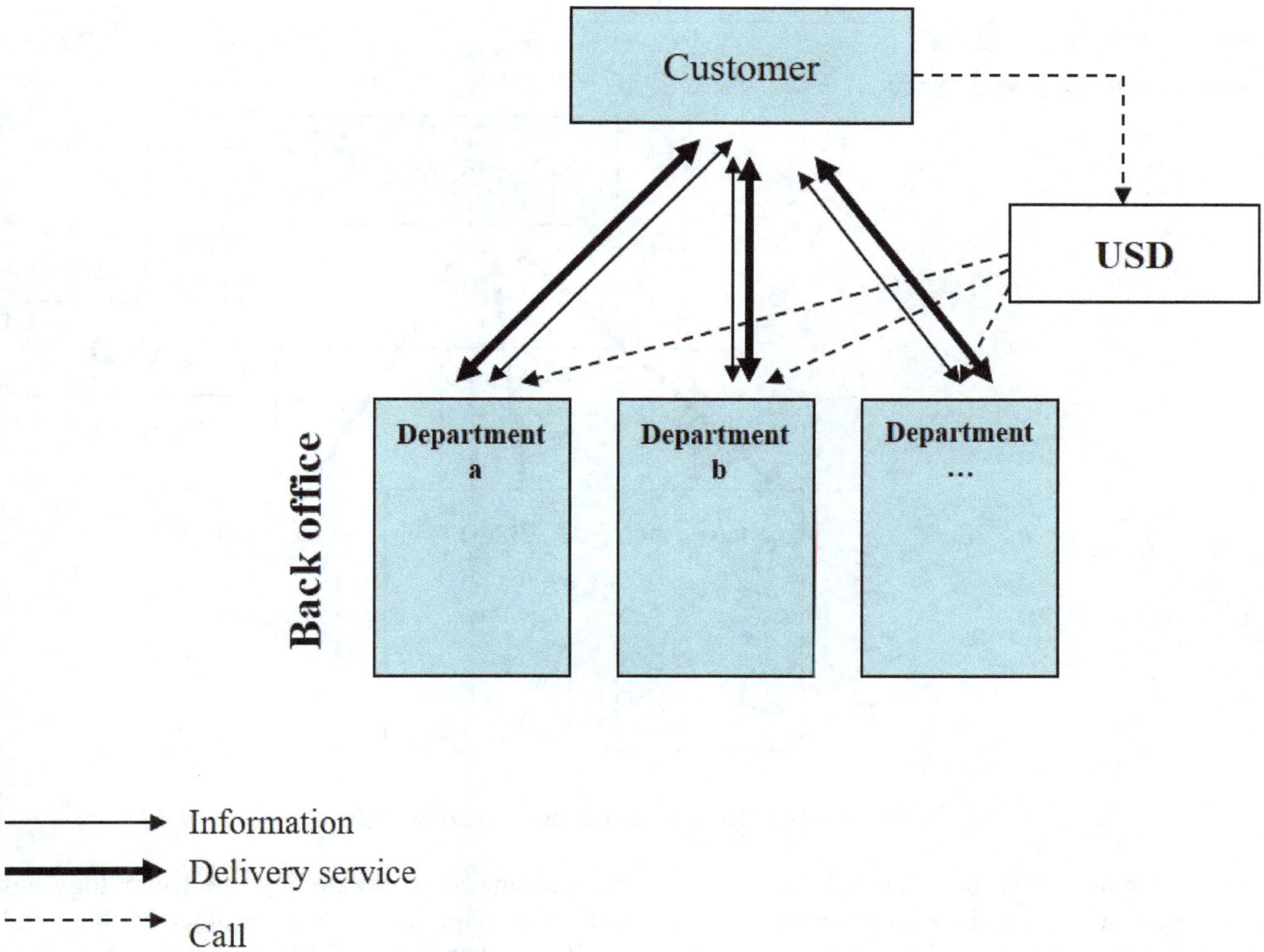

Figure 15.2: The information centre model

2. The account management model

With the account management model (*Figure 15.3*), the service request is entirely managed by the USD employees. Compared to the information counter, the following differences are apparent:

- The USD takes over the question or notification from the customer.
- The back office employee no longer deals with a customer, but deals with a request for a service or product.
- The USD will have a steering function for the performance of tasks in the back office.
- Concrete agreements are made about the time and quality of product delivery.

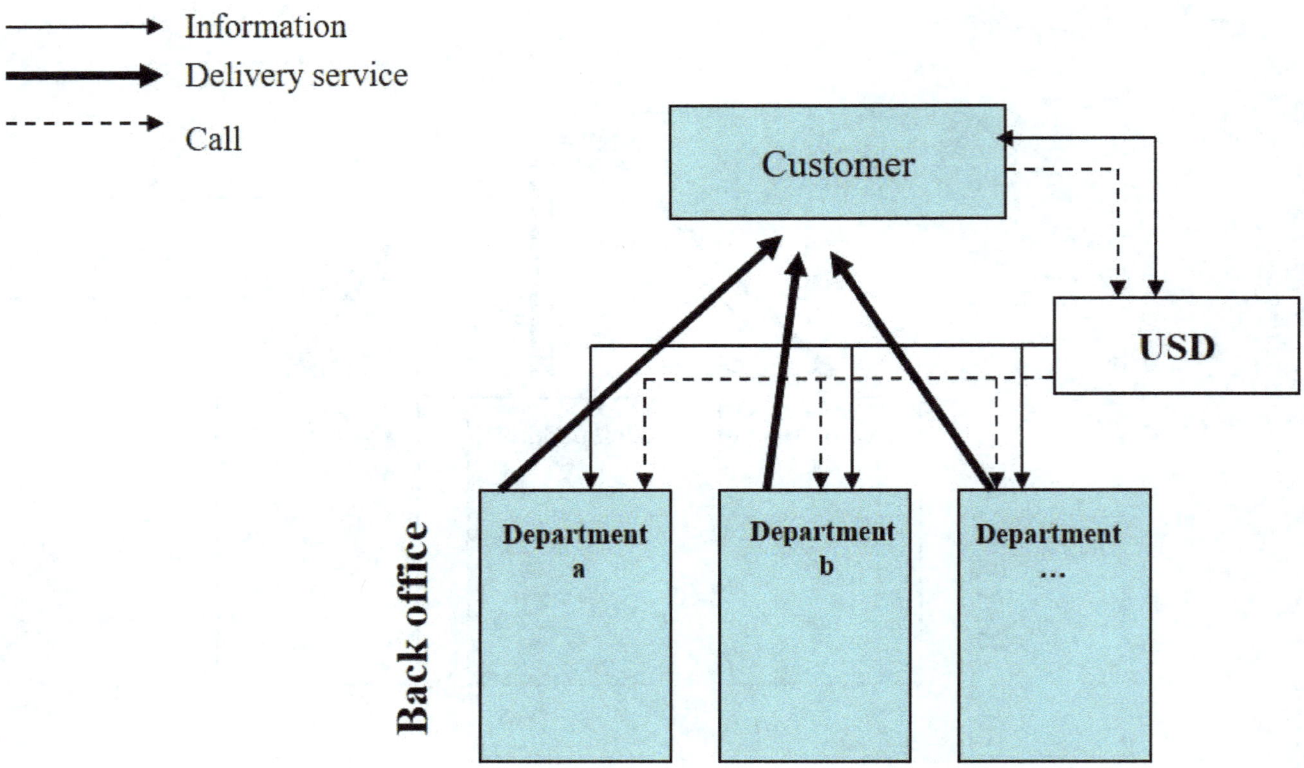

Figure 15.3: The account management model

In recent years, much has changed. The customer has become more demanding, the technology has developed (it will continue to develop as AI grows) and the experience with customer-oriented and demand-oriented working has increased considerably. Remember that the USD goal is the promotion of an efficient customer-oriented facilities or service management environment. However, it has been found that this goal is not achieved when a USD is based on the information centre model. In practice, therefore, most structures for a USD are based on the account management model.

In the context of the practical USD type approach, a distinction can be made between different variants within the account management model. The first variant is the pure, ideal type variant with one USD. In addition, two variants are divided into customer groups or departments where there is more than one USD, which is hardly universal is it? This is shown in *Figure 15.4*.

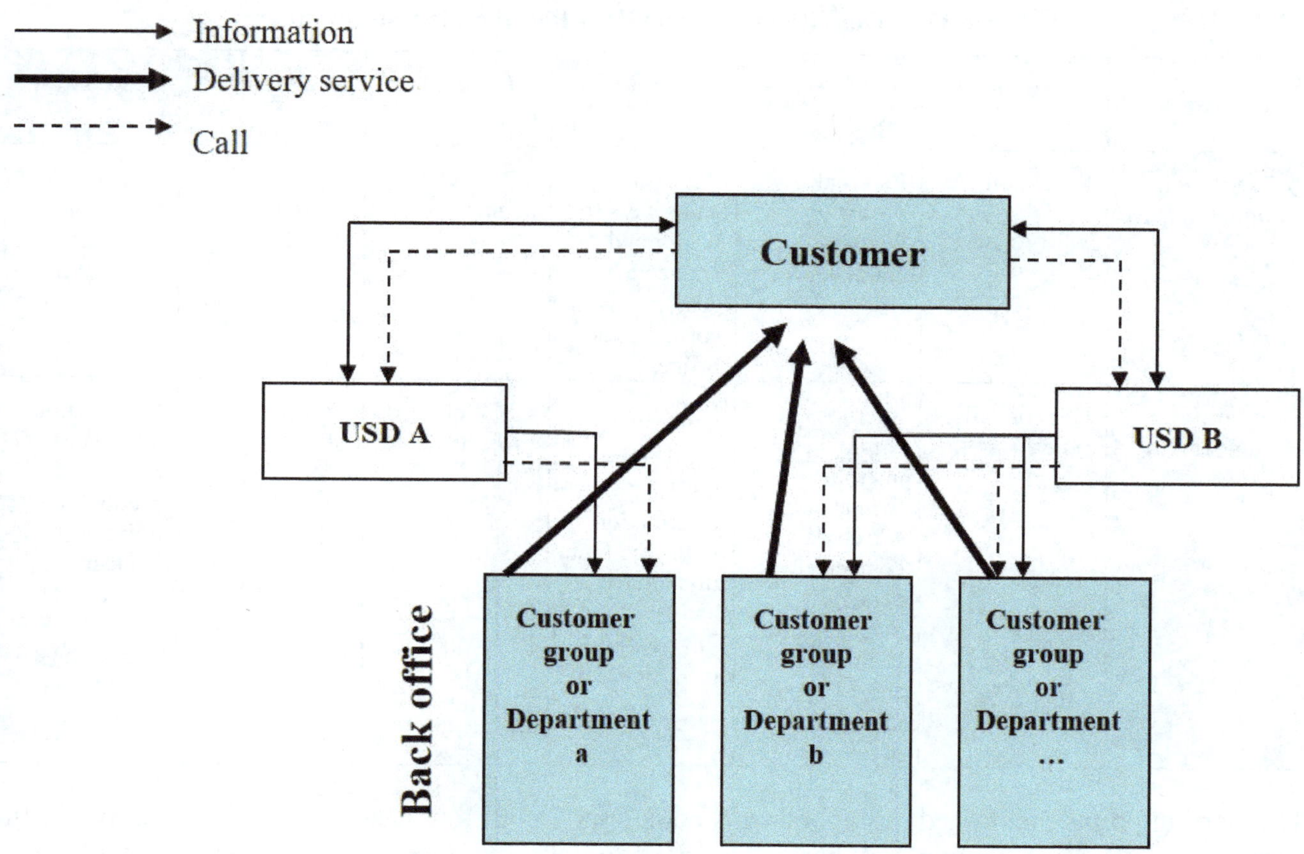

Figure 15.4: USD type categorised by disciplines, customer groups or department

In some enterprises, the presence of one USD is not sufficient, which of course means 'universal' is not always 'universal'. This can have many causes, for example, where it does not make sense to allow specific customer groups to use the same USD. For expatriates, for example, it is much more convenient to be able to go to a specialised USD for employees abroad. For drivers of fleet vehicles, they could go to the specialised USD for all transport matters. Where paper documents remain important, it may be decided to enforce application for printed matter to a USD 'repro and printed matter,' or to the help desk for ICT. Another argument may have more to do with interests and mandate.

Classification based on situation

In addition to the distinction between the information model and the account management model, the situation in which a USD is needed can also be considered. Distinction can then be made to structural situations such as customer support within an enterprise, or customer support in case of an incidental situation such as a trade show or an event. If both are compared, the following table is created with four types of USD.

Table 15.3: Classification Type USD Based on the Situation

	Structural	Type of Customer	Activities	Incidental	Type of Customer	Activities
Information Model	Reception	External visitor or internal employee.	Registration and access to visitor and connecting customer with correct back office.	Visitors desk at an event.	External and internal visitor.	Issue event badge and information about the event.
Account Management Model	USD or call centre	Internal employees, internal specialists, secretariats, contact persons, managers, back office and management organisation.	Registration, complaints, needs, information, faults/malfunc tion advice and information provision.	USD for projects.	Target group of the project.	Registration and issue of project product. First point of contact in case of incidents during the project.

The starting points mentioned throughout this book apply in all four cases and for all USD types. In an incidental situation, thought will have to be given to the elaboration of procedures, handbooks, the organisation of systems, and so on. In the case of incidental situations, scenarios will be worked on earlier, and much more will fall back on standardised systems that are directly operational without much customisation. In the incidental situation, USDs will also demand a lot more from the improvisation capacity of the employees.

15.4 Management and control

The entire USD management and organisation should be under one umbrella. This includes the virtual USD, the call centre functionality and any physical locations, such as service desks and account management.

In general, the responsibility for the Internet or intranet lies with the IT department, perhaps split between communications (for content) and ICT (for technology). Account management also often falls under the USD, though it can be set up as a separate department. This division of responsibilities is logical but it can lead to problems because the USD handles internal customer needs differently to the other departments.

Consequently, it is advisable to bring the management of the service site, the PDC and account management functions under the direction of the USD. The USD has a number of tasks and functions to enable the virtual USD (via the service page) to function properly. After all, the virtual USD is an integral part of the entire USD concept, especially in the field of accessibility. The head of the USD thus also has the functional management of the components of the virtual USD.

Management and control as the one-stop shop concept

Putting aside structural models, the objectives and consequently their associated authority and functionality, are more important than the geographical location in the enterprise in which the USD is located. When considering location think first about customer demand and how best the customer can be supported. The entire enterprise is involved in the handling of many customer questions, especially when it concerns integrated services across multiple disciplines. In which department the USD is accommodated, matters less, although an independent position is preferable. This is because the USD can draw upon support from the total enterprise more easily in an independent position, and this would not be as feasible if the USD is one part of one of support service.

This discussion is closely related to the one-stop shop concept. In many enterprises, you often find a variant of the account management model with multiple counters. For example, a desk for the facility services, repro, personnel information, help desk, a desk for the people that don't like desks, and so on.

The one-stop shop idea regularly considers combining these counters into one USD. Literally and figuratively speaking, this means that a customer can go to one counter for all products and services.

We have to ask ourselves if this makes much sense. In general, an ICT help desk mainly offers telephone and email functionality and therefore the location is not so important. A counter for parking services or chauffeur services is generally placed close to the garages so that substantive knowledge is also available quickly. In addition to practical arguments, there is sometimes also organisational resistance. Employees of the various counters often have different backgrounds, knowledge levels and cultures. What is the point of merging the work of library and facility staff?

Accordingly, it is more logical to merge the services along the line of management from the one-stop-shop concept, and to bring coherence to the various levels of service provision. Customers benefit more from considering internal service provision as a whole, rather than as separate services. One counter is therefore, in our view, the entire service that has to be offered *from the same perspective*. The service must be structured logically from the customer's perspective. This can be enhanced by placing request items that are logically connected in the same area of the catalogue (or providing support at a single location for service), using the same processes and software support systems, placing the physical counters in the same location (service area), or choosing one means of delivery or access to services.

15.5 Finances

Cost components

Different cost components

Designing and setting up a USD in abstract is fun and can lead to the most beautiful result; and it will cost a fortune. That is why it is wise to draw up a business case at the start, in which case the investment and operating costs are always taken into account.

Investment costs

The cost of investment can be very high depending on the choices made about mission and objectives. Think of the costs of organising the physical environment, the purchase and implementation of information systems, ICT, the time that must be put into the preparation, and so on.

Operating costs

Once the USD is up and running, the operating costs must be taken into account. These comprise for a large part the personnel costs. There are more costs, such as licensing costs, depreciation, (replacement costs and the costs for the use of the accommodation, energy and for maintenance). The costs must of course be calculated on the basis of agreed service levels.

Yields of the USD

Financial revenues are much less transparent, as was confirmed by a 2008 study that found that overhead costs were opaque in many enterprises (Huijben and Geurtsen).[29] The financial benefits of a USD will mainly exist in the back office and for the customers. If the USD does its job well, the efficiency and thus the productivity increase for the other two parties. The added value of a USD should therefore mainly be sought in more qualitative factors. Think mainly of higher satisfaction among employees in the enterprise through accessible and clear (and therefore measurable) support.

It is necessary to follow a growth trajectory to manage the scale of the costs and the low transparency of revenues. In general, it has been concluded that enterprises operating the so-called single-point-of-contact USD find the financial calculations more advantageous than those operating with multiple customer entries.

15.6 Capacity of the USD

Components of required capacity

Ensuring a continuous service by the USD means continuous accessibility. To achieve this, USD staffing must be in balance with the enterprise's stated ambition and objectives. Consequently, USDs will employ a large number of staff. Not least so that in case of absence the tasks can be observed, but also to provide extended hours of service, 'follow-the-sun' attendance perhaps in some enterprises. Absence has various causes e.g. meetings, consultations, client visits, illness and holidays. If continuous accessibility is to be guaranteed, take into account:

a) Productivity
b) The requested minimum capacity
c) The required expertise

a) Productivity

Employees are not always productive during office hours, because of what is called the *occurrence of friction loss*. This means that they do not continuously work on USD tasks. Employees cannot be 100% productive in the time that they are present due to multiple causes, for example the irregular spread of customer questions and the lack of clarity in customer demand and incorrect communication. Also, consider interruptions, personal time, lunch and other breaks. Don't even think about trying to assess staffing without allowing for idle time that may be as much as one third of the working day.

Consider the use of policy to manage peak traffic. Not only in contracts and SLA but think about policies that restrict counter service during times of crisis as an example.

[29] Huijben, M. & Geurtsen, A., *Heeft iemand de overhead gezien? Een beproefde methode om de overhead te managen*, Den Haag: Academic Service, 2008.

b) The requested minimum capacity

There must be sufficient capacity available at any USD counter. When answering the phone, emails cannot be handled and visitors cannot be supported at the counter. Two employees is the minimum in such a situation. Even then, this does not offer any possibility for transferring or absorbing peak traffic where work exceeds the capacity of one employee because of say, a major incident.

c) The required expertise

USD employees must have the right knowledge and skills:

- General knowledge of the enterprise and its processes and support systems
- Organisational skills
- Social and communication skills
- Product and process knowledge

See *chapter 12* for a more in-depth discussion of the expert USD staff.

Calculate the capacity

A USD's required staff can be calculated in two ways: First, by establishing a critical lower limit, through what is basically inspired guesswork; and second, on the basis of quantified information.

Calculate critical lower limit in the USD

'Critical lower limit' refers to the minimum occupation of the USD needed to guarantee an effective service but not optimal accessibility. This minimum formation is not calculated on quantity data but is based on four different components:

1. Guaranteed continuous service
2. Assessed productivity
3. Required capacity
4. Expertise level

1. Guaranteed continuous service

Continuous service at the USD means continuous accessibility. It is important to know the preferred opening hours for the USD. From 7.00 am to 19.00 pm is nice and customer friendly, but it means that more than one employee is needed to staff the USD.

The staffing can be calculated as follows: One employee corresponds to a full-time position (in this example, say 36 hours per week); therefore, a full-time employee works 2080 gross hours and 1440 net workable hours per year. This conversion of gross to net workable hours takes into account:

- Leaves of absence
- Working hours reductions
- Special leave and holidays
- Study

- Internal consultations
- Illness

This means that an employee with full-time employment (1440/8 hours a day) is productive for 180 days a year on average. Based on 250 workable days per year for an enterprise (in which a business closure is not processed), 1 full-time equivalent (FTE) provides 72% of the total opening time. For continuous accessibility, 1.4 FTEs are therefore required. This means that the occupation of the USD with one employee is just unworkable for continuous accessibility.

2. Assessed productivity

As a starting point, a 15% loss is applied to 180 productive days for each employee. Therefore, in order to realise the continuous availability of the USD, about 1.6 FTE is required.

3. Required capacity

In order to ensure that sufficient capacity is available in the USD, it must be clear that the workload is in line with the available occupancy. The capacity within the USD is determined by vulnerability and working quantity. Given that the presence of only one employee leads to vulnerability, an average attendance of 1.5 employees per FTE is assumed. That means 1.6 FTE multiplied by 1.5 FTE, or 2.4 FTE. This calculation determines the critical lower limit. However, it may be necessary to set the critical lower limit at a higher level because of the workload or because it is necessary to have an expert in addition to the required one or two employees. Next time someone asks you how many employees are needed, ask them how much work needs to be done.

4. Expertise level

Depending on the products and services and the level of handling, it must also be assessed whether the necessary basic expertise can be accommodated with one person. If this is not the case because, for example, special knowledge and experience is required which is too large to accommodate with one person, the services have to be adjusted.

The critical lower limit is determined on the basis of the assumptions and the corresponding calculation. However, it may be necessary to set the critical lower limit at a higher level because of too large a workload, or the necessary presence of expertise that cannot be combined in one or two employees.

Calculation of occupation on the basis of quantity

In order to make an accurate calculation based on the amount of work and the required staffing, insight into the various activities that determine the USD capacity requirement is needed. We can make a distinction between activities that are directly customer-related (for example, the processing of a report by telephone or desk), or activities that are not directly customer-related but necessary for the organisation of the USD, (for example coaching interviews, consultations, training, appraisal interviews).

Observing the necessary activities is the only way to know how much work is on hand and how much time is needed to complete that work.

This calculation is done in two steps:

1. We must determine the average processing time per employee per unit of time for each customer-related activity. How much time does it take to handle a telephone report on average? How much does it cost on average to help a customer at the counter?
2. If the average processing time per employee per distribution channel, and the processing time of the other activities has been determined, this average is used for the inventory of the work stock on the USD.

Step 1– Calculation of processing time per employee

Customer-related activities

In this step-by-step plan, we start with the most important customer-related activities. Assuming that all contact channels can be used by the customer, the following components can be identified: telephone, email, Internet or intranet and the physical desk.

It is important to first clarify the most common calls per component and then determine the average handling time per employee. You can then determine the total number of resolutions and escalations per hour. However, the waiting time between the calls must also be taken into account.

Activities of the USD organisation that are not directly customer-related

These activities are often overlooked but they can increase the workload considerably. These are activities that are not directly related to customers; they include work meetings within the USD, consultations with the various back offices, coaching discussions with USD employees, assessment and functioning discussions, training and participation in projects. Of course, this varies enormously per enterprise, but for capacity determination it is good to make it transparent so that you will not be faced with surprises later on.

Step 2 – Calculation of work

When the average processing time for all activities (both customer-related and not directly customer-related) has been determined, this average can be used to inventory the USD work.

First, we examine how often activities are carried out; this information may be retrieved from systems or determined by an investigation. This data is then combined with the average processing time. An example of how it can be presented is provided below.

Table 15.4: Average Handling Time and Number of Calls

	Average Handling Time	Number of Calls per Hour
Phone	0:04:30	11
Email	0:04:24	13
Intranet	0:04:30	13
Desk	0:04:30	13

We then process this in an overview per day, week, month and year (*Table 15.5*).

Table 15.5: Required Capacity Per Unit of Time

Monday	No. of Phone Calls	No. of Employee Hours Available	No. of Emails	No. of Employee Hours Available	No. of Intranet Requests	No. of Employee Hours Available	No. of Visitors at Desk	No. of Employees
8:00–9:00	5	2	10	1	3	0.5	10	2
9:00–10:00	15	2	12	1	2	0.5	12	2
…								
…								
17:00–18:00	3	1	4	1	1	0.5	2	1
Total	94	17 hours a day	83	10 hours a day	28	5 hours a day	87	17 hours a day

Then all this information can be aggregated to provide an insight into the required capacity utilisation and an indication of what can be achieved.

Help from mathematics: the Erlang-C calculation

Erlang-C is a mathematical formula that helps determine the number of employees required within the USD to handle the predicted supply of calls within the provided service level.

By means of the expected contact volume, expected talk time and handling time and the desired service level, Erlang-C calculates the number of employees to be deployed per time unit.[30]

This method is mainly used for larger call centres and is in many cases far too complicated and too heavy for a facility USD. Filling in the formula and calculating is not easy either. Fortunately, the computer brings a solution. There are many examples and tools available on the Internet to apply the Erlang-c formula (see for example *www.callcentrehelper.com/tools/erlang-calculator*).

15.7 Structure and position of the USD in the enterprise

Finally, we can roll out the enterprise's USD. Blueprint thinking (design based on the rational design and implementation of changes) and Redprint thinking (design based on cultural aspects, mutual understandings and common goals) can now be completed. Practically, this means that the following must have taken place:

---

[30] Regtop, D. (z.j.), "De Erlang-C-calculatie"; Tanner, M., "The Erlang-C Formula" 2000; Cleveland, B, *Call Centre Management on Fast Forward: Succeeding in the New Era of Customer Relationships*, Colorado Springs, CO: ICMI Press, 2012.

- Deciding on, describing and recording the position of the USD within the enterprise, (this actually defines the mandate that the USD has in respect of the complete demand settlement).
- Various levels of service provision are organised within the enterprise, for example by a single service portal and call centre functionality and multiple physical locations in cooperation with the local back offices.
- Deciding on, describing and recording the formal hierarchy of the USD, shown in the organisation chart including staffing agreements.
- Deciding, describing and recording the job descriptions, the work processes, procedures and tasks, the performance requirements and quality requirements, the way in which people work and coordinate with each other, and the way in which the relationships with other components (internal and external back office) are tuned.
- Recording the agreements on development, education and training.
- The planning of control using, among other things, the product and service catalogue, service agreements, management agreements and (multi-year) plan (including budget agreements).
- Deciding on, describing and recording the ways in which work is synchronised.
- Deciding on, describing and recording the way the relationships with other components (internal and external back office) are synchronised.
- Establishing the agreements on development, education and training.

CHAPTER 16: IT AND THE SERVICE HELP DESK – REFLECTIONS BY A PROVIDER OF MANAGED SERVICES

16.1 Introduction

The manager and a small team of analysts employed by a provider of managed services (outsourced service desk capabilities), were interviewed to discuss USD concepts such as their specific application to their 'ITIL compliant' service desk (which was one of their advertised capabilities), and the differences they observed when customers focused on IT services or wider managed services, including facilities management issues.

We wish to express our thanks to the interviewees for their time and patience.

16.2 Services

The enterprise is international, though this interview was restricted to a single facility in the UK where the outsourcer employs over 300 people in a purpose built complex that provides a range of help desk services to customers in a number of industry sectors including government, insurance, banking, retail and legal. The services range from basic capabilities such as trouble shooting generic IT problems (e.g. laptop password resets, accessibility issues), to routine but industry specific application issues often requiring knowledge of specific lines of business, and services that relate to logistics and to account management that are substantially facilities management processes.

Many but by no means all employees in the facility have taken the 'ITIL Foundation' certificate, though management positions are not dependent on the certification, because it has long been recognised that Foundation qualifications are the basis for education and not the end-goal. Management positions are entirely based on experience first and tertiary education certification second.

ITIL is considered as a useful grounding to understand process and procedure, and in the past it was considered to be a differentiator in the market. The enterprise also paid for an 'ITIL compliance' audit from a third-party company to demonstrate to prospective customers that its processes and procedures were consistent with best practice. The relevance of the compliance audit is different in each market and in each geographical location; some customers are insistent on suppliers 'having the ITIL badge' and others are only interested in contractual costs.

16.3 Process and procedure

It was widely recognised in this UK facility that the 'ITIL' processes and procedures were in effect a variation of activities that had been used by the enterprise over many years, and that ITIL 'compliance' related largely to adherence to published definitions and basic procedures in the areas of incident, problem, change and service level management. Furthermore, it was accepted that these processes were already at the core of the enterprise's managed service offerings.

The 'ITIL audits' had involved investigation (and 'approval') of many other processes deemed to be 'ITIL'. The basic processes and procedures were primarily applied to infrastructure management. To a lesser extent, they were also applied in attempting to manage application (information) issues and as a basis for the intake-like procedures needed in a true front office to back office scenario. In this particular facility, no application design services were available. A particular issue was knowledge of the wide range of applications that each customer was using in disparate markets. A further issue was the number of customers who were unaware that their information services (design and maintenance) were most often either retained 'in house' or outsourced to an application services provider with no links to the managed services activities.

Processes such as cost, configuration, availability and capacity management were not managed as ITIL processes and in many cases the processes existed only on paper. Furthermore, widespread scepticism existed in the team about the value of a generic process audit to the enterprise and its customers unless there were specific contexts focused on the services provided. It was generally agreed that IT-driven services should be designed more robustly as the driver for better services, which would largely eliminate the need to focus so much attention on operational activities to 'fix' problems.

16.4 Customer service

The SLA processes and procedures are in place largely to serve as parameters for response to events, incidents and problems. The enterprise is contractually liable to a variety of customers; as such, the nature of the contracts can vary particularly in areas of cost where 'you get what you pay for' is the basic principle. Any SLA drawn up for operational use is always a best endeavour but it is not a guarantee. This can lead to disputes when customers are not familiar with the differences between what has been contracted (at board or executive level) and what can be achieved in terms of the SLA. In general, SLAs reflect a customer 'need' such as 99.5% availability of service. However, service is not clearly defined and, as with most SLAs, the terms and conditions do not apply to information services (applications) but to the infrastructure that supports delivery. This issue is also mentioned above in process and procedure.

Such a situation is far from unusual and it reflects the lack of a common understanding of what should be underpinned in an SLA, and how such issues should be defined and communicated. Where problems arise, it is with customers that have contracts for application services support or with the wider FM issues, such as logistics or account planning. The enterprise covers these possible 'gaps' by having service managers available on site.

Account planning is a 'top of the office' service where a strategic investment has been made with the outsourcer so that the customer can shed inessential activities. It was apparent that many problems resulted from the customer's failure to ensure that key activities were understood when they required a deep knowledge of the business. In many cases, the desire to shed activities resulted in the customer's having little or no internal experience to define needs or to understand the impact of outsourcing. The 'intelligent customer' best practice would undoubtedly have been of use; unfortunately, the outsourcer's understanding is that best practice is almost entirely absent in many customer sites.

16.5 IT support

A topic that engaged the people at the help desk was the manner in which IT was perceived as a support mechanism by different customers (and how often it was also considered a painful necessity…). Generally, though not exclusively, customers restricted to services relating to events and incidents involving IT infrastructure were more likely to accept that technology invariably would go awry, and that 'fixes' could be applied to rapidly normalise events. These customers were also mostly able to get events or incidents resolved either while on the phone/Internet, or well within whatever limits were prescribed in the SLA.

Customers reliant on retrieving or processing information (including FM customers), were most likely to be dissatisfied with levels of services; they were also less receptive of explanations that involved the failure of IT components. Where the applications were to blame for problems, resolution was/is invariably slower and caused disruption and ever more scepticism in the customer about the value of the outsourced services and the value of the IT investment. This particular tension, between specific customer understanding and the need to have a cost-effective help desk for multiple customers, is an issue that cannot be solved by the help desk. It is a strategic issue that needs to be addressed at board level and it is part of the customer's cost-benefits discussion.

16.6 Help desk and FM software

The enterprise is reliant on the highly technical and expensive installation of recognised service desk software from a major international vendor. After a competitive tender, this software replaced that of another well-known supplier. The previous software was considered 'end-of-life', and the enterprise wished to upgrade a number of service components to take advantage of AI and of perceived opportunities to build a more automated response.

The vendor provided excellent support, though the cost of the services needed to make full use of the software, exceeded the actual cost of the software by so great a margin that only part of the capabilities were actually put in place. These included many that would be considered to be truly business-led and many that would enhance the FM activities in the strategic sector. This again is a widespread experience. Using the standard software versus applying process specific made solutions leads to principal questions about the costs of configuration, versus the added value for the business.

An additional issue is that the software suite offers many sophisticated capabilities but the enterprise does not have sufficient skills to make full use of them. Furthermore, as ever, the definition of 'automated' leads to disputes. Automation may comprise integrated call centre telephony allied to web-based services, but the definition becomes irrelevant when customers insist on talking with trained operatives because they believe that customer service is about communicating with people rather than technology.

In some cases, this has led to dissatisfaction with customers because communication is more distant and less personal than in the past where in-house employees were at the end of a phone line. Depending on the role of the caller, the outsourcer has found that self-service IT is not even considered as a benefit. Furthermore, the concept of automation (and what that really means for some processes), is ridiculed by business leaders. Saving money is the only reason for considering both outsourcing and automation (despite of course eulogies about efficiency, effectiveness and the 'benefits' of having to do everything yourself, rather than explain issues to a friendly clerical contact). The fundamental difference between the strategic users of the IT services and the operational level users is that for many FM-focused tasks, IT support is secondary whereas at operational level it is not simply the primary focus, it is the channel from which there is no other option.

It is well understood that the tasks of intake (obtaining the needed information to be able to act on enquiries or incidents), is no different in FM or IT. Even the level of detail is not considered an issue, nor is the opportunity to use IT for self-service, using the web or mobile phone or using the multiple choice voice-automated menus in modern telephony.

It is worth mentioning that many customers expressed (and continue to express) their discontent about menu-driven telephony. The incidence of circumventing all menus by discovering the code (often '0') that will allow access to a person has increased year on year. This is, of course, a widely known issue.

16.7 The USD

As a concept, the USD was welcomed by management and operatives. The vast majority of employees were in favour of streamlining processes and adopting a generic approach to all enquiries and incidents, a united approach aligned to an organisational commitment to a superior definition of front office to back office processes.

A number of operational personnel, employed by the outsourcer as a result of staff transfer under Transfer of Undertakings (Protection of Employment) Regulations 2006 (TUPE), also stressed that the 'Intelligent Customer' process needed to be better understood and established in their parent organisations.

The UK implemented TUPE, the United Kingdom's implementation of the European Union's Transfer of Undertakings Directive. It is an important part of UK labour law, protecting employees whose business is being transferred to another business.

The difference between FM and IT operations was considered to be more of a scaling issue than a major problem. It was agreed that ITIL or similar best practices could be adopted more widely if more emphasis was placed on the different needs of business and technology. It was also widely understood that older concepts like front office to back office and account management did not depend on any form of IT best practice, though it was, of course, recognised that employing IT could increase practicality and efficiency.

Specific FM software did not exist in this environment and it was considered to be unnecessary if sufficient attention was paid to proper adaptation of the current IT software suite. A somewhat subjective review of FM software on the market did not alter that opinion. It was considered that there was more in common between FM and IT software than there were problematic differences.

16.8 Next steps

The team was enthusiastic about organising a concept of universal service with greater emphasis on cross training to enable integration between IT and FM activities. It was perceived that improving the design of the services offered (the capabilities), would assist in streamlining operations and training, and lead to stratification of activities that would be based on experience rather than simply process models. Process models and procedures would then be mapped to the activities at different levels, which would allow an improved approvals model to be put in place.

Closer cooperation with customers would also be instigated as a 'pilot' by this team so that it could be demonstrated that contract and SLA provisions and therefore compliance, would benefit both customer and supplier.

SUMMARY OF PART 2

The design and construction of the USD are described in fifteen steps divided over five phases. Some steps are sequential while others can be executed in parallel. The different parts of the USD, which have to be developed and set up in different steps, are explained separately in part 2. There we cover the service or facility management information system (FMIS, SMS or ITSM Tool), the virtual USD, the call centre functionality, the account management, the interest of expert employees, the way in which the processes between the USD and the back office are designed and secured, and the structure and organisation of the USD.

Methods of settlement can be divided into two classes: those requiring physical contact between the service management functions and the customer, and those that entail no physical contact. There is clearly no direct contact on the intranet. The telephone is already interactive but it can be separated geographically, and email does not require direct contact but the customer does expect a response. Physical contact between a USD employee and the customer is necessary when setting up the counter and account management.

The information services focus on the functionality required for the USD's effective and efficient operating. In addition, they often also offer facilities to provide self-service options as standard. Whether an enterprise makes full or partial use of it depends on whether it wants to offer the USD functions separately, or if it wants to integrate them into their own intranet site.

The second level of service is the call centre functionality, which focuses on telephone handling, email and other digital mail. At this level, specialised software makes phone and email handling easier and faster.

In addition, a USD is sometimes a physical presence. Both the design of the service desk and the organisation of account management must fit in with the overall coherence and ambition for the USD. Points of attention during construction are function, identity, technical possibilities, economic considerations, aesthetic aspects and finally organisational requirements.

Account management within the service organisation is managing, supervising and developing the internal customer relations. Account management functions as a bridge between the internal facilities offered and the customer.

The questions and notifications that the USD receives must be forwarded to the back office. The split in the process between the USD and the back office depends on the level of handling per product and service. When this is determined, different methods can be chosen to structure its coordination. These methods consist of organisation and competencies, procedures and practices, and cooperation.

With a professional USD, a service organisation strives for a customer-oriented attitude. In order to be able to make this happen, expertise must be available and one must have the powers to have a good management function and sufficient capacity to handle the client's questions. The USD employees must therefore be sufficiently competent to realise the ambitions of the USD. Requirements for the competence of the USD employees are:

- General knowledge of the systems and the enterprise
- The ability to organise the USD substantive knowledge areas
- Good communication and social skills

- Product and process knowledge

Finally, all these aspects and their choices must be implemented in their context. The minutiae of discussions and considerations exceed the scope of this book.

The following issues may give rise to change considerations with regard to the design:

- USD type;
- Structure and management;
- The USD location within the enterprise;
- Finances; and
- Required capacity.

SECTION FOR YOUR NOTES

Part 3: Development and improvement of the USD

INTRODUCTION

Part 3 deals with various topics related to the functioning and improvement of the USD. In these chapters, topics are covered in the context of the USD, but are not directly part of the design. Such topics are:

- The USD as part of management and control;
- Implementation and further development;
- The quality of service; and
- Quality improvement and practical improvement of returns.

Part 3 ends with a look into the future:

- Sourcing of the USD;
- The rise of the IoT; and
- The possible development of the USD as an 'intelligent hub'.

CHAPTER 17: THE USD AS A KEY TO MANAGEMENT AND CONTROL

"How do we support the mission and objectives of the enterprise by using USD concepts?"

The answer to that question provides the basis for a mission statement and it requires the creation of a strategy to fulfil that mission. The service management strategy should not be limited to IT or facilities; it must identify the means to fulfil the whole enterprise's needs. The first step is to understand and influence the enterprise's functioning. The second step would be to take responsibility to steer overall service management, and therefore this concerns controlling service and facilities functions in their entirety. The decision to embrace both internal customer service and external customers is one of the key strategic points, as is the decision about what services should be brigaded under FM and/or service management.

After reading this chapter, the reader will better understand how the management of facilities and services takes shape within an enterprise and what position the USD must, by necessity, adopt.

17.1 Management and control

Control provides insight into the customer demand, the package of services on offer, the internal processes, the processes in the information partner and supply chains, the quality indicators and the costs and the relationship between these elements. Management implies movement and direction. The services manager operates in accordance with the set corporate governance policies on the basis of customer expectations. The customer groups determine to a large extent the nature of the services provided, and how the quality of service is valued.

Controlling the service organisation is closely related to the way in which the services and service organisation can respond to the expectations of the customer and the timely deployment of new products and services. The service organisation has administrative capacity if it is able to formulate clear objectives for itself and to realise these. The management and control concepts determine the steering power. Such concepts include the strategic services plan with its vision and mission, the front office to back office principle, procurement management, internal management functions, client mandate, account management, culture, competencies, marketing, budget, performance indicators and management information.

Understanding the service organisation's position within an enterprise is essential for interpreting the USD role in the management and control mechanism. The service organisation can be positioned between the various stakeholders in the enterprise.

The position of the service organisation is approached from stakeholder management perspectives (Freeman[31]; Mastenbroek).[32] The stakeholder approach emphasises the importance of investing in relationships with those who have an interest in the stability of these relationships. These stakeholders

---

[31] Freeman, R.E., *Strategic Management: A Stakeholder Approach*, Cambridge: Cambridge University Press, 2010.

[32] Mastenbroek, W.F.G., *Conflicthantering en organisatie-ontwikkeling. Proefschrift Leiden, vierde herziene druk*, Samsom, Alphen aan den Rijn, 2005.

are groups within the enterprise or in its environment and that have an effect on the enterprise, or are affected by its objectives. Networked enterprises are based on the cooperation between rival units with different interests. The relationships between these parties are characterised by simultaneous co-operation and competition. In other words, in some activities the emphasis is on cooperation, in other cases mutual competition is dominant and the separate interests of units play a greater role.

Consult IT Governance Publishing Ltd's *Collaborative Business Design* (Johnson and de Rouw) for a detailed study of the issue of stakeholder relationships in the design of business services.[33]

The mutual dependence between the parties is evident. Examining the perspectives help us understand the tension between supply and demand. The service organisation can be positioned from this perspective between the four main parties dealt with in the intermediary role on a daily basis:

1. The general management or board, also called 'clients'
2. The clients, also called 'customers'
3. The users, also called 'consumers' or 'customers'
4. The service providers, both internally and externally (the various suppliers)

This is shown in *Figure 17.1*.

[33] www.itgovernancepublishing.co.uk/product/collaborative-business-design.

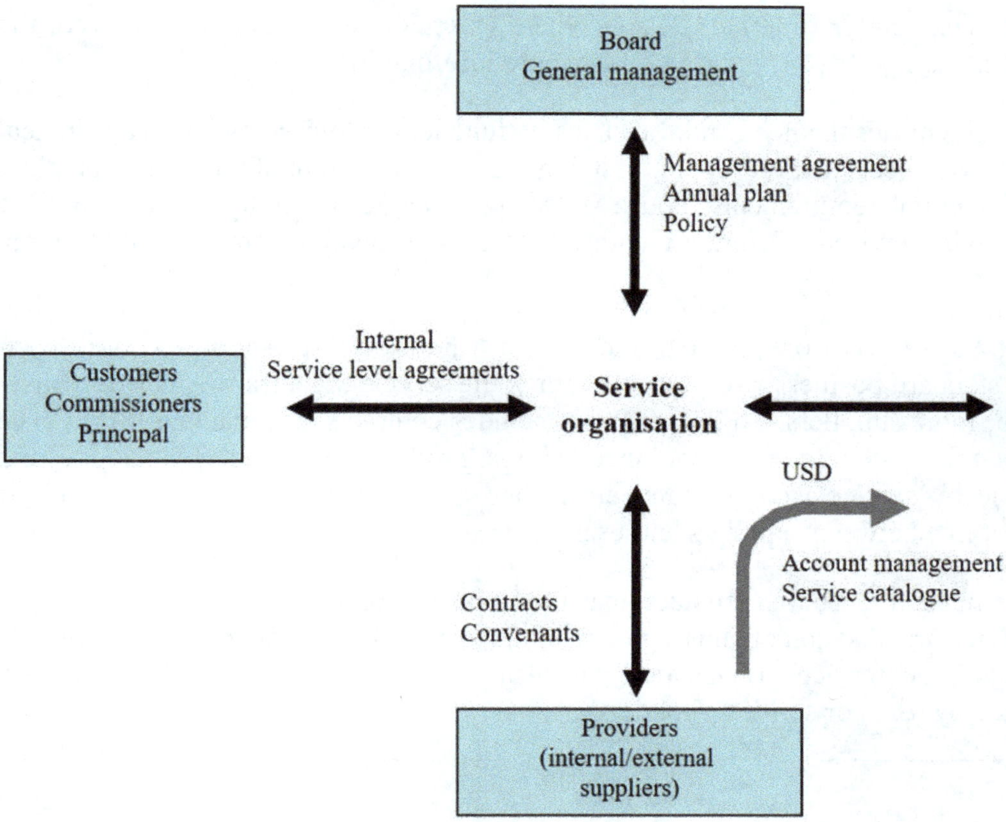

Figure 17.1: Four important parties for the service organisation

As shown schematically in *Figure 17.1*, the service organisation brings supply and demand together. On the demand side, the service organisation has three parties:

1. General management
2. Customers
3. Users

Customer versus users

For a good understanding of the management cycle, a distinction must be made between the customers of services (the users) and those from whom the service organisation receives money. In general, the customer can dictate because they pay. Thus, we speak of customers when there is some degree of control. Users in this model have no control, they do not pay.

However as already indicated at the beginning of the book, users will often be referred to as customers. The distinction between customer and user/customer is important in stakeholder analysis. Sometimes this distinction is solved by speaking of contractor and user, or of client and contractor.

The service organisation's services are purchased for users so that they can perform their work. With the clients or customers, the service company makes agreements based on the needs and/or priorities of the users about the price that has to be paid in order to be able to deliver the services. The most important customer or client is generally also in the management board or general management with the portfolio for business operations. They pay for the generic or basic services. These needs are often laid down in service agreements or (internal) SLAs. Where external customers are concerned, the documents will be contractual, perhaps supported by the more informal SLAs.

The service organisation identifies the need and translates its functional requirements into a technical package of requirements that meets market supply. In doing so, it takes account of requirements set by the board such as architectural requirements, house style and strategic principles. In addition, the service organisation will also advise the board on matters such as new developments, standardisation, policy and costs.

Where services cannot be offered from internal sources (or where external supply is more cost-effective (sometimes a standard business word for 'cheaper'), the service organisation then purchases the services from one or more suppliers. To this end, it concludes contracts, covenants or SLAs. The service is provided to the customers in accordance with a product and service catalogue and maintained, for example by service/account management and a USD desk. In *Figure 17.1* this is represented by the direct line between suppliers and users.

On the basis of measurements (e.g. audits, satisfaction surveys, panels) and performance management on the contracts, the service organisation obtains a picture of the quality. Results are reported to general management and clients. The service organisation can also take the initiative to advise on new developments (motivated by users or service providers).

Example:

Some service management systems offer automatic surveys after calls. Customers can provide feedback about their support experience by rating their solved tickets. When customer satisfaction ratings (CSATs) are enabled, end users receive an email 24 hours after the ticket has been solved that asks them to briefly evaluate their experience.

The service organisation therefore maintains various relationships with the various parties. Sometimes these are instrumental relations, such as contracts or work agreements. In addition to these, other relationships can also be distinguished such as social, power, dependency and negotiation relationships. The nature of service is generally supportive within the enterprise. A characteristic of this type of work is that they are primarily a cost centre.

The choice to translate needs into a concrete range of products and services mainly concerns the use and distribution of scarce resources. Therefore, the service organisation seeks an optimal relationship between wants and needs and the available services in the market. Of course, the wants and needs of buyers, clients and management are not necessarily the same. Users want maximum support, regardless of the costs. Clients will evaluate costs in relation to the quality of service. In addition to its organisational objectives, management (sometimes general management) has social and political interests. This means, for example, selective cost reduction or standardisation. The service providers (suppliers) want to earn as much as possible from the contracts with the customer organisation, or seek reinforcement of the contracts as the preferred supplier.

Critically, the service organisation must coordinate these sometimes conflicting interests of supply and demand so that all parties are satisfied. For example, sole focus on cost reduction will ultimately frustrate the suppliers, which means they will focus mainly on minimal costs and less on quality. Another example is that it is not possible to allow users' free choice at the expense of the desire for cost control and standardisation. Furthermore, ultimate standardisation may interfere with the ability of the business to develop new markets and it may alienate users and customers.

This means that the service organisation sometimes has to balance similar and different interests. In practice this translates into an effective function through a mixed approach to the relationships: on the one hand demand or customer-oriented, on the other hand by acting as the manager and conscience of the enterprise, and through monitoring and prescribing.

17.2 Nature of work

There are four types of activities that typically occur between the service organisation and the four most important stakeholders:

1. Operational services (operation and delivery)
2. Demand management (orchestration/operating model)
3. Strategic services (governance)
4. Audits, training and pilots (quality)

These activities are shown in *Figure 17.2*.

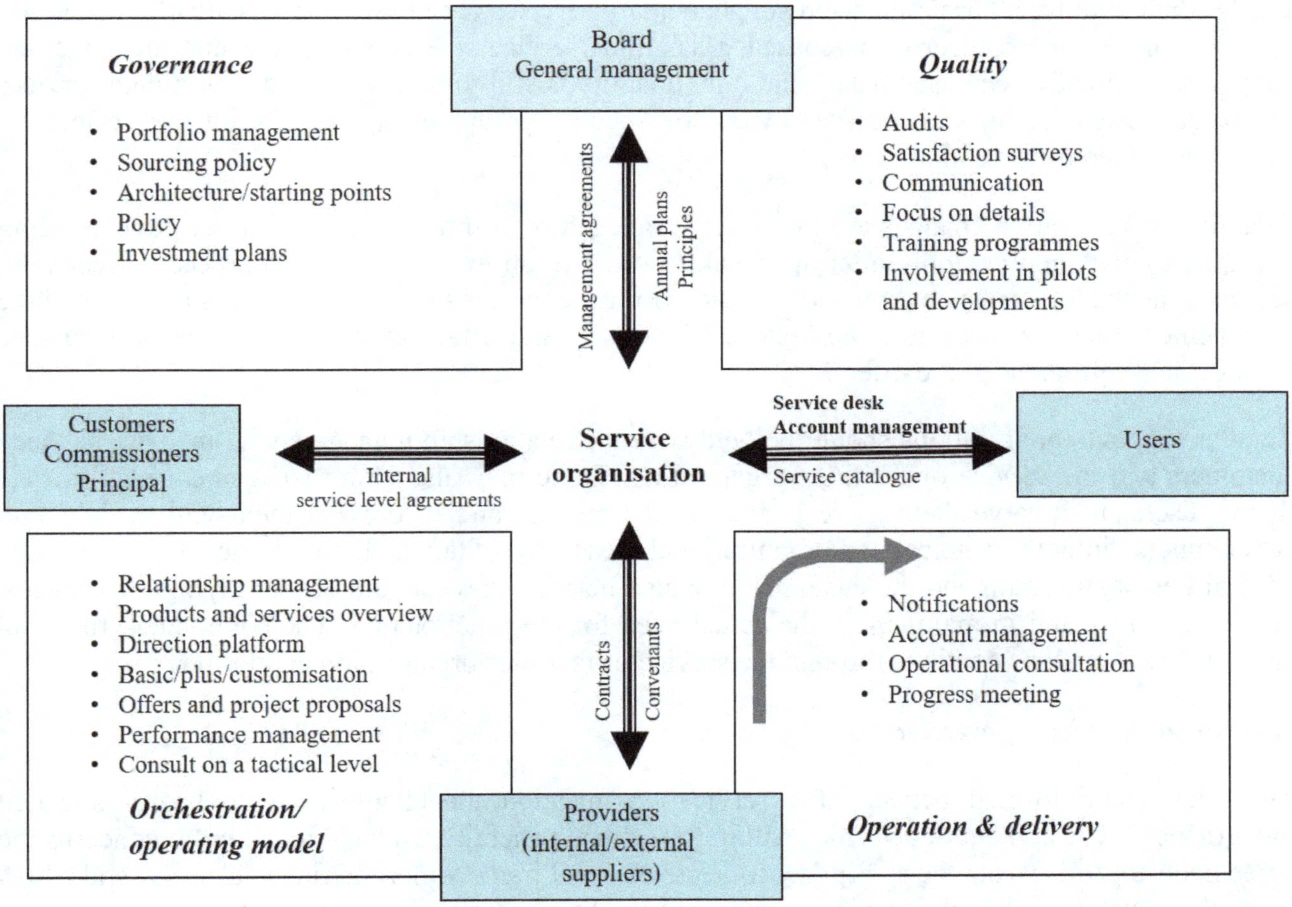

Figure 17.2: Primary activities

1. Operational services (operation and delivery)

In this area, the relationships between users, suppliers and the service organisation are maintained, but the focus is on service delivery. This also concerns the actual execution of agreed projects and changes to which offers have been issued. This means that the products and services to be supplied are known and recorded in a products and services overview. Through service management, a USD or help desk, the supplier ensures that complaints and reports are channeled and solved smartly and efficiently.

Processes and procedures are largely known and transparent, and the service organisation is kept up-to-date with reports. Sometimes it is necessary to carry out audits. Several forms of consultation monitor the operational process; these include operational consultations between customers and suppliers, regular progress consultations between the suppliers and the service or facilities organisation, and consultations regarding programme management between project managers and service organisations.

2. Demand management (orchestration/operating model)

This area focuses on maintaining the relationships between customers (clients), service organisation and suppliers that relate to the agreements made between functional requirements and the supply of the products and services on the basis of price, time and quality. This means that the service organisation has understood the current and future needs and has translated supply agreements with the suppliers. The service organisation keeps regular contact with the decision makers in the customer organisation through its relationship managers. To streamline the different groups of needs, it often divides them into basic, basic-plus and supplementary services. The basic services are often centrally budgeted and are compulsorily purchased. Basic-plus services are services in which the price and quality have already been established and only quantity is still to be determined. Additional services can be requested within specific frameworks by specific groups of clients. To this end, offers are usually provided by the suppliers.

Adaptive or innovative changes are preferably managed on a project basis, with the projects being executed by the suppliers only after approval. In order to allow this process to proceed effectively, several consultations must be arranged. Consider for instance consultations between suppliers and the management function to discuss the (external) contracts and SLAs, quality of service (performance management), progress of the offers.

Regular account conversations should be held with the relationship managers who mediate between customers and the service or facilities organisation. There may also be a management platform for 'heavy users' to involve them more in the service process and to provide them with insight into developments in both technical and organisational areas. Consultations between the supplier, service or facilities organisation and the customers are also helpful; they can aid in identifying efficiencies, obtaining clarity and in maintaining the actual need for the functionality. The contractual, financial and legal relationships continue through the service or facilities organisation at all times.

3. Strategic services (governance)

The relationship formed between the service organisation, its clients and the board is called 'governance'. The content of activities within this area is generally strategic in nature. It concerns the agreements that arise from the enterprise's objectives, legal frameworks and financial space, and which guide the development of the service provision in the longer term. Think of architectural agreements and sourcing policy, housing policy, portfolio management and policy objectives.

The service organisation also has to account for its performance annually, and to draw up annual investment plans. The role of the manager includes monitoring the effectiveness and efficiency of the provided services. It differs in every enterprise whether this is exclusively focused on business operations, or that the support is enterprise-wide.

4. Audits, training and pilots (quality)

The fourth plane is formed by the relationships that the service organisation has with the customers and the management. The quality of the service is a result of the agreements made with the customers and suppliers and the method of delivery. The general management or the board mainly benefits if the employees can perform their work undisturbed. If their employees are satisfied, they are also satisfied. There may be tension because customers are not directly confronted with the costs, and that is why they will be more inclined to maximise their wishes and demands. Certainly in times of cost rationalisation, the discrepancy between wishes and needs and available possibilities will increase. This makes it more difficult for the services/facility organisation to directly influence the satisfaction of customers.

Effective management can be achieved by taking note of the following:

- Ensure that their suppliers' service provision is good;
- Carry out regular satisfaction surveys or customer panels;
- Consider developments and their consequences for employees (in its strategic advisory role);
- Offer training programmes that are related to the nature of activities; and
- Actively involve customers in pilots or innovative developments.

17.3 The USD in the demand and supply process

As the service organisation improves the cohesiveness of its relationships with the various parties, its service provision will improve in consequence and customers will appraise it differently. Customers' wants and needs will maximise and often differentiate. Customers who have to pay for services will seek to obtain maximum service at minimum cost. The service or facilities organisation can increase cohesion through standardisation and by making strict agreements with suppliers. In doing so, it must again ensure that the suppliers' involvement is maintained. If a situation eventuates in which suppliers feel they cannot earn more, they will focus on minimal effort. In this situation, partnership is preferable.

Management and control of the supply and demand process is now conducted via the USD with the products and service catalogue and through service agreements. The package of services forms the core of the products and service catalogue, and of service provision agreements, also known as SLAs. The service package is the required instrument for top management for the effective and efficient support of the primary process. This package is in line with the vision and strategy of the enterprise. In addition to the basic package, additional products and services will be requested as necessary. Depending on the way in which the service organisation is placed within the enterprise, the additional costs will be allocated centrally or distributed to different parts of the enterprise.

These service agreements are made with the customers and as defined earlier, this refers to those who pay money to the service organisation. Furthermore, the agreements are made within the frameworks (for example the housing policy, the house style or the desired image), that have been established by the management team. Often the most important customer is also a member of the management team, with the business operations in his portfolio.

On the basis of the available budget and the agreements made, the service organisation can make agreements with suppliers (contracts or covenants). This leads to the delivery of the products and services in accordance with the agreed quality levels in the service agreements. The service organisation takes care of the composition of the service catalogue, the guideline for the users in determining the services to be purchased by them. Many of the services are delivered via the USD. The USD is thus located between the users (the customers), the suppliers and the service organisation.

The products and service catalogue

The purpose of the service catalogue is to inform the users (internal and or external) about the services provided. Simply put, the service catalogue is the 'window' of the enterprise for its products and services. In addition to a description of a product or service, it also describes in which way and under what conditions the users can purchase the services and at what quality level the products and services are delivered.

Today, the service catalogue is often made available via the Internet or intranet. In some cases, forms are also linked to the products and services so that users can not only consult the service catalogue, but can also place an order directly via the Internet or intranet. The service catalogue is established on the basis of the service agreements and the experience of the USD employees (and account management), in combination with the requirements for clear communication. Identify the communication mechanisms that are most used. For example, if it is well known that the intranet is not widely used, you should not make the intranet the sole source of information.

Table 17.1: Required Classification Per Product or Service in the Products and Services Catalogue

Required Classification
• Description of product or service. • Basic package of services: description of the basic package (for a discussion and definition of these terms, see section 3.2.). • Plus package: description of the basic-plus package with accompanying price (see section 3.2.). • Additional services: description of additional services (see section 3.2.). • Authorisation/delivery conditions: explains who is entitled to purchase a product or service. • Settlement level: the level at which a service can be handled (levels comprise information request, request, settlement within the USD and settlement with waiting or lead time). • Information about obtaining/contact person: explains who or what should be approached in order to obtain the service. Additional information (e.g. legal framework). • Quality criteria: the quality of the service and the fulfilment of the service provision agreement are managed using quality criteria.

The products and service catalogue can serve multiple purposes; it may be:

- A means of communicating to customers (i.e. the display window);
- A marketing tool;
- A means to make the added value of the services or facilities organisation transparent;
- A handle for the collection and classification of management information; and
- An instruction tool for USD employees.

SLA

Where the products and service catalogue functions as a range of offers for the users, the internal SLA is a formal contract between management and the service organisation. This contract sets out the conditions under which products and services are supplied. The SLA generally records:

- Type of service provided

- Level of performance achieved
- Conditions of service provision
- Availability and accessibility of support
- Associated costs
- Available staff
- How quality is guaranteed

Due to its contract status, the SLA has a more formal language than the products and service catalogue. The basic service package outlined in the catalogue is presented in less detailed form in the SLA and is formulated more from the objectives of the management. This means that the products and services are delivered from a vision related to business operations.

An internal SLA offers tools to provide the desired services, taking into account cost control and quality control. The SLA thus also provides the input for capacity calculation and the connection of services to the budget. A normative amount can be determined with the aid of the basic package of services and the associated work processes. Coupled with standard numbers, these form the basis for the calculation of a normative capacity.

In addition to the products and service catalogue, the SLA also contains the conditions under which the service organisation delivers. This makes it possible to discuss aspects like mandating, the work to be performed and the manner of handling complaints.

The basic service package, the corresponding capacity and the requested quality level are a tangible tool for the manager who has to defend the occupation and activities of service management to executives. It is wise to link capacity to basic service.

The SLA has several functions and can serve as:

- An informal internal contract;
- A document to record the products and services in relation to resources;
- A starting point when calibrating the objectives of the service or facilities organisation in relation to the business strategy;
- An instrument for determining formation;
- An instrument to decide the 'criticality' of an application or request based on its business impact; and
- An instrument for determining effectiveness and efficiency.

Registration and monitoring

The services requested by customers and offered by the service department should be documented and monitored within the management and control system, and they should form part of the management information.

Based on this information, it can be verified whether the services, products and budgets are sufficiently in line with user needs. After all, if additional services are requested more than what was expected, this may be a reason for the management to include these additional services in the basic provision.

Also, this information offers management guidance to make the costs arising from the desired service provision visible. By organising the administration in accordance with standards like ISO 20000 or ISO 41001, better overviews and benchmarks can be implemented.

CHAPTER 18: CONTRACT MANAGEMENT AND THE USD

Enterprises purchase many types of movable goods, including deliveries of everything from flowers for the boardroom, to building materials and services. This will also cover office furniture, cleaning and catering, management, maintenance and the hiring of external personnel, organisational advice, and ICT services or accountancy services. Contract management plays the leading role, though the USD has an operational role in contract management.

18.1 Purchasing and contract management

Every enterprise arranges purchasing differently. In large enterprises, there are separate purchasing departments. For example, one enterprise may have multiple 'category' managers with substantive knowledge of their particular market and the needs of their own enterprise. Small enterprises can work together to share knowledge, organise joint assignments or assign tasks to a shared service centre. Tender boards can be set up for a large tendering process but also for multiple purchasing processes within an enterprise.

In purchasing, a distinction is made between strategic, tactical and operational purchasing. Strategic and tactical purchasing are about purchasing policy, specifying purchasing needs, selecting suppliers and contracting suppliers. Operational procurement is concerned with purchasing activities; it includes calling about and ordering purchased goods and services, monitoring delivery times and monitoring the correctness of delivery and aftercare.

Figure 18.1 illustrates the purchase cycle. The purchasing cycle runs from strategy to tender execution to selection and may include a revised purchasing strategy based on performance. After the enterprise has followed the purchasing process with the selection of the supplier and the contract, the execution phase starts. This is shown in the ordering cycle. In this phase, it is important that the execution be monitored. This task belongs to contract management and supplier management.

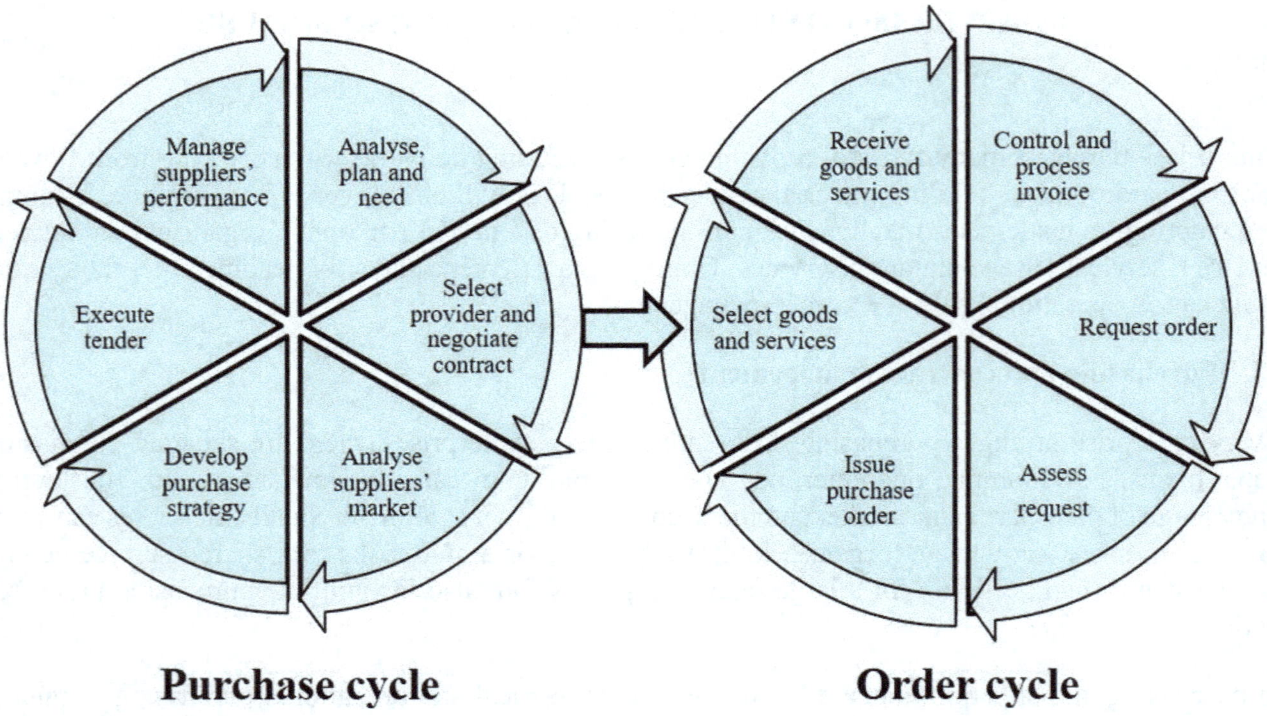

Figure 18.1: Purchasing and ordering cycle (based on Noorlander, Alleijn, 2009)[34]

The ordering cycle starts with the selection of goods and services within the agreed contract or within the agreements for one-time purchases not covered by an overall contract. The order is requested and goes through the process of purchase order, receipt of goods and services, and invoice processing.

Contract management begins after the purchasing process is completed, after the negotiation and conclusion of contract agreements. It is up to contract management to ensure that all parties to an agreement fully comply with their obligations, so that the operational objectives of the contract and the objectives of the enterprise are met. For example, catering supplies the agreed commitment in accordance with quality within the set conditions. This does not only concern monitoring the agreements made but also maintaining the relationship: 'relationship makes the performance'.

Managing contracts and contacts with external suppliers is aimed at the sustainable guarantee of the quality, stability and continuity of the services provided by the suppliers to the internal customers and the reduction of the costs thereof. Contract management is also involved in negotiating the expansion of tasks (e.g. higher volume due to the expansion of locations or changes in demand as a result of the introduction of new services). Supplier management is often part of contract management and assesses the performance of the suppliers.

18.2 Management of the service

Obtaining a new service can be difficult and time consuming. The signing of the contract is only the beginning for contract management. After the signing of the contract, ordering can begin; at this point,

---

[34] Noorlander, R., Alleijn, S., *Inkoopsoftware P2P: een goede voorbereiding is de voorwaarde voor success*, Blog, www.logistiek.nl/, Vakmedianet, 2009.

it must be clear how and under what conditions an order or assignment can take place. The securing of the ordering cycle determines contract management's work area.

After concluding the contract, contract management is still responsible for monitoring the preconditions within which the service must be performed. The contract manager is also expected to make sure that the client's obligations are fulfilled; this may include making capacity and space available, among other things.

The main tasks of contract management are:

- Ensuring service is provided
- Providing contract administration
- Managing and maintaining the relationship
- Securing 'value for money'
- Seeking and implementing improvements
- Implementing management changes
- Providing continuous analysis of the customer enterprise's needs[35]

Several parties are involved at the strategic, tactical and operational levels, both on the client's part (the customer enterprise) and on the service provider's part. This is shown in *Figure 18.2*.

[35] Beckum, J. van en & Vlasgeld, G-J., *CATS CM editie 2014: Contract management voor opdrachtgever en leverancier*, Zaltbommel: Van Haren Publishing, 2014.

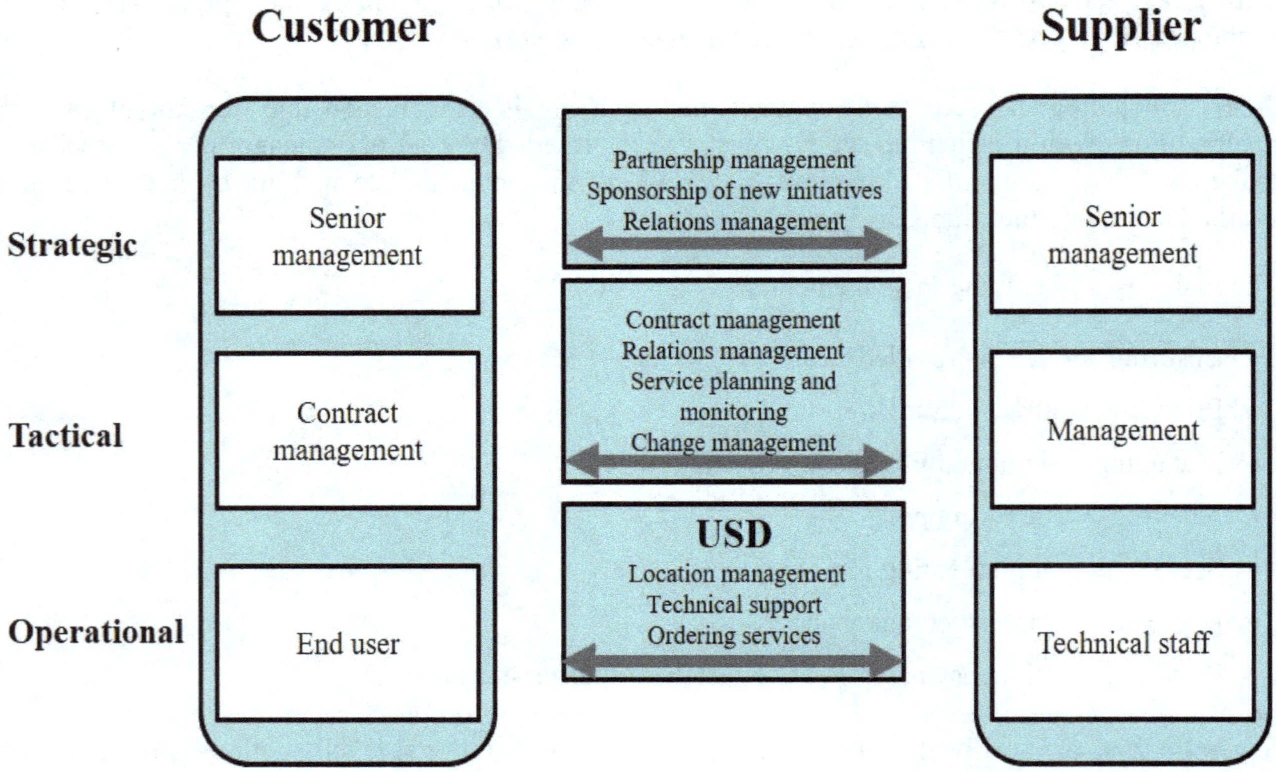

Figure 18.2: Contract management setup at three levels

Contract management is organised on three levels:

1. **The strategic level:** The client's management maintains the relationship with the service provider's management. This relationship not only focuses on existing services but also on new initiatives.
2. **The tactical level:** Contract management deals with the core task, as well as management, relationship management, managing and checking the contract, and possibly processing adjustments in the contract.
3. **The operational level:** This is where the products and services are actually delivered. The service provider delivers within the contract agreements. Daily issues are solved at this level; when that is not possible, the issue is escalated to the contract manager.

The main tasks translate into the following activities that belong to contract management in the client enterprise (*Table 18.1*).

Table 18.1: Tasks That Belong to Contract Management in the Customer Enterprise

Task	Explanation
Initiation and tendering	Preparation, organisation and start of the purchase specification (requirements).
Contract context (internal and/or external)	Who is involved in the contract? who replaces whom? Composition, consultation with client, relationships with subcontractors and other contracts.
Keep track of contract risk profile	Contract file must be fully up to date.
Monitor contract risk profile	Insight into risks and implementing mitigating measures.
Monitor the billing process (budget monitoring)	In consultation with finance, monitor the quality of the delivered invoices and payment orders respectively. Review of cash flows, remaining budget, outstanding and unpaid invoices.
Status, implementation and progress reporting	Keeping an overview of the status of the contract implementation, the extent to which the contract has been successfully implemented and the aspects where further actions must be set out for the short term.
Guard and maintenance contract calendar	Delivery dates, scope changes and monitoring the total package.
Periodic contract assessment	Monitoring whether the service provider adheres to the contract, providing timely identification and taking corrective measures for compliance.
Periodic consultations	Operational consultation with project members, facility managers, etc.; operational consultation with the contractor; tactical consultation involving the contract manager consulting their own organisation about status, progress, risks, financials, issues and tactical matters; strategic consultation with client or contractor.
Monitoring and coordination of the contractor	Insight and guardianship in relation to customer satisfaction.
Completion and retender monitoring	Introduce expertise and operational coordination to support the phasing out of existing service providers and the transition to a new service provider.

It goes without saying that the contract management for the service provider has similar tasks. However, we said it anyway.

18.3 The USD and contract management

The operational contract management for the implementation of the service organisation's services includes the service desk and location management or service management. Furthermore, this concerns more products and services than you might think. *Table 18.2* provides an overview of the possible products and services for which a contract may be concluded and with which the service desk may be related. In most cases, the service desk should have a central role. However, if departments order and receive for themselves, it is difficult for a service desk to play a role.

Table 18.2: Facility Procurement Packages at the Service Desk[36]

Product or Service	Contract About
Building and installations	Building-related maintenance, maintenance of technical installations, facade cleaning, system walls and floors, greenery and paving.
Device	Furniture, loose furnishings, art, wall decorations, plants and containers.
Housekeeping	Catering, landscaping, waste disposal, transportation, company clothing and linen supply.
External staff	Advisors, temporary workers, secondment and security.
Logistics services	Courier services, postal services and passenger transport.
Office supplies and printing	Multifunctionals, office supplies, paper and printed matter.
Automation	Hardware and software maintenance and telephony (smartphones etc.).

The purchased services are delivered against agreed performance requirements, often laid down in an SLA as part of the contract. *Table 18.3* contains an overview of indicators and requirements on which agreements can be made and where monitoring for all levels of contract management is required.

Table 18.3: Possible Agreements to be Monitored

Indicator	Requirement
Quality	• Quality delivered products and services • Quality control in general
Finance	• BID • Price-quality • Delivery and costs
Risk	• Implementation of improvement measures • Risks during execution
Organisation	• Organisation of the supplier • Attitude – customer-friendly, reliable, transparent • Honesty
Information	• Timely delivery of documentation • Appropriate appointments • Reporting problems in a timely manner • Insight into the state of affairs

[36] Lennartz, R.E., Trompetter, A. & Veeke, R.A.F., *Inkoopmanagement in facilitaire omgevingen; ... stevig faciliteren noodzakelijk, Inkoopmemo's*, Alphen aan den Rijn: Samsom, 2000.

Indicator	Requirement
Time	• Timely delivery in accordance with the state of affairs • Timely milestones achieved

18.4 The USD and associated activities for the services provided

The USD can be tasked with almost all operational services. This may include precontracting, the precise specification of operational and implementation requirements, and the acceptance of reports in the transfer of requested services to contract partners. During execution, the service desk will have regular contact with the implementers (either their own back office staff or the service providers of the external party), to report progress or problems, or to provide notification of readiness. Within large enterprises or where complex contracts are in place, the external service providers will have their own employees on site. They will generally have close contact with the employees of the USD. For the sake of clarity, in general, the service desk is mainly involved in dealing with parties where the price is fixed in the contract, and not where a requirement includes assessment of quotations.

Employees who are involved in the supply and demand side must be able to cooperate well and they must know who is responsible and what to do in case of daily problems. It is therefore important that the roles are well established. The USD and those involved in executing actions must be aware of their specific roles, and the relationship must be stable and workable. A good working relationship with the contract partner often lies at the basis of a successful execution of the contract, and the USD plays a key role in this. Sometimes there is tension at commercial level and renegotiations are needed. Operations must ensure that the impacted service continues uninterrupted. Nevertheless, problems in the contract relationship at management level can have a negative impact on implementation. Internal customers will become aware of such issues and service desk personnel will need to keep them informed.

The USD also becomes involved when it is necessary to integrate services or products into a single customer service or product. Consider the example of a renovation where several service providers will be involved; these could include telecom, a construction company, a mover, a cleaner and a mechanical and electrical engineering company.

In addition, the USD shares a joint role with the service provider in seeking practical improvements and in finding solutions when applications do not align with existing contracts. The USD will also participate in quality management as part of contract management and, consequently, it can indicate in concrete terms whether the service provider delivers in accordance with agreements. After all, the USD is often the first to discover when a service is not going smoothly.

When a contract ends, procurement and contract management generally take measures to ensure that it is retendered. This process will involve the subject matter experts. These are often experienced USD employees who have substantive process knowledge and who can make valuable contributions in this phase.

Table 18.4 summarises the USD tasks in operational contract management.

Table 18.4: Summary of USD Tasks During Operational Contract Management

Operational Contract Management Tasks	USD Task
Ordering services	Exhausting contract.
Checking services	Part of quality assurance, management reporting, performance declaration, performance evaluation of contractor (in terms of providing feedback on response times), SLA reports, etc.
Executing services	FAQ for service provider and help in solving problems.
Integration of different services into a composite product	Service desk performs operational coordination.
Provide additional services during implementation	Support during implementation. For example registration, keys, issuing job orders.
In tender or retender	Introduce expertise. Coordinate the transition to a new supplier and phase out the existing supplier.
Relationship management	Operational relationship management.
New services or improvements	USD meets new demands or identifies improvements needed.

CHAPTER 19: SUCCESS CRITERIA

The structure and functioning of the USD determine the extent to which success factors can be met. Factors for a successful USD are related to good accessibility, accurate information, effective and efficient operation and the conviction among customers that they have been effectively helped.

After reading this chapter, the reader can identify factors that describe a successful USD.

19.1 Added value of the USD

The impact of a USD service depends in part on its interaction with customers. Often customers will actively participate in the service process and their experiences are in part determined by the interaction with those who provide services. The result is that often the enthusiasm or disappointment of customers determines the quality judgement. Bad experiences linger a long time and are passed on to others, therefore quality control in services for the service organisation is of great importance. This means that not only the physical handling of a demand must be carried out properly, the contact with the customer also determines the ultimate experience of the way someone is helped. How the customer experiences the services is therefore decisive for the image of the service organisation and thus the quality of service provision. The perception of the USD as the first point of entry for customers is a determining factor.

19.2 Success factors of an effective and efficient USD

In previous chapters, we described how a USD's financial advantages mainly benefit users and departments outside the USD. If the USD works well, it means that other parties, the customers and back offices, can concentrate better on their own activities and have no loss of time as a result of the front office tasks such as taking telephone calls, talking to people they cannot immediately help and providing support services themselves. For a successful USD, the following needs to be in place:

a) The USD is easily accessible
b) Customers are well informed and effectively helped
c) Customers are convinced that they will receive excellent service
d) Cooperation between the USD and other organisational units focuses on optimal service provision
e) Processes support the service effectively
f) The USD works adequately within the available budget

a) The USD is easily accessible

In the first place, accessibility entails providing sufficient staffing to manage the different points at which the USD receives customers including counter, email and telephone. The USD must have sufficient staff capacity to:

- Accept phone calls;
- Process emails in a timely manner;
- Receive customers at the counter;
- Process requests; and
- Perform other common tasks.

In the second place, the USD must respond quickly to a customer request. Service standards can help; for example, they may specify that telephone calls be recorded within 30 seconds or emails be answered within one hour. When customer questions cannot be handled immediately, the customer must be informed that their incident or enquiry has been logged.

On occasion, it is inevitable that workload will mean that customers cannot be served quickly at a counter. At that moment, the customer must have the choice to return or wait. In order to shorten the experience time (which is often different from the actual waiting time), so-called 'waiting softeners' can be deployed. Waiting softeners are information brochures or a seat at the desk; similarly, telephony can be used to play music or offer information.

b) Customers are well informed and effectively helped

In the first place, an expert intake of customer demand means that USD employees:

- Know the content of the products and services and the enterprise's structure;
- Are able to translate a customer's demand into products and services;
- Are able to ask the right questions; and
- Have written and oral communication skills for customer contact.

This means a *professional* intake. Professional refers to the attitude of the employees at the USD. A demand-oriented organisation starts with employees who are intrinsically customer-oriented. Such employees understand that statements like "I do not know" and "I cannot help you" must be avoided in all interactions with customers.

If it is not possible to respond immediately, the employee must tell you that the incident/enquiry is being examined and the customer can expect a call back later. The characteristics of a professional attitude are:

- Displaying an open and interested demeanour;
- Accurately informing customers, either directly or by calling them back later;
- Always keeping promises;
- Never making promises that cannot be fulfilled or for which no authority exists; and
- Knowing "what you do not know" and asking questions when in doubt.

Of course, customers should be reasonable. The customer is king, but only as long as they remain polite and fair.

Finally, customers will be helped effectively when there is a *successful* intake. Remember, that the primary task of the USD is to properly take and process customer demand. Customer questions must be correctly translated into concrete products and services and directed to the appropriate back office or to third parties.

c) Customers are convinced that they will receive excellent service

Quality of service is defined as the way in which the customer has experienced services. This means not only effective handling of a customer request, but also that the customer has the conviction that the help was effective. The customer must feel that the USD has dealt with and responded to their incident, request or enquiry efficiently and effectively. Where the processing of a request is perfectly business-like, but the customer has a negative experience with the way they are treated, the services' image will be negatively influenced. The customer handling by the USD therefore has two aspects: the actual and the emotional handling of the request.

d) Cooperation between the USD and other organisational units focuses on optimal service provision

After the customer request has been made, it will be decided whether it can be handled within the USD or whether the request must be passed on to other parts of the service, facilities organisation or to an external party. When the USD serves as more than a channel for customer questions, it will also have to monitor the entire work process. This means:

- Controlling the process of transferring requests to the correct party;
- Ensuring progress and performance;
- Ensuring agreements with customers are kept;
- Ensuring that both the enterprise and third parties provide correct provision; and
- Informing customers of issues when necessary (for example, a delay in the delivery process).

The cooperation between the USD and other organisational units and third parties requires attention. Cooperation must be aimed at optimal service to the customer. In order to achieve this, the USD needs knowledge of the tasks, expertise and skills of the other components. Due to various causes – varying from personal arguments to complex organisational processes – this knowledge is not always present at the USD. The management concerned must be aware of this and cooperate closely with each other.

e) **Processes support the service effectively**

The organisational structure or the functions in the enterprise are not the starting point for setting up the process from customer demand to completion; processes should describe the relationship between the different actions and activities. In concrete terms, the processes behind the products and services are set out and then from there the responsibilities and activities are assigned. It may be that some tasks do not always fit well within a department, because these have been laid down from historical, cultural and positional perspectives.

Management must recognise exceptions and indicate that certain existing processes must be retained; this will result in a recalibration of activities. The advantage of this approach is that:

- It aligns with modern systems' approaches to enterprises;
- It aligns with the prevailing quality systems, such as the European Foundation for Quality Management (EFQM) model, Lean Six Sigma and the ISO 9000 series;
- It creates room for employees where customs, procedures and traditions are clearly established; and
- It takes the service and therefore the customer and their needs as the starting point when dealing with issues.

The quality of the products and services provided are highly dependent on the quality of the USD information with which the USD works. Quality is determined by the purpose for which the services are provided ('fitness for purpose'). The users of the services, and therefore the information, are the users of the USD (see also *BISL-Next- A framework for Business Information Management: Second edition* Johnson et al.).[37] Improving the efficiency of the USD should therefore not only be sought within the USD or in the service delivery chain (front office back office), but also in the environment in which the USD is connected to the important processes. There are various best practices or standards (such as BISL-Next, ITIL and ISO standards) that categorise these processes. Each organisation will use its own categorisation (which in practice obviously looks very similar to the aforementioned standards).

The reader should translate and adjust the management processes mentioned in the next chapter for their own situation.

f) The USD works adequately within the available budget

On the basis of the available budget and the agreements made, the service or facilities organisation can make agreements about the scope and content of products and services. This ensures the delivery of the products and services in accordance with the quality levels agreed in the service agreements. The quality that the USD can deliver is largely limited by the available budget. There will always be a 'threshold' below which good quality can no longer be delivered even if maximum effort is provided by the USD employees. This threshold value depends, of course, on the nature and size of the enterprise. In a professional environment, managers should be able to make an estimate using historical data.

[37] Johnson, B. et al., *BISL-Next- A framework for Business Information Management: Second edition*, Zaltbommel: Van Haren Publishing, 2018.

CHAPTER 20: QUALITY IMPROVEMENT

In order to guarantee the quality of service, you need to understand the activities and their consequences and this insight helps an organisation make the right decisions. But what does this mean and how do you organise this?

After reading this chapter, the reader will better understand the need for quality management in the USD. Examples will provide insights on how to deal with criteria and standards, and how these can be translated into a USD staffing occupation requirement.

20.1 Quality management in the USD

In order to safeguard or realise the goals of a successful USD, the assurance and improvement of quality is required. According to Philip Crosby, "Quality is free,"[38] and by that he means that every mistake you have to correct incurs costs that you could have prevented. By preventing errors in the USD, added value for the enterprise is created:

- Additional costs for the business are prevented
- The USD will be more efficient and can handle more with the same resources
- The back offices work more effectively and efficiently

Within the USD, therefore, a process must be set up with the aim of collecting data, processing and analysing the data and making decisions on the basis thereof. This process is also known as the quality management process. One of the most common methods for implementing such a process is the Plan-Do-Check-Act cycle (PDCA cycle), also known as the Deming or Shewhart quality circle.

This method is intended to pursue continuous improvement. On the basis of this cycle, the services from the USD in relation to the tasks can be made transparent. *Figure 20.1* shows the PDCA cycle applied to the management and control within the service organisation (as discussed in *chapter 16*).

[38] Philip Crosby, *Quality Is Free*, McGraw-Hill, 1979.

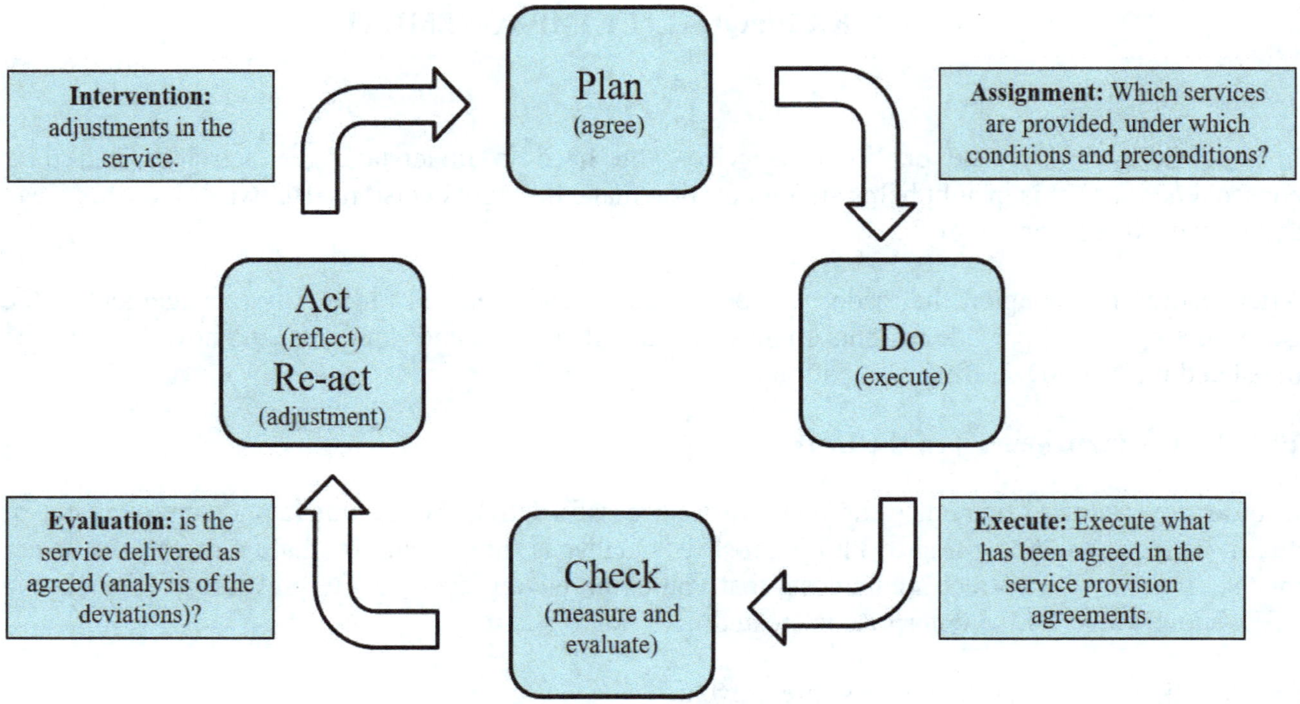

Figure 20.1: PDCA cycle for management and control within the service organisation

Plan

In the plan phase, we focus on the services that must be provided and under what conditions and preconditions. If changes to the basic package (including the basic plus and/or plus package) are set out in the SLA, this will have consequences for the USD activities. As a result, changes can be made to the service offering, prices, performance standards, etc., and the catalogue will therefore also have to be adapted.

Do

The products and services provided by the USD are covered by the service organisation's internal SLA. These products and services can be offered in various ways:

- On request via the USD (only services from the internal SLAs)
- On request via account management (services from the internal SLA and questions for services that are not included in the internal SLAs)
- Based on agreements in the internal SLAs (secondment, periodic activities and the like)

Check

During the check phase, the service is monitored in various ways. Monitoring means regular and periodic exchange of progress and performance information. Available management information provides insight into the nature and scope of the service to the USD. This means that the registration of specific data yields important information about the number and type of customer questions, as well as about the connection between supply and demand (including progress and capacity requirements). Measuring performance remains a difficult issue and often the best solution is found by combining different methods. Methods include the use of software support systems, annual reports, telephone records (often a standard option in telephony installations), quality measurements, customer and complaints surveys, invoices, records of absenteeism due to illness, stakeholder research and the simple counting of occurrences such as the number of visitors to the desk.

Act

During the act phase, the deviations observed during the execution are analysed and their causes are investigated. The results of this phase form the input in the plan phase. After all, it may be that the results of the analysis are reason to adjust the product and service offerings. This closes the cycle.

20.2 Criteria and standards help to identify deviations

In order to be able to measure and compare whether the desired objectives are achieved (for example optimal staffing, a fast processing time, expertise of the USD), it is necessary that the objectives are concrete (criteria on which you can measure objectives), and that insight is provided into the scores of these criteria. This section deals with the first point: realising the objectives. The trick is to set the most essential criteria for our own USD, the so-called critical success factors (CSF) with corresponding performance indicators.

CSFs are issues that are crucial for the successful functioning of the USD, as expressed in the ambition. The CSF is then translated into a KPI; subsequently, the KPI identifies the measurement method that the CSF quantifies and thus makes measurable. Definitions of KPIs and CSFs vary considerably. Some consider KPIs to be CSFs. To avoid confusion, clear agreements are needed about what you need to achieve and how you can translate this into the USD objectives. For example, Stuart Emmett and Barry Crocker summarise performance indicators into these main groups:

- Quality (customer and user satisfaction)
- Quantity (number of services provided and number of notifications received via telephone, email, Internet and counter)
- Price (cost per hour or total project cost)
- Location (level of support on location, sufficient occupancy)
- Time (first-line processing time, average time for resolving a report and average time from request to resolving a report)[39]

Finally, the desired standard must be set for each performance indicator. For example, the balanced scorecard is useful for this process of determining CSFs, performance indicators and the associated standards.

---

[39] Emmett, S. & Crocker, B., *Excellence in Supplier Management: How to Better Manage Contracts with Suppliers and Add Value*, Cambridge: Cambridge Academic, 2009.

Table 20.1: Examples of Performance Indicators Applied with the Balanced Scorecard

Perspective	Goals	CSF	KPI (with norm)
Internal customer	• Demand oriented (customer first). • One-stop shop.	• Quality of service. • Service agreements are clear, efficient, relevant, consistent and maintainable.	• Customer contact standards applied (customer satisfaction measurement, mystery guest). • Reporting and evaluation in accordance with agreements. • Satisfaction (>7). • Number of complaints (<2%).
Suppliers' perspective	• Contracted suppliers are reliable partners whose services are as agreed.	• Price and quality of services provided is in accordance with contract. • Delivery reliability.	• Current contracts with all suppliers. • Reporting in accordance with agreements.
Innovation and growth perspective	• Meeting current objectives for current tasks. • Meeting objectives for future tasks.	• USD develops with demonstrably more experience.	• Assessment of general management, customers and users (>sufficient). • Concrete improvement and innovation activities.
Financial perspective	• Maximum service at minimal cost. • Contributes to efficiency.	• Adequate use of business economic resources. • Financial policy is clear and consistent.	• Products and service catalogue and internal SLAs in order. • Insight into portfolio (quantitative and qualitative). • Budget exhaust transparent.
Employees' perspective	• Employees are professional, result-oriented and customer-friendly.	• Keeping employees competent. • Employees are informed about their tasks and roles and about the trends and developments in these.	• Performance interviews (all are held). • Personal development (POP plan). • Low absenteeism rate.

These criteria and standards are agreed and recorded in internal SLAs (see also *chapter 17*).

20.3 Measuring is knowing

Now that we know which criteria and standards are used for the USD, we can start measuring to determine whether the objectives for the set criteria are met. This section makes it clear how information gathering can be used to determine the necessary number of people on the USD and how to subsequently act on possible deviations. The calculation method is discussed in *chapter 15*.

The analysis and calculation is done in two steps:

1. To determine the average handling time per employee
2. To calculate the average workload

Step 1 – Average handling time

In order to make a good calculation about the required staffing based on the amount of work that ends up in a USD, we need to have insight into various components that determine the capacity requirement of the USD. There are two components:

1. Capacity utilisation through activities that are part of the handling of customer requests
2. Capacity utilisation as a result of day-to-day overhead tasks in the USD

Activities that are part of the handling of customer demand

Assuming that the customer can use all contact channels, information about the components is required (telephone, email, intranet and the physical desk).

In the first instance, the most common calls per component are made transparent. The exceptions are, of course, important but they have little or no influence on the work stock calculation. If this data cannot be retrieved from the existing systems, there is nothing to worry about. The essential thing is to get an estimate of the average processing time per component. Tabulation (and aggregation) of activities and processes through use of a stopwatch is often necessary to identify handling times for most categories of enquiry. A number of examples are mentioned below.

There are a number of common reasons for telephone enquiries:

- Reserve meeting rooms
- Report visitors
- Report minor disruptions
- Make IT service requests (frequently these regard locked accounts, forgotten passwords and accidentally deleted documents)
- Request information
- Discuss back office issues (both internally and externally)
- Report serious incidents (elevator confinement, leaks and uncompleted work)

Email is commonly used to make the following enquiries:

- Reserve meeting rooms (often term reservations as well as standard single reservations)
- Report visitors (especially the larger numbers for meetings and events)
- Report minor disruptions
- Make IT service requests (frequently these regard extra space on the team media drive or applications)
- Request information
- Discuss back office issues (both internally and externally)
- Make complaints

Through the intranet, the following types of requests are common:

- Reserve meeting rooms
- Register visitors at meeting rooms
- Set up a new employee's user account
- Make other reports
- Make complaints

The following types of enquiries are common at the physical counter:

- Collect access pass
- Collect IT products (including smartphones and laptops)
- Collect business cards
- Request information

Clearly, this list is not complete and it will differ between enterprises. When all these notifications are registered in the support software, it is relatively easy to determine the processing time. This is calculated for telephone in *Table 20.2*.

Table 20.2: Handling Time for Telephone Notifications (example)

Number of Telephone Reports	1	2	3	4	5	6	7	8	9	10	11
Employee											
John	0:02:45	0:03:45	0:05:45	0:01:45	0:04:45	0:02:45	0:03:45	0:05:45	0:01:45	0:04:45	0:05:45
Claire	0:03:45	0:04:45	0:06:20	0:02:30	0:05:15	0:03:45	0:04:45	0:06:20	0:02:30	0:05:15	0:06:20
Simone	0:02:15	0:05:20	0:06:45	0:02:45	0:05:45	0:02:15	0:05:20	0:06:45	0:02:45	0:05:45	0:06:45
Mary	0:04:45	0:03:55	0:05:50	0:02:15	0:05:15	0:04:45	0:03:55	0:05:50	0:02:15	0:05:15	0:06:55
Average per Call	0:03:23	0:04:26	0:06:10	0:02:19	0:05:15	0:03:23	0:04:26	0:06:10	0:02:19	0:05:15	0:06:26
Average Total	0:04:30										

In this example, the average handling time for phone enquiries is 0:04:30; this is based on the assumption that all calls are handled well by the employees and that they are recorded in the SMS.

The results can be used to determine how many telephone reports can be handled per employee per hour. In this example, this is 13 calls per hour if the employee answers the phone continuously. However, this is not realistic as there will always be a waiting time between calls and this example assumes a 1:00 waiting time. This becomes 05:30 per notification when the average handling time is added to the waiting time. So, this amounts to a maximum of 11 telephone reports per employee per hour.

Calculations should be similar for the other components. You can measure the time from the moment the email is opened (by means of a read receipt) until the customer has received the confirmation of their enquiry. The time from the opening of the email to the customer confirmation is the total handling time of the request. You can determine which and the number of employees you involve in this study in the same way we described for telephone enquiries. A customer questionnaire should also be drawn up in the same way.

Email notifications

A common problem with email notifications is that the initial report is incomplete or inadequate in some way and the USD employee will pose additional questions in a response. This can lead to lengthy email correspondence after which both parties no longer know what the original report was about in the first place. It is preferable to contact the customer by telephone to ask the additional questions to make a complete report. This factor is an important component in the research; how many email notifications can be handled immediately and how many emails require further contact with the customer.

Intranet messages can in principle be accessed in the same way as email. The processing time is from the moment of opening the message until the customer receives confirmation or receives a response that they can see by logging into the intranet. Which and how many employees you involve in this study can of course be determined in the same way as described earlier. The customer questionnaire is also drawn up in the same way. Below is an example of how you can process the collected data.

The physical desk, in particular, can have many activities that do not require entries in software support and, therefore, are not reported. Such tasks must be identified because they affect the workload. The total handling time begins at the moment the customer is greeted at the counter and ends when all administrative actions have been completed successfully.

Capacity utilisation as a result of organisational tasks in the USD (overheads)

In addition to the customer's perspective, enterprise tasks also have to be calculated to determine staffing. These are activities that are not directly related to the customers. You can think of work meetings within the USD, consultation with the various back offices, coaching interviews with the USD employees, assessment performance interviews, training sessions and participation in projects.

Step 2 – Assessing the workload

If the average processing time per employee per distribution channel and per activity within the USD organisation has been established, this average can be used to assess the USD workload.

Customer

For this example, we assume that the customer can use all contact channels. If the information cannot be properly derived from available systems, the numbers can be made transparent by means of score tables (perhaps a tally). The period of the study must be at least four weeks, preferably six weeks. It is important to ensure that the chosen period is representative of the research, so do not measure in a period with many holidays.

Once the period has been determined, it is important that good, clear and unambiguous score or tally tables are created and used. For this research, it is important that the score or tally table is drawn up per hour to cover the USD's entire opening time. In order to properly determine the USD capacity, calculating the data per hour will be essential. Simple numbers, like 85 phone calls and 55 emails, do not say much about how much effort is needed to deal with enquiries. It is important that you know when these 85 phone calls and 55 emails have been offered and what the peak moments are. This is imperative because you must have the average total processing time to accurately determine what capacity you need where.

This research will show which days are busy and which are less crowded. If, for example, it appears that the number of visitors at the physical counter is high between 12:30 and 13:30, it is not convenient for customers if all employees of the USD have lunch between those hours.

Process the data from the score or tally tables accurately and quickly. If you have questions to ask employees, it is easier to get answers relating to a question about yesterday's events than it is to ask them to cast back their minds two weeks. When you have inventoried the entire period and have processed the data correctly, the total picture can be constructed.

Below is an example of what it can look like:

Table 20.3: Capacity Requirement of the USD (example)

Monday	Phone	Email	Intranet	Desk	**Tuesday**	Phone	Email	Intranet	Desk
8:00–9:00	5	10	3	10	8:00–9:00	6	12	2	10
9:00–10:00	15	12	2	12	9:00–10:00	22	16	3	14
10:00–11:00	18	6	2	8	10:00–11:00	17	8	3	12
11:00–12:00	12	6	2	8	11:00–12:00	20	8	2	8
12:00–13:00	5	8	4	14	12:00–13:00	8	12	4	16
13:00–14:00	5	8	4	12	13:00–14:00	8	10	5	14
14:00–15:00	12	10	2	5	14:00–15:00	14	10	2	8
15:00–16:00	10	12	6	6	15:00–16:00	12	8	6	8
16:00–17:00	9	7	2	10	16:00–17:00	8	7	4	12
17:00–18:00	3	4	1	2	17:00–18:00	5	4	1	2
Total	94	83	28	87	**Total**	120	95	32	104

These are the average numbers for the different contact channels from the six-week study. It is sensible to see if there have been any major incidents in this period of six weeks, that have greatly affected the numbers of one of the contact channels. An example might be when there has been a major data corruption incident reported by all customers; leave these numbers out of the investigation otherwise it gives a distorted average picture.

Now we can link the average numbers to the average total processing time; this is demonstrated in *Table 20.4*.

Table 20.4: Average Handling Time of the USD (example)

	Average Handling Time	**Average Number of Calls per Hour**
Phone	0:04:30	11
Email	0:04:24	13
Intranet	0:04:30	13
Desk	0:04:30	13

Table 20.5: Total Requirement (example)

Monday	Phone	Employees	Email	Employees	Intranet	Employees	Desk	Employees
8:00–9:00	5	2	10	1	3	0.5	10	2
9:00–10:00	15	2	12	1	2	0.5	12	2
10:00–11:00	18	2	6	1	2	0.5	8	1
11:00–12:00	12	2	6	1	2	0.5	8	1
12:00–13:00	5	1	8	1	4	0.5	14	2
13:00–14:00	5	1	8	1	4	0.5	12	2
14:00–15:00	12	2	10	1	2	0.5	5	2
15:00–16:00	10	2	12	1	6	0.5	6	2
16:00–17:00	9	2	7	1	2	0.5	10	2
17:00–18:00	3	1	4	1	1	0.5	2	1
Total	94	17 hours	83	10 hours	28	5 hours	87	17 hours

These numbers represent the required number of employees per hour. This clearly shows the minimum occupancy needed to achieve good accessibility, though there will always be exceptions.

Other activities

As explained earlier, these are activities that are not directly related to the customers. Think of work meetings within the USD, consultations with the various back offices, coaching interviews with the USD employees, assessment and / or performance interviews, training sessions and participation in projects. It is important for capacity calculation to make this transparent. You can of course make good use of the overviews that have just been described so that you can use the quiet moments of the week and day for meetings, coaching conversations and participation in projects.

Based on the data, we can decide in advance about the staff levels within the USD over the year.

20.4 Acting on research results

For all criteria that determines the capacity requirement, research must take place and the results must be analysed. In our example, we perform research into the handling time and the work backlog over a certain period with consequences for the necessary staffing.

Of course, in practice, activities can be merged, such as email and intranet processing, but for now it is more important that the methodology of research is clear. In this example, it is wise to organise employees to use telephone service, email / intranet service and physical counter service.

Finally, you can observe deviations from the norm. For example, in the above with respect to the average processing time and the quality of the report. Subsequently, the causes of the deviations can then be identified and measures can be taken such as increasing the number of staff, changing the opening hours and specific training for employees.

The idea of the quality/continuous improvement cycle requires that these activities are iterative.

CHAPTER 21: IMPLEMENTATION AND FURTHER DEVELOPMENT

Successful implementation and further development of an existing USD will only be achieved if the consequences of the adjustments, and therefore of the improvements have been carefully considered beforehand. This means that the project team responsible for the design and final construction of the USD must first take into account the environment in which the USD operates, and the parties involved. This requires management involvement and a strategic approach.

After reading this chapter, the reader will have insight into the way in which the implementation of a new USD, and further improvement of it can be tackled systematically. Attention must be paid to the support of general management, and to a continuous improvement process based on good practices for a project-based approach to change.

21.1 Stakeholder interests and USD development

In order to achieve a successful implementation or further development of the USD for the services/facilities organisation, the following must be taken into account:

- The USD ambition must align with the service organisation's organisational structure.
- It is important that employees be involved in the USD development and that their motivation can be maintained. This means ensuring a clear vision and approach, good communication, and emphasising the involvement of employees in the improvement process.
- Customer motivation is also important. Innovation means change and they may have to drop existing methods of making service requests. The biggest change takes place where a USD is set up for the first time. Internal customers must focus on the USD and they can no longer go directly to involving the back office by default. The USD will only be a success if the customers make use of it and continue to do so.
- Finally, management must be fully informed of the changes and endorse the proposed developments.

This can be achieved by taking into account at least the following starting points:

- Management sponsorship
- Incremental growth
- The use of good practices for a project-based approach

21.2 Align with management

We described the first step in the total phasing of the design and construction of a USD, as the formulation of the mission and objectives. This step is often underestimated. In this phase, we not only formulate the mission and objectives, but we also generate support from management. This is less difficult in situations where the ambitions for the USD are low. Think, for example, of an information desk with little influence. Where the aim is for a full USD to have an influence beyond the boundaries of its own department, management or unit, management sponsorship is absolutely essential for the acceptance of the USD. An all-encompassing variant of the USD has far-reaching consequences for the entirety of the enterprise. It is therefore not uncommon to find that up to 30% of the total turnaround time from idea to realisation, is spent on obtaining approval from management.

Management may be involved in the process in many different ways:

- In formulating the USD development strategy.
- Through an explicit management mandate, for example a project letter or initiation document.
- By receiving regular feedback regarding project results.
- By receiving feedback following the completion of each step in the project including a justification and a proposal for the next step.

There are a few other related matters that must be considered. Customers must receive periodic feedback when changes are made. Nothing should be promised to either customers or management that cannot be fulfilled. Above all, it must be ensured that service continues as usual, irrespective of changes.

21.3 Incremental growth

During a USD implementation, project leaders or service managers sometimes become embroiled in discussions regarding considerations and dilemmas relating to the design and layout of the project plans. The desire is that everything has to be done at the same time, yet the opposite is true. It is good to understand the fundamental principles that show how a USD should be developed and what is involved however, the implementation does not so much require technical (and therefore substantive) professional knowledge, but more so an approach of leadership and persuasion.

The beginning is the absolute commitment of management. This is gained by having a clear picture of the USD ambition and associated mission and objectives. There are two aspects to which management is allergic:

1. Unrest that can be caused.
2. The fear that once a decision has been made, it has a negative domino effect.

In order to achieve the desired final situation, it is wise to follow a steady development process in which different growth or development phases are followed. The ambition for the USD development will then be reached over time. It is therefore advisable for the designer to outline a final situation, and to indicate that the road to this is comprised of stages with well thought out 'go/no go' moments.

For the project manager, firstly this means that they need to know what the USD should ultimately entail for the enterprise and, in the second place, that they must think carefully about how this is achieved. It is unlikely that everything will be implemented in one go. In practice, elements of the USD (the USD as a concept consisting of a call centre, intranet portal, counter, account management), are not thrown together immediately.

All enterprises will differ, but in a situation where there is already a USD or where there is the desire to follow an implementation path, a possible growth path could be as outlined in *Figure 21.1*, where it is assumed that there is already a simple USD with sufficient employees.

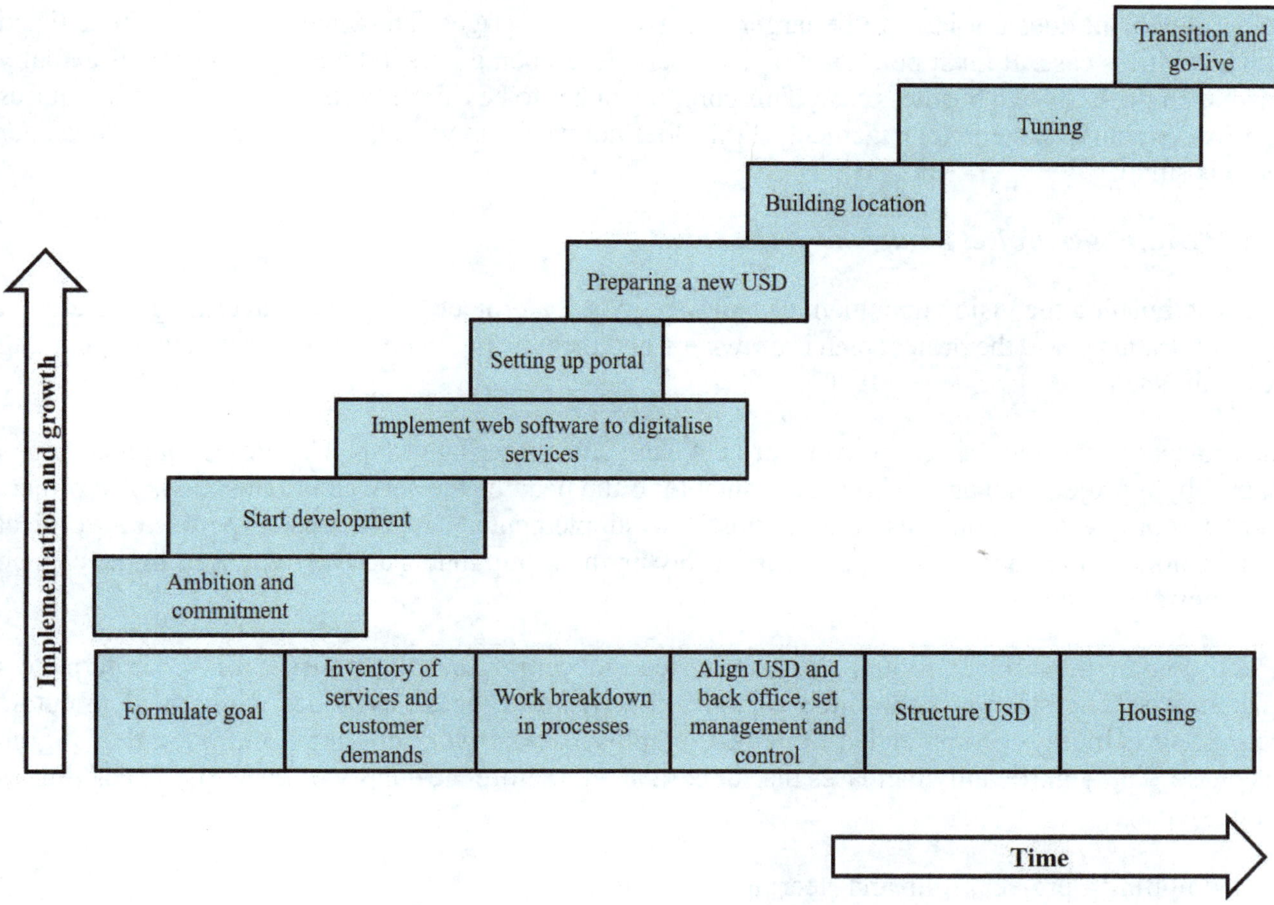

Figure 21.1: Growth scenario for a USD

21.4 Use a project-based approach

There are various methods for project design and construction of the USD. Different good practices are available which are easy to use for example PRINCE2®, PMI, PRAXIS. Whichever is chosen, a project-based implementation process, including planning, comprises the following eight components:

- **Part 1:** Preparing a vision document or policy intention, objectives and business case
- **Part 2:** Drafting a project group and project plan
- **Part 3:** Inventory of supply and demand in products and services (handling levels)
- **Part 4:** Redesign of work processes
- **Part 5:** Coordinate and manage the USD
- **Part 6:** Setting up USD functional requirements
- **Part 7:** Implementation
- **Part 8:** Aftercare and completion

Part 1: Preparing a vision document or policy intention, objectives and business case

In this step, the starting points for a service organisation's USD are based on the results of interviews with managers and the project group. Subsequently, it is possible to create a global design, vision document or a policy proposal containing the objectives. These proposals are formulated and elaborated in SMART terms (Specific, Measurable, Identifiable, Realisable and Time-related). This vision document does not have to be larger than two to four pages. The vision must be substantiated with a business case. It must be clear which objectives are being pursued and whether this is actually feasible on the basis of a business case. This component has to be carefully followed because it requires the involvement of general management. If this does not work out well, the chance of success in a later phase is small.

Part 2: Drafting a project group and project plan

After establishing the vision document or policy proposal, a project group and a steering group are put together. In this phase the project plan is drawn up, and then the project organisation and work planning are established.

The project organisation is set up with a project team and a steering group. The project organisation is chaired by a project manager who is accountable to the head of the service organisation. The project team comprises of employees and is possibly supplemented by external expertise. A project organisation is not necessarily large, it can simply be the group that is actively engaged in the change and renewal of the USD.

In addition to the project group, there is a steering committee that consists of the enterprise's stakeholders. The steering committee supports the change process, provides advice and monitors progress. It is highly recommended to involve employees who work or start working on the USD in this phase. This significantly increases the support, and therefore the quality of the USD. The activities in this step are:

- Compiling a project group and steering committee;
- Determining the resources of the parties involved (including their time and money);
- Obtaining support amongst employees;
- Taking care of the processes from reporting to management;
- Operationalising the vision document within the framework and the available resources;
- Determining the completion date;
- Identifying risk factors and possible interventions; and
- Planning the work.

Part 3: Inventory of supply and demand in products and services (handling levels)

Next, an inventory is made of both the supply of products and services and the customer's need for them. Per product and service it is determined whether the settlement takes place within the USD or in cooperation with the back office/account management (handling level). If necessary, a products and services overview can be drawn up. Employees of the USD must after all be aware of the product to be delivered. In this section, involve the customers in drawing up the functional requirements. The activities in this phase are:

- Identifying new or changed products and services;
- Identifying new or changed questions and customer needs for integrated products and services;
- Establishing the relationship between supply and demand;
- Determining the level of handling for products and services;

- Determining separation in product or service settlement between the USD and back office;
- Drafting or adjusting a provisional products and services package;
- Drafting a basic, basic-plus and supplementary package description for the products and service catalogue; and
- Conducting a strategic discussion about basic, basic-plus and supplementary packages.

Part 4: Redesign of work processes

By subsequently identifying the relationship between supply and demand, the relationship is established between the single products offered and composite customer products. For each service define which processes are followed. Depending on the type of process, decide whether or not to redesign.

Part 5: Coordinate and manage the USD

Based on the mission and the objective, choices can be made for the size, scope, responsibility and positioning of the USD. This determines the actual demarcation line between the USD and the back office (the handling levels). The activities in this phase are:

- Determining which choice is made for the processing of customer questions (choices include information models and other variants);
- Designing the 'redprint' (powers, responsibilities, coordination mechanisms and client-contractor relations);
- Drafting the assessment parameters for quality control, work management and result measurement; and
- Determining the relationship and responsibilities between service counter, call centre, virtual USD and account management.

Part 6: Setting up USD functional requirements

A customer can submit requests to the USD in various ways (telephone, email, mail, visiting the desk). This section specifies which distribution channels are used, which systems are used and the way in which the USD connects to the back office.

The activities in this phase involve:

- Choosing products and services through a distribution channel (intranet, telephone, email, post, desk or account management);
- Preparing technical and functional requirements;
- Determining the formative content with job descriptions and job requirements;
- Determining the distribution channels available for the USD;
- Determining the processing method for answering a request; and
- Establishing a cooperation programme between the USD and back office.

Part 7: Implementation

In this section, the USD is implemented either as 'big bang,' or in phases. For a good transition between the current situation and the new situation, it is sometimes useful to work with a transition document. This document specifies which products and services are available through the USD and how the alignment takes place within the relevant organisational units. This can be implemented within the existing structures. Also, in this phase it is wise to involve the most important customer group, or a representative group in the progress. The management must of course be regularly informed about the progress. The activities that must be carried out are:

- Drafting a transition document;
- Determining the introduction date;
- Building a new organisational structure;
- Opening up positions and vacancies;
- Appointing employees;
- Providing training and education;
- Making agreements with customers about the size and quality of service;
- Communicating about the new form of service; and
- Guaranteeing aftercare (maintenance and management).

Part 8: Aftercare and completion

Upon completion of the project, the project can be signed off. If necessary, a small team will remain available during the initial phase to ensure that necessary adjustments are made to aspects like organisation, the use of resources and agreements with customers. By defining the starting points in SMART terms, the USD goals can be translated into concrete results. On the basis of management information, it can be periodically verified whether these results have been achieved. Where goals are not achieved, interim adjustments can be made, or expectations can be adjusted. It is important to periodically review which developments are affecting the current situation and the desired goal achievements. These developments should lead, where necessary, to the adjustment of the USD and to the improvement of results arising therefrom. In this way, management can make timely adjustments.

CHAPTER 22: IMPROVEMENT POSSIBILITIES

22.1 Four themes and associated tips

In the previous chapters, many ideas and examples have been given regarding how new ambitions may lead to adapted designs and, therefore, to structural changes. However, this is not always possible and sometimes quick and dirty improvements and solutions are required. In this chapter, thirty different ideas are offered and suggestions are presented; these are divided into four themes:

1. Quality
2. Employees
3. Delivery
4. Orchestration and policy

We do not aim to provide an exhaustive list because every situation is different. Use these ideas as a source of inspiration and as starting points for your own USD. Be well aware of the issues and priorities of your own situation so that you use the ideas at the right time.

Table 22.1 gives an overview of the four themes and the associated tips. The tips are listed by theme and are in a random order.

Table 22.1: Improved USD – 30 Tips to Consider

Quality	1. Improve interaction with customers and users 2. Enhance knowledge of the software 3. Be accessible 4. Ensure that the physical location is easily accessible 5. Identify needs accurately at the time of reporting 6. Make the service site visible and more user-friendly 7. Improve your image 8. Be aware of stakeholders and priorities 9. Remember, account management is not just a function 10. Management sponsorship helps 11. Create methodical work processes
Employees	12. Have employees participate 13. You cannot always choose your staff 14. Recruit trainees, students and starters 15. Training and coaching
Delivery	16. Make more efficient use of available support 17. Do not let the system dictate the method 18. Improve back office transfer processes 19. Make good use of the contracts 20. Assess the workload 21. Standardise and automate processes when you can 22. Close the door to the back offices 23. Use fact sheets 24. Pay attention to details 25. Avoid concurrent telephone service and email handling

Orchestration and Policy	26. Products and services from other departments 27. Know your mandate 28. Innovate 29. Do not automate everything 30. Support the primary process

22.2 Quality

Tip 1 – Improve interaction with customers and users

The employees of a USD are often swamped with work and mostly exist in a closeted environment. In a situation such as this, the business world seems to exist as a cultural mismatch. The result is that the business world forms a critical view of the USD. The solution is simple. Connect with customers; initiate conversation in the first instance and do not make promises that you cannot fulfill. See if you can quickly solve problems for customers.

Tip 2 – Enhance knowledge of the software

Effective use of the available software engenders considerable productivity improvement. Train or simply guide users to make best use of the software. Guarantee in the enterprise that there is knowledge and expertise of the application and look together for opportunities to improve the software and make it more user-friendly. Involve users and suppliers actively.

Tip 3 – Be accessible

If it exists, the service counter must be easily accessible. This means, for example, that waiting times are short, opening hours are chosen in a practical and logical manner (for example ensure counter staff are present during lunchtime or in the morning), and the physical and virtual accessibility is well coordinated with matching service levels of response times and self-service options.

Make sure that the USD employees can help users with self-service notification. They should also be familiar with the service and products catalogue which must be easy to find and read.

Tip 4 – Ensure that the physical location is easily accessible

Make sure it is clear to the customer where the counter is located, and if there is no counter and instead an office space is the workplace for the USD, make sure that the customer knows at which workplace the requests/incidents can be reported.

The physical location of the USD is the calling card of the service management facilities. Consider a physical location that may be less attractive, but which is centrally accessible within the enterprise.

Tip 5 – Identify needs accurately at the time of reporting

Good understanding of customer demand at the USD saves time and effort. Make sure staff are trained to obtain all the information they need at the first point of contact whether in person, by phone or by software forms. Understanding the customer demand in one go and processing it properly saves a lot of extra search and inquiry work, and it increases the chances of good execution in the back office.

Tip 6 – Make the service site visible and make it more user-friendly

Marketing self-service to users can be simply achieved by making the intranet landing page interesting and useful. In some enterprises, the virtual USD or portal is named after the software supplier, for example Ultrability or Service Yesterday. Names like this will be of no interest to customers. In other enterprises, the USD service site is hidden behind pages other people deemed more interesting. By highlighting this page (preferably at least with a link on the home page), users can find it more quickly and it presents an image of being important.

The quality of an application or website is not only determined by its functionality but also by its usability. Working with a user-friendly service site makes it easy to learn. The actual use, and therefore the success of the service site, depends on it. Certainly, in enterprises with many different locations, a good service via the intranet offers great efficiency benefits.

Tip 7 – Improve your image

A courteous and service-oriented attitude works wonders. That is why there are several arguments that users of the facility services should be regarded as customers. After all, you have a different conversation with a customer than with a colleague. Customers expect a service, colleagues do not.

Tip 8 – Be aware of stakeholders and priorities

Obtain insight into your customer groups so that you know who you need to pay attention to. Time is scarce, know when you need to be flexible and when you do not. The more flexibility you provide, the more work you will need to perform. Flexibility inevitably diminishes efficiency.

Tip 9 – Remember, account management is not just a function

Even though there may not be a formal function, the role of an account manager can still be used. Talking with users, meeting with them and taking time to listen to their issues works better than sending emails or making phone calls.

Tip 10 – Management sponsorship helps

Management support will encourage customers so that they report problems in a timely fashion and make use of the service organisation. It also means that possible problems as a result of errors or miscommunication are recognised in time and that the customer, as a result of the personal relationship, shows more understanding and is more flexible. It is essential to establish mutual trust.

Tip 11 – Create methodical work processes

The USD often works ad hoc. This is not uncommon, because many problems and requests are unpredictable. This situation causes work pressure and chaos. Always look at processes and procedures, and identify employees that have different skill sets that can help with structuring how the USD operates. For example, some employees handle phone calls more quickly than others. This results in shorter conversations, reducing the pressure on the telephone and requiring little repeat traffic.

Agree email response time with the customer and make sure employees follow the policy. People have a strong tendency in email to handle everything as quickly as possible. This is laudable but can lead to unnecessary work pressure and unreasonable expectation where major issues are reported.

If there is also a physical counter, make sure that there is sufficient occupancy and that all necessary products and services are available and located as close to the counter as possible.

22.3 Employees

Tip 12 – Have employees participate

It has been said before that people form the enterprise. It is evident that employees want and need to be involved in changes and innovations; they know the situation best and often informally have the top contacts and ideas. Always respond to proposals and ideas, even if the proposal is not feasible.

Be aware, you will not get everyone onboard and conflicts can be unavoidable. Create a solid basis of involvement if you want to successfully implement innovations and changes, then small improvements also have a direct effect.

Tip 13 – You cannot always choose your staff

Working in the USD is a profession, but not everyone has chosen to work on the USD within the service and facilities team. Particularly in the public sector, people are often simply assigned to a position. Make sure USD employees are adequately trained and coached for their tasks when it comes to customer-friendly behaviour, being the expert about questions, referrals and feedback.

Tip 14 – Recruit trainees, students and starters

The USD often offers the ideal starting position for graduates in service and facilities management because, within a short time, they will deal with all facets of the enterprise. Contrary to some beliefs, high quality individuals should be recruited to the positions. Furthermore, any marketing for the positions should emphasise the importance of their tasks.

Employees may need to be able to carry out projects such as supervising a relocation, organising meetings or arranging facilities for a new employee. After a period, they can move on to other functions. The USD also offers an excellent internship for students or trainees for vocational training. The USD is able to quickly incorporate new employees into the enterprise, and it benefits from the new knowledge and expertise of both trainees and new employees. With trainees, the USD can be filled to better absorb fluctuations in capacity requirements, and starters and trainees benefit from practical work experience.

Tip 15 – Training and coaching

Invest in employee training and coaching in the USD in order to create a better understanding of the products and services and the manner of processing. Know what is necessary to keep the PDC in order and to keep it up-to-date, monitor the handling of telephone conversations, and so on. It does not always have to be expensive on-site training, visits to colleagues and interventions can also help. Any improvements in conversation techniques yield multiple benefits. Call times are reduced and the right questions are asked, leading to better quality and completed reports.

Significantly, confident employees increase customer satisfaction. Coaching regarding confidence can be done by the team leaders and by senior employees, and team leaders can also lead sessions about using software.

22.4 Delivery

Tip 16 – Make more efficient use of available support

Telephony services can be set to manage peak traffic by creating a call-back appointment. You can often choose other settings that change the routing, or you can obtain overviews from the system about how it is being used. Routing calls to specific employees or ensuring an even spread of calls can be programmed.

There is most likely a need to examine the waiting times of callers, and calls that were cancelled ('abandoned call'). Team leaders and managers should be aware of the features of the support systems and services.

Tip 17 – Do not let the system dictate the method

A 'brown field' USD does not always have a system that allows notifications to be made and handling to be tracked. Renewing or purchasing a new system takes time and money, and that is not always available. Thus, it is most practical to find processes suited to your conceptual ideas that can already be adequately supported with the available system. As a result, you may work less 'state of the art' but you can work better in a way that fits the available capacity, resources and expertise.

Tip 18 – Improve back office transfer processes

Many errors arise in the transfer of incidents, problems and requests to the various back offices. Incorrect information that is passed on means that the back office has to respond with additional questions which takes time, or they fail to ask questions and the request is handled incorrectly (again taking time to correct). Results are of course, a lot of time loss and annoyed customers.

Make an inventory of transfer processes that cause problems (employees will be happy to improve the processes), and initiate a discussion about this together with the USD staff and back offices; even talking is an initial improvement.

Tip 19 – Make good use of the contracts

Often the contracts are concluded in large tendering processes and then deposited with the USD for operational management. Closer cooperation with the service providers' service managers and site managers always helps. Good knowledge of the contracts also makes collaboration easier. For example, create fact sheets with the issues that are important to the USD, including reaction times, expectations that have been set in stone and delivery times. USD employees should be members of the tendering team. Practical experience and ideas can then be incorporated in the functional requirements at an early stage and included in the contract.

Tip 20 – Assess the workload

In order to quickly gain insight and get a feel of the amount of work in a USD, you can count the number of client inquiries via the various distribution channels for two to three weeks. You will get a general idea about how many calls are received, how many people come to the counter and how busy it is during the course of the day. Based on these figures, you get a better impression of the required staffing at the various levels of service. You also get a better idea about the available and required capacity and in which direction possible problems point.

Tip 21 – Standardise and automate processes when you can

Try to further standardise processes and see if the handling levels were well chosen. Look carefully at the entire process between supply and demand and assess whether links between the USD and back offices can be simplified. Further simplify services from a tactical level or to standardise and/or automate processes. By shifting the handling of products and services from a tactical to operational level, it is also easier to place them in the 'basic' bucket (i.e. centrally funded).

Tip 22 – Close the door to the back offices

Prevent customers from going directly to the back offices. Electric fences are unsightly, so simply communicate that services are now dealt with centrally. Make agreements with the employees of the USD and back offices to ensure that people are aware of the need to abide with policy.

Tip 23 – Use fact sheets

An easy way to establish the various objectives is to make a practical set of agreements for both the demand side (the customer side) and the supply side (enterprise side) concerning categories of products and services. Agreements are made per group about the way they are handled and under what conditions. Based on the groupings, consideration can then be given to how products and services can be requested, how they can be delivered and how they relate to each other.

Tip 24 – Pay attention to details

Despite the small risk of misunderstanding simple questions, the account manager must remain alert. In the case of inadequate handling, whereby a customer at a given moment gets the feeling of being ignored or minimised, small questions suddenly become very large.

Tip 25 – Avoid concurrent telephone service and email handling

Customer satisfaction surveys show that this method does not always work well. Employees who handle email and who are subsequently 'disturbed' in that work by an incoming telephone call may be less well-focused. Try to separate call and email work. The advantage is that the employee can in principle process the emails undisturbed. The disadvantage is that the work on a USD is generally so hectic and diverse that it is difficult to achieve.

Size matters, with larger USDs it is easier to create a separation between email handling and telephone service. It is a good way to help new employees get used to the type of questions. Moreover, by processing these in the support software they can also learn how to become familiar with the system.

22.5 Orchestration and policy

Tip 26 – Products and services from other departments

A well-functioning USD may have the opportunity to organise and execute other USD-type tasks for products and services from other disciplines that were excluded in the original plans. A trend among many enterprises is further consolidation in business operations and this sometimes leads to merging ICT help desks, P&O help desk tasks and other facility tasks.

Tip 27 – Know your mandate

No, it has nothing to do with the various dating applications. It often happens that there is insufficient clarity about the division of responsibilities between the USD and the various departments. This should be discussed within the management team. If the relationships are good, practical arrangements can be made quickly to suit the current situation. Structural changes take time and need to be well prepared. Ensure that these agreements are subsequently followed up by translating them into working agreements between the departments.

Tip 28 – Innovate

You do not immediately have to think about the latest technology; innovation can also be about using resources that have not been thought of before. How about an inventory of your current support software's unused features to see where use can be initiated or improved?

As the USD becomes more expansive and money becomes available, more advanced technology can be purchased, such as newer telephony software. With this software, the planning of the USD can also be made on the basis of historical data and the achieved results of the day. Often electronic 'wallboards' are installed to broadcast 'how things are going.'

Tip 29 – Do not automate everything

There is a tendency to automate everything that moves (and, yes, we have repeatedly mentioned automation), but sometimes you have to accept that it is easier to do things the 'traditional way'. Not everything should be automated; consider the multiple products and services from chapter three (*Table 3.3*), such as bringing in new employees (onboarding), or organising a reception.

Tip 30 – Support the primary process

Sometimes the USD has the ability to make it easy for the employees in the business using primary processes. A good knowledge of the enterprise, insight into its processes and knowing what is current helps to assess the priorities and their urgency. For example, if an important project with firm deadlines, or a crisis team is at work, it helps if the USD handles reports quickly and effectively. Think of arranging extra rooms, telephone facilities, solving defects and so on.

Finally, the USD can have a useful signalling function because it collects data on costs and customer satisfaction. This information may be a reason to adjust the range of services or the service provision.

CHAPTER 23: THE USD OF THINGS

The classic boundaries of enterprises are fading under the influence of technological innovations, cultural changes and globalisation. As a result, in some enterprises the support services will change substantially in the coming years, and with them the role of the USD.

After reading this chapter, the reader will better understand how new ideas will change the USD, perhaps as an 'intelligent hub'.

23.1 A focus on personal work environment

In the previous chapters, the USD position within the enterprise's management was established based on sound principles and the concept of building blocks. The USD was positioned as part of the service management concept of the enterprise, more or less within the classical boundaries of an enterprise. But the classical boundaries of enterprises are fading due to technological innovations, cultural changes and globalisation. Many researchers have been conscious of this trend for a long time, "The developments in the field of ICT will continue at lightning speed and ensure that we can do our work better, easier and faster. ICT will ensure that we fundamentally change basic office processes".[40]

However, changes are more radical than supposed at that time, and are not limited to office environments. No one was able to foresee that the new technological possibilities would structurally change our economy and the way in which we deal with each other.

Technological changes have affected every part of life, including through the rapid rise of Internet shopping, Internet banking and insurance and the use of social media such as Facebook, Twitter and LinkedIn. Innovations have consequences for the way we deal with our work and how enterprises are organised. Hodge, Poglitsch and Ankerstjerne note that facilities management increasingly focuses on integral service provision in the work environment (Hodge, Poglitsch and Ankerstjerne).[41]

This corresponds with the contemporary vision of the workplace of the future, which perceives that the traditional office structure is shifting from a network of people in a central physical location, to a virtual network of people in various locations (ISS, 2013). Where physical locations are standardised, the virtual work environment is becoming more digital and personalised. This is a challenge for service and facilities management, and it may be met by developing the USD into the integral supporter in a virtual network of work environments.

23.2 The new work environment is virtual and individual

Although the 'classic' working environment will still continue, the new work environment is no longer limited by physical offices. Supported by new technological possibilities such as smartphones, laptops,

---

[40] Veldhoen, E., *Kantoren bestaan niet meer, versie 2.0*, Rotterdam: Uitgeverij 010, 1998.

[41] Hodge, G., Poglitsch, R. & Ankerstjerne, P., "Perspectives on the FM market development", *ISS White Paper*, 2014.

tablets and broadband services, people can sit anywhere and work together. The Martini feeling of 'anytime, anywhere, anyplace' is becoming a reality today.

Driven by competition, new ways of doing business, new ways of earning money and new forms of collaboration, enterprises want to be able to respond quickly to changing environments. Helped by technology, a virtual environment is created in which new organisational forms arise. Video conferencing makes it possible to meet with people who are on the other side of the world, and collaboration can take place in digital spaces where multiple users can work simultaneously in the same document. Time differences between locations become less of an obstacle. Collaboration with other enterprises takes different forms and leads to network enterprises, where it is not always clear whether an enterprise offers a platform or offers services via the platform itself. Borders between enterprises are fading, and at the same time, startups and small companies get opportunities that they did not have before. The physical reality thus shifts to a virtual reality.

Modern employees have less trouble separating work and private life. In order to improve the balance between the two, more and more enterprises have made flexible working hours possible, and they often try to organise the workload in such a way that it no longer needs to be physically carried out in a traditional workplace.

The working environment takes shape through combinations of work at the office, rented or temporary locations (café, hotel, rental office) and at home. At the office, the workspace varies from private spaces, open office space, temporary workspaces, touchdown points or landing areas and project spaces. Use is made of various (mobile) devices. At the moment these are laptops, smartphones and tablets. There is already considerable experimentation with wearable technology and in extreme cases, technology embedded in humans. Think of devices in clothing (wearables), in watches (smartphones), in glasses (Microsoft® HoloLens) and in virtual reality.

23.3 Technical developments

The Internet of things (IoT) is a collective name for five technological developments that make it possible to interactively connect the physical world with the digital world. The IoT comprises of:

1. Cloud technology;
2. Mobile technology;
3. Development of social media;
4. Analysis of large amounts of data (big data); and
5. Sensor technology.

In this context, 'things' refers to physical objects with built-in sensors that collect and send environmental and status information, receive instructions and which may act autonomously to varying degrees.

Examples:

The IoT leads to entirely new applications. Clothing producers follow the retail route of their denim jeans thanks to a tiny chip that they have hidden. Farmers use 'smart sensors' to monitor their harvest via the Internet. Meteorologists predict hurricanes by monitoring stations around the world. Car manufacturers work on cars that can drive independently with the aid of sensors. Advertising boards make contact with passersby and adjust their advertising immediately, and 'smart' pills are introduced into the body and are able to tackle specific diseases at specific locations.

When it comes to the possibilities that technology offers, creativity is the limiting factor. Significantly, we consider an object or application to be 'smart' in relation to the richness of the information and use of the software and sensors provided. Six types of application may be distinguished with each type performing a different function[42]; these applications:

1. Monitor the behaviour of people, objects or place them in a central position. This type includes inventory management, as well as insurance companies that place sensors in cars and set the level of their premiums based on drivers' behaviour ('presence-based advertising');
2. Strengthen insight into environments; this includes sensors within infrastructure (roads and buildings) to measure conditions in the environment (pollution, humidity and weather);
3. Facilitate sensor-driven decision-making analysis and direct interventions in 'real time'. This type of application includes the continuous monitoring of chronic diseases that helps doctors choose effective treatments. Chain stores also use this technology to follow the behaviour of buyers so they can improve the layout of their stores;
4. Optimise processes. This type combats the wastage from automated processes and provides more refined tuning of operations on assembly lines;
5. Optimise consumption. This type provides more detailed insight into the consumption of resources (for example, energy and electricity) so that appropriate action can be taken. Think of 'smart' electricity and gas meters in houses that show real time consumption and costs; and
6. Provide complex autonomous systems. This type of application may, for example, prevent collisions or coordinate the use of independent robots to clean up hazardous material.

The IoT also enables two developments that are directly related to the development and innovation of the working environment: smart buildings and smart cities. The use of sensors in buildings leads to completely new insights into improving their infrastructure and how they are used and maintained. Data on and in buildings are collected and used to gain awareness into the condition of the buildings themselves (e.g. climate, energy consumption, maintenance), and the use of the buildings (e.g. occupation, use of spaces, walking routes). The possibilities are many:

- Assess the use of rooms. For example, data relating to self-flushing toilets may permit cleaning schedules to be effectively adjusted;

---

[42] Chui, M., Löffler, M. & Roberts, R., "The Internet of Things", *McKinsey Quarterly*, March, 2010.

- Determine whether a dispenser needs to be refilled;
- Provide technical information about the state of maintenance;
- Ensure that system faults are immediately reported, including their nature and location;
- Notify motorists which parking spaces are free (this is often done via smartphone);
- Measure whether plants have enough nutrients and moisture;
- Save energy;
- Track rent and contributions for tenant use;
- Track space usage (presence and behavioural detection may be used to explore future use);
- Keep inventories; and
- Monitor compliance. This can apply to health and safety regulations, noise levels, CO_2 levels, temperature and obstacles in evacuation routes.

Managers of smart cities are also looking for ways to further develop using the IoT.[43] Research and experiments take place to promote self-sufficiency of citizens, good coordination of care provision and need (the nurturing city), improving government services, improving the quality of education, strengthening safety features, stimulating activity through regulatory pressure, and the development of future-proof industrial sites. A concrete application is already in place that connects companies in a city via a network for information exchange and cooperation, which gives a new dimension to the new way of working (Or Big Brother…).

23.4 The USD as an intelligent hub

All of these developments make it possible to think about enterprises, work and living in a completely different way. Organisational structures change and with them, the ways in which work is completed, decisions are made, processes are managed, work environments are set up and large or even global projects are organised.

What does this mean for the USD? Thanks to these developments, services can be delivered across borders, continents and countries; a larger and more diverse clientele is in range; customisation is possible and greater efficiency can be achieved. The unity of the working environment is changing from the physical workplace to an environment consisting of smart buildings and smart cities. If the working environment arises from a network of locations in buildings and cities, the service organisation's focus is to bring three components together. Accordingly, enterprises are always looking for the most effective and efficient strategy to manage the working environment. This focus translates into solutions for the smart and practical use of available workspaces: limiting vacancies, making optimal use of rented environments, limiting travel costs and providing optimal support for knowledge workers and employees in projects.

As a result of these changes, a USD must deal with:

---

[43] Manen, T. van, Bloem, J. & Doorn, M. van, "SMACT and the City", *VINT onderzoeksnotitie 4*, The Sogeti trend Lab VINT, 2014.

- New opportunities and developments;
- Working environments in smart buildings and smart cities;
- Flexible possibilities to setting up working environments (think of rented locations, including office hotels);
- Users' physical and digital needs and desire for support from users (they must respond proactively to these);
- The smart and flexible use of existing contracts;
- The organisation of infrastructures for collaboration; and
- The consequences of managing and setting up working environments in multi-tenant and multi-client buildings.

Supply oriented service organisation	**Demand oriented service organisation**	**Integrated facility management of total facility management**	**Integral management of the work environment**
USD as a takeaway counter.	USD as a central helpdesk, technically oriented.	USD one-shop-stop for service organisation, technically oriented.	USD as an intelligent hub, business oriented.
USD exists only as a desk or takeaway.	USD is part of the service concept of a customer-oriented service.	USD is outsourced and is part of the provider's service concept and works for several customers.	USD to support multi-client and multi-tenant.

Evolution of the USD

Figure 23.1: The evolution of the USD

How this USD looks has yet to be discovered and explored. The possibilities are many, but much is still in the phase of experimentation and discovery. Some enterprises are working on the development of use-cases. Others experiment on a small scale with the use of QR codes, smartphones and sensors that can measure the conditions of the building and installations.

Developing the infrastructure to make maximum use of the possibilities takes time and money. Much is not yet fully developed, such as further refinement and improvement of software and sensor equipment. In the economic and legal field too, much remains to be determined. Consider, for example, the new license and contract conditions or consequences for the privacy of employees.

Start by building insight into the necessary technology. Experiment on a small scale and look for practical possibilities with a big impact. These are often found in reducing waste, measuring and reducing energy consumption and the maintenance of installations and buildings.

23.5 The USD as a hub or platform

What are the attributes of a USD as a platform or a hub? Exactly how this USD looks is still to be discovered and explored. The possibilities are many, and much is still in the phase of experimenting and discovering. Some enterprises are working on the development of use cases. Other experiments revolve around the use of QR codes, smartphones and sensors that can measure the conditions of the building and installations. Several providers are developing their management information systems into a platform that can be used to transform traditional services into the extended services, to be used in a hub.

Based on these initiatives, we can gain insight into the characteristics of a USD as an intelligent hub. These aspects are explained in *Table 23.1*.

Table 23.1: Possible Features of a USD as an Intelligent Hub

Attribute	Explanation
Information	Availability of information about the entire value chain (knowledge centre).
Technology	Availability of a platform where information is provided in real time. The platform must be able to connect users and internal and external facilitators. The platform can take different forms, on the one hand, to connect different subcontractor services and various groups of users and, on the other hand, to act as an intermediary between these parties that make transactions possible on the basis of the agreements made previously.
Service providers and value chain	Control and knowledge of all service providers, services and the value chain. The value chain can also display characteristics of dynamic contracts that differ from the traditional chains. Easily scalable.
Integration in the service organisation	Has a position in the enterprise that is independent of the other service providers. Self-organisation, exhibits characteristics of organic developments, as close as possible to the customers.
Management and employees	Management and employees have competencies that fit with high-quality service and hospitality. Employees are professionals who have to work independently. Management creates the preconditions so that professionals can perform at the optimal level. Self-management optima forma is the key to making this possible. A wide range of reports and problems will require creative solutions.
Service landscape	Flexible and individual. Users expect more customised services and more options that are continuous or easily available no matter where and how they work. Recognise and apply a service landscape philosophy.

As can be seen from these characteristics, the USD as a hub comes from existing forms of USD organisations. The introduction of new technology simultaneously with other forms of working and living has consequences for how we look at and apply service provision. New technology now has a major impact on how we can request service and get service, how we look at enterprises, hierarchy, management and what we expect from employees. Think of smartphones, tablets, IoT, big data, social media, cloud computing, business intelligence, virtual reality, NAN technology, business intelligence and robotics.[44]

[44] ISS 2020 Vision, "Future of Service management", *Copenhagen Institute for Future Studies*, Whitebook, 2018.

Figure 23.2, on the basis of these characteristics, sketches a framework that gives the manager a handle to think practically about the further development of the USD to a hub.

The USD is in the middle of a web consisting of six axes. These axes show the development direction of six aspects that form part of a USD as a hub.

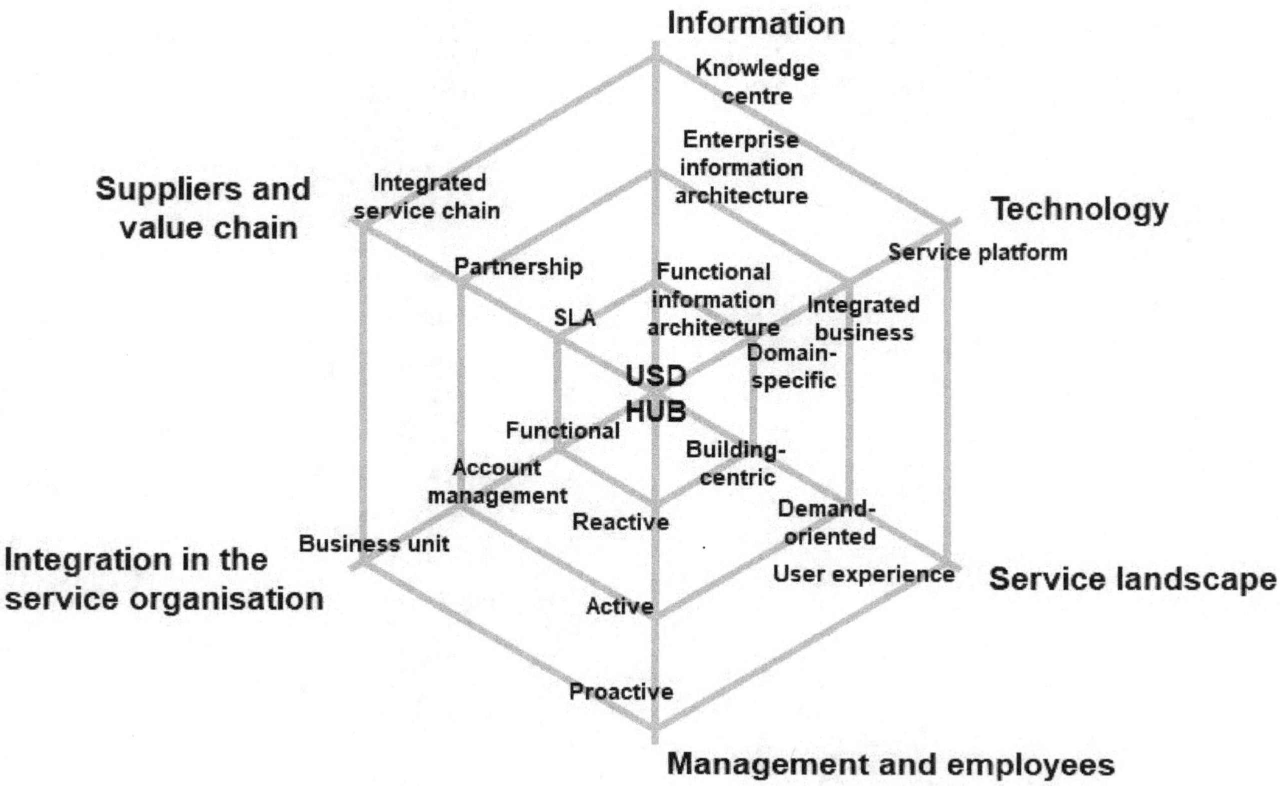

Figure 23.2: Framework for the USD as an intelligent hub

The two inner circles indicate the core features of the USD as they have been discussed so far. On the outer line, the contours of the USD become visible as a hub.

Developing the infrastructure to make maximum use of the possibilities costs time and money. Much remains to be developed, and not only technically such as further refinement and improvement of software and sensor equipment. In the economic and legal field too, much remains to be determined. Consider, for example, the new license and contract conditions or consequences for the privacy of employees. Start by building insight into the necessary technology and experiment on a small scale. Look for practical possibilities with a big impact and recognise opportunities and use them.

Although the consumer pioneers or futurologists like to talk about a total turn and innovation, there will be a new possibility that exists in addition to the traditional forms of organisation. Our working environment is constantly changing and because of this, our service requirements will also differ. A products and service catalogue that is made up of a static group of services is hopelessly outdated. We need flexibility and to renew the service landscape, depending on individual users, so that it is situation-specific.[45] It is no difference that it will have consequences for the organisation and operation of a USD.

[45] ISS 2020 Vision, "Future of Service management", *Copenhagen Institute for Future Studies*, Whitebook, 2018.

CHAPTER 24: A CASE STUDY FROM THE UK GOVERNMENT

24.1 Introduction

One of the key reforms in government was to brigade a number of government agencies (departments that were staffed and run by public servants, but were not funded by the public purse and were expected to charge other government departments for their services), under one commercial structure.

The purpose of the new organisation was to support the procurement and acquisition process of public sector organisations in the UK through policy and process guidance, and the negotiation of overarching service and provision frameworks. This was intended to improve value for money for the taxpayer, optimising the level of taxpayer's equity directed towards the delivery of services.

The organisation supported initiatives to encourage better supplier relations, sustainable procurement, the benefits of engaging smaller suppliers and the potential of eProcurement.

The combined agencies included a government department, which focused on IT best practices and technology innovation; an FM organisation, which focused on supplying everything from building works to carpeting; and a body that managed all aspects of building works in the Civil Estate from creating project management best practice through to the management of programmes and projects.

It had been decided that each of the agencies had similar processes and procedures; for example, each one used a products and service catalogue to showcase what it offered and each used a help desk or service desk arrangement. Additionally, it was widely understood that consolidation would reduce overheads and offer the opportunity to significantly improve services to the government at large. One obvious example was that instead of working with multiple agencies, a one-stop shop could be created where a department could make procurement and planning arrangements for a new office that included everything from IT to office premises, tables and chairs, carpets and blinds, even to pens and paper. Services could extend to the wider government that would make, for example, building a provincial new hospital cheaper and more efficient.

24.2 FM or IT?

Every organisation arranges purchasing differently. One of the early considerations was the issue of IT being the focus for best practice (because modern business is IT), or building management where many years of experience of very large scale project management existed. IT project management was deemed no different to any other form of project management.

A similar argument existed over the definition of 'best practice'. Large-scale building works had clearly been managed with best practices that had evolved over many years, and a controversial decision was taken by the government body to term all IT guidance as 'good' practice and reserve the 'best' terminology for long-proven practices (which, incidentally, included facilities management). It may be of interest that the government body was the Office of Government Commerce (OGC), which has created some of the most widely used best practices like inter alia, portfolio management, programme management, PRINCE2 and ITIL.

A result was that all best practices, from procurement to the use of various goods or service catalogues and any form of advice regarding process work, were forensically examined and where possible integrated, or at worst, aligned as far as possible. At the highest level it was decided that 'best practice' would apply to buildings and office equipment and that IT would be considered a subservient arrangement, served by its own specific 'good practices' that would be derived from the afore mentioned 'best practices'. For example, portfolio or project management best practices in the building and construction area would be used to derive 'good practices' for managing IT. Similarly, a process such as incident management would be created for large construction projects and adopted by IT if appropriate. So, to further clarify the organisation's distinction between primary and secondary departments: based on their connections with the primary building works function, construction work, buildings maintenance and office provisioning were all designated as part of facilities management, and were, therefore, considered primary level processes and subject to OGC's best practice regulations.

The OGC also demanded cross-training in the government organisations where there were separate purchasing departments for example, with multiple 'category' managers with substantive knowledge of their particular market and knowledge of the needs of their own organisation. Over time, it became very clear that IT was (and is) different from 'standard' business FM and that it would be a retrograde step to attempt to enforce a single approach to procurement because expertise was so obviously specialised in many areas of business and IT.

Instead, it was decided to establish FM as an overarching principle of governance and to combine similar management processes and techniques under a business-first approach with specialist IT knowledge being 'subcategories' of best practice.

Additionally, substantial investment was made in contract management best practice. This decision was made in accordance with the basic principle that managing contracts and contacts with external suppliers aims at the sustainable guarantee of the quality, stability and continuity of the services provided by the suppliers to the internal customers and at the reduction of the related costs. It is worth noting that contract management is also involved in negotiating the expansion of tasks, such as higher volume due to the expansion of locations or changes in demand as a result of the introduction of new services. Supplier management is often part of contract management because it assesses the supplier's performance.

24.3 Transformation: governance and strategy

The new agency decided that a key service for government customers, particularly in the light that the agency would be offering a range of services previously obtainable from other agencies, would be a business service desk that would immediately direct callers/enquiries to the party that could provide assistance. FM activities would be passed directly to the part of the new organisation, that in the past was a separate entity. Customers however, would be unaware of the procedure. This was simply a means of retaining specific knowledge under a new label, and promoting an air of harmonious service delivery.

In fact, although the departments in the new agency were effectively no longer in existence, their respective databases and intranets were entirely retained for the staff and access only changed to the degree that it was directed via a new 'corporate' interface.

As an initial step it was clear that the large scale developments would have repercussions all across the business departments of the agencies, and an approach was agreed to define governance and strategy and from there examine the improvement that would be possible as a result of the well-defined developments required. The first decision was to create a service desk that would be predicated on a 'one-stop shop' for all customers, old and new, and an overarching account management structure/function (the foundation), that would handle large customer departments (accounts). As a result, account management was largely a business level activity irrespective of whether or not IT was involved. Two major services, the Government Catalogue (GCAT) and the Service Catalogue (SCAT) were created as a means of managing the various services to be offered to government customers.

Operation needs would be recognised early in the lifecycle of development. The definition of KPIs and CSFs, would drive the outcomes required with regard to training (particularly for the putative service desk, given the decision that the new service desk was to be the flagship 'front office' for the brigaded departments).

It was recognised that good governance required the creation of a strategic direction that aligned with policy. The agency's CEO directed that best practice principles should apply to all policy making regarding the services to be built and deployed. In addition, the CEO directed that customer-centric policies regarding information management and help desk management must be created by the business and supported by IT (via inter alia).

Business information management led directly to the policy that individual ministries should not order and receive products or services themselves. This policy was based on the principle that a single negotiating body with full knowledge of all data points regarding negotiations was a powerful engine for cost savings and efficiency.

Stakeholder analysis was key to determining the needs of the varied customers of the organisation. In addition, the concept of collaborative business service design (CBSD) was deployed as the best means of defining the business drivers (need, value, mission and capability elements) that would apply to the overall design of the service desk. Need (for the services provided by the service desk) and value (both actual and perceived), were carefully considered in the context of the business demand from customers; if a service had no value, it was unlikely to be needed and vice versa.

24.4 Business management or IT?

For many years, one of the brigaded agencies had operated as a buying agency for government departments across the country. Although purchasing of specialist IT software for the service desk would be an important technology component, it was decided that procurement of the entirety of the service desk project would be run under business procurement auspices with IT taking a subordinate role for specific elements.

As a by-product of these considerations, the agency made the controversial decision mentioned earlier: to term all IT guidance as 'good' practice and reserve the 'best' terminology for long proven business practices. In this context, it became clear that the new service desk was the precursor of the important decision to integrate all business and IT practices (necessitating additional policy development), under one strand of management.

CBSD provided the necessary strategic guidance to establish sensible overarching principles and policies for the complex transformation of multiple enterprises. The guidance was also central to the overall programme being designed in such a way that appropriate best practices and expertise were available to manage and control the different facets of the overall design.

Service desk issues were guided primarily by existing published best practices (and a number of these publications were IT focused). USD guidance has by and large been built from long standing front office/back office guidance that is in turn the fundamental basis for all business FM and IT focused service desk/incident management guidance, allied to knowledge gained from the practical implementation of such guidance.

24.5 Practical implementation

As an improvement measure, it was decided to establish FM as an overarching principle of governance and to combine similar management processes and techniques under a business-first approach, with specialist IT knowledge forming subcategories of good practice.

It was necessary to analyse the need and value of managing contracts and contacts with external suppliers. In this, the aim was to ensure that management targeted the sustainable guarantee of the quality, stability and continuity of the services provided by the suppliers to external customers and to reduce the associated costs. Contract management also involved negotiating the expansion of tasks, including higher volume due to the expansion of locations, or changes in demand as a result of the introduction of new services. Supplier management became part of overall contract management and was used to assess suppliers' performance. In each case, the information and data were analysed to ensure their completeness and the identification of dependencies. The results were described and accepted as 'best of breed' contract management.

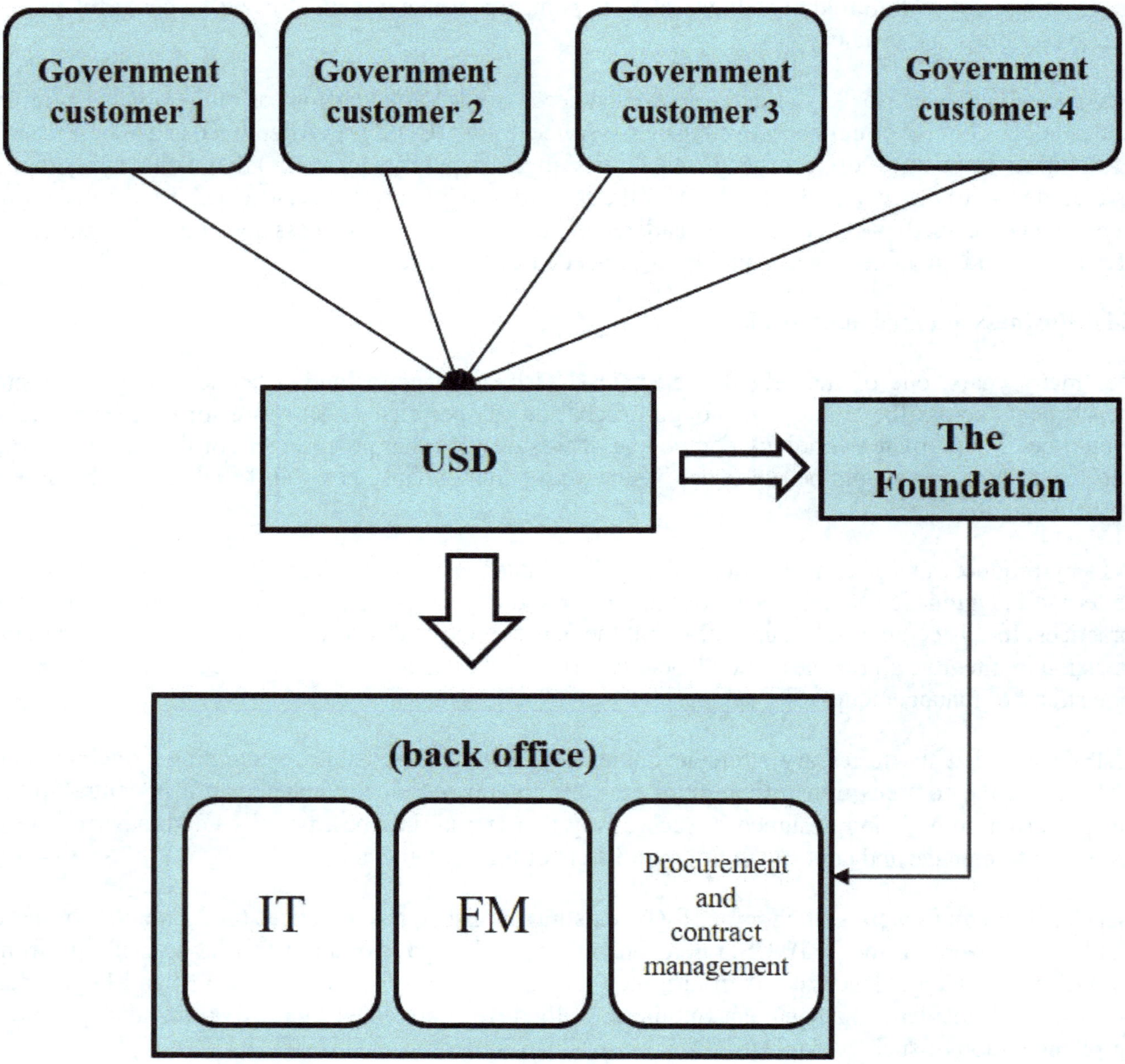

Figure 24.1: Setup of the service provisioning

24.6 Providing the services

Business information design involved the extensive interviewing of representatives from numerous government ministries and agencies at all levels to properly define and design the new or improved services to be offered to the ministries via the service desk. The 'soft skills' described in our sister publication *Collaborative Business Service Design* were used as a template for an adapted skills matrix for current and future employees; similarly, the workload calculation guidance was used to determine staffing levels. Based on all of the evidential criteria, staff training and development plans were drawn up and training was planned just-in-time to be available as the service design was completed and in plenty of time for go-live rehearsals.

Some activities were managed in the fashion termed 'Agile', for example creation of training packages and staff training. The method of development and deployment was assessed on the basis of risk and complexity. For example, the following activities need to be designed commensurate with the information needs:

- Monitoring to ensure that service is provided as described and agreed in the SLA with the customer;
- Providing contract administration where suppliers are involved;
- Managing and maintaining relationships with customers;
- Securing 'value for money' through the use of the departmental products and service catalogue;
- Seeking and implementing improvements;
- Managing improvements; and
- Performing continuous analysis of the new or changed needs of customers and supplier organisations.

The service desk was required to be available continuously from 7:30 am to 17:00 pm; (unusual for government and therefore subject to trade union key stakeholder approvals). The usual telephone answering services were to be in place plus electronic services via email and the secure information portal used for intra departmental communication. Librarians were heavily involved in the information design aspects of 'help' scripts and adaptation of IT 'service desk' software to support mostly IT-driven business information services, and also services peripheral to these such as answering FAQ and managing general enquiries. Such enquiries were wide-ranging, including ministerial enquiries about how to locate the CEO!

Service management was established on three levels:

1. **Strategic level** – the management of the customer maintains the relationship with the agency. This relationship not only focuses on existing services, but also on new initiatives.
2. **Tactical level** – contract management deals with the core tasks: relationship management, managing and checking the SLA or contract and possibly processing adjustments to the SLA/contract.
3. **Operational level** – where the products and services are actually delivered.

The account management team (the foundation) was drawn from a range of experienced people and led at a very senior management level. The purpose of this was to ensure that senior government figures would understand the scope of major services, such as GCAT and SCAT, and the expertise available to plan and project manage major building and office works.

In all cases, the service desk was the initial point of contact, except where the director of the foundation or its immediate senior staff initiated contact with existing or potential customers.

Over time, the success of the business service desk led to the expansion of services, to greater responsibilities and, of course, to increases in staff. The initial operational contract management for the enterprise's services included the service desk and was soon expanded to location management and overall service management. This embraced more products and services than you might think.

SUMMARY OF PART 3

Part 3 deals with the aspects that affect the USD but which are not directly part of its design. These aspects encompass the service desk's place as part of management and control, the quality of service, quality management for the service desk and practical quick wins to achieve efficiency improvements within the service desk. A number of implementation issues were also discussed.

Service agreements (internal SLAs) are made with the customers, i.e. with those who have the budget. These agreements are made within the frameworks (for example the housing policy, the house style or the desired image) that have been determined by the management. Often the most important customer is also a member of the management, with the business operations in his portfolio.

On the basis of the available budget and the agreements made, the service organisation can make agreements with suppliers. This leads to the delivery of the products and services in accordance with the quality levels agreed in the internal SLAs. The service and facilities organisation produces the products and service catalogue, which serves as the guideline for users in determining which products and services they will purchase. Many services are provided through the service desk so it is located between the users (the customers), the suppliers and the service and facilities organisation.

It is the experience of the customer that determines the degree of the quality of service. In addition to a defined handling of a customer demand, the feeling that the USD has dealt with the service question efficiently and effectively is an essential criterion. The process, the nature of products, the services and the manner in which the services are provided via the intranet or by the desk employee, play a role in the customer experience.

In order to guarantee the quality of service, decisions must be based on insight into the activities and their consequences. Within the service desk, a process has to be arranged aimed at collecting data, processing and analysing the data and making decisions on the basis thereof. This process is also known as the quality management process and one of the most common methods to regulate such a process is the PDCA cycle. The core of this method is to strive for continuous improvement. On the basis of this cycle, the services from the service desk in relation to the tasks can be made transparent.

The various interests within the enterprise must be considered in order to successfully implement a service desk for the service and facilities organisation. Important factors include the involvement of general management, understanding the evolution for the design of the service desk and the use of a project-based approach.

A total of 30 tips are included, divided among the four themes of:

1. Quality;
2. Employee;
3. Delivery; and
4. Policy.

What is the future for the USD when working environments change from a physical environment, to a virtual one, and therefore completely separate from a specific location? The new ICT, imagined in the IoT, will make this possible. This can mean that the service desk evolves into an 'intelligent hub'.

SECTION FOR YOUR NOTES

CHAPTER 25: FINALLY ... FOR THE CUSTOMER: THE USD AS AN INTERFACE

If you have read right through this book, you have discovered that behind something as simple as a USD is a complex world of pain... This book is not an instruction manual but a book about the different ingredients required and how these ingredients interact. It is up to you to assess which parts apply to your own situation. There are examples, tips and practical advice, but in the end you need to decide for yourself what will or will not work in your own environment.

An important feature of enterprises is their interaction with customers. This interaction has become increasingly complex over the years. Significantly, it has become increasingly difficult to maintain individual contact with customers because enterprises have become substantially larger. Just think of the development of the grocer on the corner, to the supermarket in the district to the hypermarkets in France. Customers were recognised as having individual needs and consequently, increasing thought was given to creating systems for improving the relationships between customers and enterprises.

The purpose of these systems was to make complex relationships simple and intuitive for customers. By providing the system as an interface, the enterprise's actual internal complexity can be mitigated for customers. A very simple interface is the button in the elevator, or the receptionist who greets the visitor and directs them. The telephone exchange is an interface both in terms of technology and staffing. An interface can therefore be purely technical or purely human.

As service departments continue to develop into demand-oriented organisations, the need for a good interface between the internal customer and the various back offices has increased. The interaction between customer and service support became increasingly complex due to multiple processes. As the services and facilities organisation outsourced more and more services such as IT, HR, cleaning, catering and security, the different contacts between customers and the different parties increased. Although the customer had less need for different contact points, the number of 'counters' increased. To ameliorate this situation, the idea of the USD was developed as a single entry for enquiries and requests.

The USD is an interface that streamlines the customer demand for services based on the front office to back office principle. In its simplest form, the USD answers this demand in the form of information; in a more developed form, the USD takes over the customer request and ensures that it is resolved through one or more processes in the back office.

The USD as a concept

A service organisation's USD can be arranged in many ways. Some enterprises choose to make a central information number available, while others provide a number for external customers and a number for internal customers (or any combination of numbers fronted by increasingly long and annoying menu selections). Some enterprises offer a complete 'service plaza', supplemented by an intranet site and account management. The reasons for this are diverse, in many cases the current USD has grown through 'trial-and-error'. Sometimes good thought has been given to the requested products and services, the desired level of service, necessary cost reduction or even the data needed to provide better services.

Consider the USD as a concept that comprises a service site on the intranet (the virtual USD), the call centre functionality (telephone, email and post), physical contact points (one or more service counters) and account management.

Considering the USD as a concept has several advantages. In the first place, freedom arises to think about the logic of the layout and function. In the second place, the discussion is separated from departmental interests. After all, the purpose of a USD has to do with the customer need for easier access to the products and services. In the third place, this approach makes the translation of the one-stop shop idea into concrete results easier. The point is that a customer is optimally helped by the logic of the service. This means that an ICT help desk and facility USD may fall under one management but are physically separated and have two separate telephone numbers. Time and again the right mix of components of a USD has to be used for the best possible service. Fourthly, considering the USD as a concept allows management to assess the individual components of a USD within their context, in relation to the desired USD target within the enterprise. This also drives the decision that sometimes only a virtual USD is chosen, while another enterprise will opt for all distribution channels.

General management and the USD

The explanation of the USD as a concept fits in well with the world of senior management. The discussion about the interaction between customer and enterprise is well known to many project managers, and service managers have big plans for the design and development of the USD. But soon three things become clear.

In the first place, an important step is easily skipped: thinking and formulating the mission and the objectives. Once these have been established, they will often have consequences for the design of the USD. Not enough attention is paid to this first step in many cases.

Secondly, general management often has different ideas than those of the service/facility management team. It is important to be clear about expectations and mandate, otherwise this will lead to unpleasant surprises.

Thirdly, it is important that general management realises that the objectives for the new USD will not be achieved immediately. In addition, they should understand that important requirements can also be imposed, such as higher competencies or more capacity (i.e. more costs), or a radical renovation or a change in mandate, i.e. a change in the balance of power.

Match between specific demand and generic supply

After the objectives have been determined and they have been endorsed by general management, inventories can be made of both the offered products and services and the needs of customers within the enterprise. However, the experience of the customers is completely different from that of the employees of the service organisation. A customer speaks about a meeting for training, not about the need for a room for a whole day with IT set-up, projector, coffee and tea, and which also needs to be cleaned in advance (and afterwards), or to register a new employee. The USD is the designated organisational unit that can translate the demands for a range of activities. In the more developed role of the USD, the customer demand is actually disconnected from the underlying process within the back office.

By managing customer demand, another advantage is created. Customer questions are generally specific in nature. The decoupling creates the possibility to standardise partial services, products or components, so that efficiency gains can be realised.

"Come together"

John Lennon's song works for USDs as well: ultimately, all parts of the USD must "come together" within an enterprise. However, the extent to which the different parts can be brought together depends on many factors. These include how the various components are implemented, how the quality of service is determined and how far the authority of the USD extends (is it just an information desk or does it also control the handling process?). It also depends on where the account management function is positioned and whether it is integrated within the USD, the capacity of the USD, and so on.

From thinking to doing

Once all of these myriad issues have been contemplated, the construction of the USD can begin. The design can be realised, for which various activities are started such as building a service site on the intranet, creating a physical location, installing and implementing systems and staffing the USD organisation.

It is advisable to think about how and at what speed the implementation of the USD takes shape. Implement the ideas and tools that you need from this book. Maintain focus on the way in which your internal clients are addressed, the speed at which matters are handled, possible developments within and outside the enterprise and the expansion of digital possibilities.

Keep in mind that the classical boundaries of enterprises are fading through technological innovations, cultural changes and globalisation. This may mean a greater ambition and therefore a different interpretation of the USD.

Therefore, the USD is an important tool in a customer-oriented, or better, demand-oriented service/facility organisation. Relatively small adjustments to the accessibility and functioning of a USD do wonders. They contribute to a positive image of the service/facilities organisation.

Above all, service to customers (internal or external) is improved. This leads to efficiencies and greater customer satisfaction. And after all, that is the ultimate goal of the USD.

BIBLIOGRAPHY

- Beckum, J. van en & Vlasgeld, G-J., *CATS CM editie 2014: Contract management voor opdrachtgever en leverancier*, Zaltbommel: Van Haren Publishing, 2014.
- Bernard, P., *IT-service management op basis van ITIL® 2011 Editie*, Zaltbommel: Van Haren Publishing, 2013.
- Bloem, J., et al., *Things – internet van businesskansen, VINT onderzoeksnotitie 1*, The Sogeti trend Lab VINT, 2013.
- Bon, J. van, Polter, S., Verheijnen, T. & Selm van, L., *ISO/IED 20000; een introductie,* Zaltbommel: Van Haren Publishing, 2010.
- Boomsma, S. & Borrendam A. van, *Kwaliteit van dienstverlening,* Alphen aan den Rijn: Samsom, 2000.
- Bos, P., *Handreiking contractbeheer en contractmanagement*, Den Haag: Vereniging van Nederlandse Gemeenten, 2014.
- Bos, R., Luchtenberg, B. & Schulte, R., *Wegwijs in accountmanagement. Echte accountmanagers golfen niet*, Zaltbommel: Uitgeverij Thema, 2002.
- Buitelaar, S., "Dienstverlening – Doodlopende telefoontjes", *Binnenlands bestuur* 50, p. 28–29, 2006.
- Chui, M., Löffler, M. & Roberts, R., "The Internet of Things", *McKinsey Quarterly*, March, 2010.
- Cleveland, B., *Call Centre Management on Fast Forward: Succeeding in the New Era of Customer Relationships*, Colorado Springs, CO: ICMI Press, 2012.
- Computable, "Helpdeskmedewerker is moeilijk te vinden", *Computable* 41(6), 2008.
- Crosby, P.B., *Quality is Free. The Art of Making Quality Certain*, New York: McGraw-Hill Book Company, 1979.
- Deming, W.E., *Out of the Crisis*, Cambridge, MA: MIT, 1982, 2000.
- Doorn, M., Duivestein, S. & Smith, P., *The unorganization; design to disrupt, report 5 of 4*, SogetiLabs, 2015.
- Drucker, P.F., *Management: tasks, responsibilities, practices*, 5th print, New York: Harper Business, 1973.
- Emmett, S. & Crocker, B., *Excellence in Supplier Management: How to Better Manage Contracts with Suppliers and Add Value*, Cambridge: Cambridge Academic, 2009.
- Evans, P.C. & Gawer, A., "The Rise of the Platform Enterprise A Global Survey", *The Emerging Platform Economy Series*, New York: The Center for Global Enterprise, 2016.
- Fikkers, H.J, Nieuwenhuizen, L.R., Nijssen, J.P.J. & Schaap, H.A., "Op weg naar werken met BIM", CUR Bouw & Infra en de Bouw Informatie Raad, 2012.
- Freeman, R.E., *Strategic Management: A Stakeholder Approach*, Cambridge: Cambridge University Press, 2010.
- Gartner, *How to Determine Social Media's Role in Your Customers' Journeys*, May 2018.

- Gartner, *Magic Quadrant for IT Service Management Tools and Magic Quadrant for IT Service Management Tools*, August 2018.
- Grönroos, C., *Service Management and Marketing: A Customer Relationship Management Approach*, Chichester/Hoboken, NJ: John Wiley & Sons, 2000.
- Hardjono, T.W. & Bakker, R.J.M., *Management van processen. Identificeren, besturen, beheersen en vernieuwen*, Deventer: Kluwer, 2006.
- Hodge, G., Poglitsch, R. & Ankerstjerne, P., "Perspectives on the FM market development", ISS White Paper, 2014.
- Huijben, M. & Geurtsen, A., *Heeft iemand de overhead gezien? Een beproefde methode om de overhead te managen,* Den Haag: Academic Service, 2008.
- ISS 2020 Vision, "Future of Service management", Copenhagen Institute for Future Studies, Whitebook, 2018.
- ISS 2020 Vision, "New Ways of Working–the workplace of the future", Copenhagen Institute for Future Studies, Whitebook, 2013.
- Johnson, B. et al., *BISL-Next- A framework for Business Information Management: Second edition*, Zaltbommel: Van Haren Publishing, 2018.
- Johnson, B. & Rouw, de L.P., *Collaborative Business Design: Improving and innovating the design of IT-driven business services*, Cambridgeshire, ITGP, 2017.
- Johnson, B. & Rouw, de L.P., *Collaborative Business Design: The fundamentals Improving and innovating the design of IT-driven business services*, Cambridgeshire, ITGP, 2018.
- Kaplan, R.S. & Norton, D.P., *Op kop met de balanced scorecard. Strategie vertaald naar actie*, Amsterdam: Business Contact, 2000.
- Knapp, D., *A Guide to USD Concepts*, Boston, MA: Course Technology, 2010.
- Kwaliteitskeurmerk ITO, "Klantgerichte certificering voor telefonie, e-mails en webforms", Brochure, Houten: ITO, 19 maart, 2007.
- Lee, M. van der & Rappard, A., *Innovatie met IT. Een must voor facility management*, Alphen aan den Rijn: Kluwer, 2007.
- Leeflang, P.S.H., "Account management, een zaak die aandacht verdient", Bedrijfskunde 1991(1), p. 99–111, 1991.
- Lennartz, R.E., Trompetter, A. & Veeke, R.A.F., *Inkoopmanagement in facilitaire omgevingen; ... stevig faciliteren noodzakelijk, Inkoopmemo's*, Alphen aan den Rijn: Samsom, 2000.
- Manen, T. van, Bloem, J. & Doorn, M. van, "SMACT and the City", *VINT onderzoeksnotitie 4*, The Sogeti trend Lab VINT, 2014.
- Mastenbroek, W.F.G., *Conflicthantering en organisatie-ontwikkeling. Proefschrift Leiden, vierde herziene druk*, Samsom, Alphen aan den Rijn, 2005.
- Mintberg, H., "The Manager's Job: Folklore and Fact", *Harvard Business Review*, March-April 1990, p. 1–13, 1990.
- NEN 2748, Nederlandse norm, *Termen voor facilitaire voorzieningen; rubricering en definiëring*, Delft: Nederlands Normalisatie-instituut, 2001.

- NEN 15221-4, Nederlandse norm, *Facility Management – Deel 4: taxonomie, classificatie en structuren in facility management*, Delft: Nederlands Normalisatie-instituut, 2011.
- Noorlander, R., Alleijn, S., *Inkoopsoftware P2P: een goede voorbereiding is de voorwaarde voor succes*, Blog, www.logistiek.nl, Vakmedianet, 2009.
- Obers, G-J. & Achterberg, K., *Grip op processen in organisaties. Analyseren, ontwerpen en inrichten van bedrijfsprocessen*, Zaltbommel: Van Haren Publishing, 2014.
- Office of Government Commerce, *How to Manage Service Provision: the IS management and business change guides*, Norfolk: Format Publishing Limited, 2002.
- OL2000, *Van loket-idee naar implementatie. Reeks Resultaten onderzoeksprogramma*, Den Haag: Programmabureau Overheidsloket, 1998.
- OL2000, *Van vraagpatroon naar loket*, Den Haag: Programmabureau Overheidsloket, 1997.
- Rayport, J.F. & Jaworski, B.J., *Best Face Forward: Why Companies Must Improve their Service Interfaces with Customers*, Boston, MA: Harvard Business School Press, 2005.
- Regtop, D. (z.j.), 'De Erlang-C-calculatie'.
- Rouw, L.P. de& Verhoef, C., *Het regiebureau. Kernprincipes voor sturen op resultaat*, Zaltbommel: Van Haren Publishing, 2015.
- Schiffman, L.G., Kanuk, L.L., & Wisenblit, J., *Consumer Behavior*, French's Forest, NSW: Pearson Australia, 2010.
- Shakir, A. & Haider, S., "Towards Designing a Course for the Front-office Department Staff at Pakistani Hotels", *Journal of Research, Faculty of Language & Islamic Studies*, vol 4, p. 45–57, 2003.
- Shostack, G.L., "Designing Services that Deliver", *Harvard Business Review*, January-February 1984, p. 133–139, 1984.
- Tanner, M., "The Erlang-C Formula", 2000.
- The Erlang-C Formula, http://erlang.chwyean.com/erlang/erlangC.html.
- Veldhoen, E., *Kantoren bestaan niet meer, versie 2.0.*, Rotterdam: Uitgeverij 010, 1998.
- Waard, J. de, Godding, B., *Coaching aan de lopende band; leidinggeven aan mensen die het doen voor de poen,* Zaltbommel: Haystack, 2010.
- WRR, "Het borgen van publiek belang", *Rapporten aan de regering nummer 56*, Den Haag: Sdu Uitgevers, 1995.
- Zeithaml, V., Parasuraman, A. & Berry, L.L., *Delivering Quality Service: Balancing Customer Perceptions and Expectations*, New York: Free Press, 1990.
- Zwart, A. de, "Presesponsieve gemeente als facilitaire dienstverlener", *Facility Management Handboek*, 1.2.1, artikel A3, Nieuwegein: Arko Uitgeverij, 2000.

FURTHER READING

IT Governance Publishing (ITGP) is the world's leading publisher for governance and compliance. Our industry-leading pocket guides, books, training resources and toolkits are written by real-world practitioners and thought leaders. They are used globally by audiences of all levels, from students to C-suite executives.

Our high-quality publications cover all IT governance, risk and compliance frameworks and are available in a range of formats. This ensures our customers can access the information they need in the way they need it.

Other resources you may find useful include:

- *Collaborative Business Design – Improving and innovating the design of IT-driven business services* by Brian Johnson and Léon-Paul de Rouw, *www.itgovernancepublishing.co.uk/product/collaborative-business-design*
- *IT for Business (IT4B) – From Genesis to Revolution, a business and IT approach to digital transformation* by Brian Johnson and Walter Zondervan, *www.itgovernancepublishing.co.uk/product/it-for-business-it4b*
- *PRINCE2® in Action – Project management in real terms* by Susan Tuttle, *www.itgovernancepublishing.co.uk/product/prince2-in-action*

For more information on ITGP and branded publishing services, and to view our full list of publications, visit *www.itgovernancepublishing.co.uk*.

To receive regular updates from ITGP, including information on new publications in your area(s) of interest, sign up for our newsletter at *www.itgovernancepublishing.co.uk/topic/newsletter*.

Branded publishing

Through our branded publishing service, you can customise ITGP publications with your company's branding.

Find out more at *www.itgovernancepublishing.co.uk/topic/branded-publishing-services*.

Related services

ITGP is part of GRC International Group, which offers a comprehensive range of complementary products and services to help organisations meet their objectives.

For a full range of resources visit *www.itgovernance.co.uk*.

Training services

The IT Governance training programme is built on our extensive practical experience designing and implementing management systems based on ISO standards, best practice and regulations.

Our courses help attendees develop practical skills and comply with contractual and regulatory requirements. They also support career development via recognised qualifications.

Learn more about our training courses and view the full course catalogue at www.itgovernance.co.uk/training.

Professional services and consultancy

We are a leading global consultancy of IT governance, risk management and compliance solutions. We advise businesses around the world on their most critical issues and present cost-saving and risk-reducing solutions based on international best practice and frameworks.

We offer a wide range of delivery methods to suit all budgets, timescales and preferred project approaches.

Find out how our consultancy services can help your organisation at www.itgovernance.co.uk/consulting.

Industry news

Want to stay up to date with the latest developments and resources in the IT governance and compliance market? Subscribe to our Weekly Round-up newsletter and we will send you mobile-friendly emails with fresh news and features about your preferred areas of interest, as well as unmissable offers and free resources to help you successfully start your projects. www.itgovernance.co.uk/weekly-round-up.